Flexible Church

Flexible Church

Being the Church in the Contemporary World

Helen D. Morris

scm press

Published in 2019 by SCM Press
Editorial office
3rd Floor, Invicta House,
108–114 Golden Lane,
London EC1Y 0TG, UK
www.scmpress.co.uk

SCM Press is an imprint of Hymns Ancient & Modern Ltd (a registered charity)

Hymns Ancient & Modern® is a registered trademark of
Hymns Ancient & Modern Ltd
13A Hellesdon Park Road, Norwich,
Norfolk NR6 5DR, UK

British Library Cataloguing in Publication data

A catalogue record for this book is available
from the British Library

978 0 334 05813 7

Typeset by Regent Typesetting Ltd
Printed and bound by
CPI Group (UK) Ltd

Contents

List of Figures

Introduction

Church of the Apostles, Seattle

Around 35 people enter a coffee shop at 5pm on a Sunday evening. Ambience is created by incense, a crucifix propped on a sound speaker, candles, projected videos, and jazz-style music. There is sung worship, and a Bible verse (unreferenced) is placed on a screen for people to discuss. The person leading the meeting shares their thoughts on the passage, talking about exposing sin and bringing it into Christ's light of truth. A few respond to a call to write their sins on a piece of paper and place it in a plastic bowl, symbolic of casting their sins onto Jesus. There is a dramatic reading of the story of Jesus healing a blind man, followed by 'Open Space', within which some talk to a friend, others make coffee, some light a candle, others pray, and some journal. Communion is shared, led by lay leaders within the group. At the end, there are notices and an invitation to newcomers to join the community of faith.[1]

Kahaila Café, London

Another café, and it is Wednesday evening. Twenty-five regulars and 15 visitors gather for a weekly church service. Some of the visitors are café customers, who heard about the church gathering and decided to come along. Others are people who used to be involved in church, but have since drifted away. The meeting is led by a Baptist minister. The corporate worship is varied in style and there is a time of teaching followed by discussion. The teaching style is interactive to enable non-believers to contribute their opinions and feel a sense of belonging. The website describes the group as: relational, not religious, and a family, not an institution; those who seek to live life in its fullness and believe that Jesus' teaching brings that fullness; imperfect people, who promise not to judge newcomers and ask that they in turn are not judged.

This evening gathering is part of a café project, launched in 2012, in response to the observation that thousands visit the local market on Sunday mornings but, although there were Muslim evangelists and people doing tarot cards, there was no Christian presence. All the Christians were at church. The café project was started to facilitate community and, through building relationships, provide an opportunity for those working at the café to talk about Jesus and offer prayer. The evening gathering aims to help those interested in exploring the Christian faith to find out more. The café functions ethically and provides good quality service so that the good news of Jesus is evident in its working practices alongside its workers' spoken witness.[2]

Messy Church Fiesta, Shetland

Balloons and artwork decorate a small rural Methodist church. A church with an average Sunday attendance of 30 people squeezes in over 60 for craft activities, a cooked meal, and an interactive all-age Bible-based talk. The age range includes newborns to a woman in her 90s. Some of those present are regular members of the Methodist church but others found out about it through a work colleague. Leaders mingle with newcomers to build relationships and make those attending feel welcome. The atmosphere is bright and lively. The Christian content has provoked interest from some of the adults in attendance. A monthly café church will soon be started, in addition to Messy Church, to give these adults the opportunity to explore the Christian faith more fully. Children's interest has also been piqued and attendance at the weekly 'Sunday Club' has increased from 6 to 15 since Messy Church was launched. Messy Church has prompted wider interest too, with one attendee submitting an article to the local press in praise of the initiative. Leaders of Messy Church say the name itself is a strength; it communicates that everyone is welcome, regardless of how messy their lives are, and speaks of a Jesus who reaches out to a messy world.[3]

Re-Contextual Church

The communities described above are examples of what I refer to in this book as 're-contextual church'. 'Re-contextual church' is the umbrella term that I use to describe both communities and authors who are rethinking the form and role of church in light of cultural change. Re-contextual authors include the proponents of Church Next, Missional Church, Emerging Church, Emerging Missional Church, Emergence Christianity, Flat Church, Mission-Shaped Church/Fresh Expressions, New Contextual Church, The Church Beyond the Congregation, Deep Church, Messy Church, Multi-Voiced Church, and Liquid Church, to give an indicative but not exhaustive list.[4] These authors highlight changes in Western culture and urge the Church to engage more effectively with its new context.

Their goal is more substantial than surface-level alterations. They aim to reimagine church away from old (and, they would argue, failing) paradigms and towards new and fresh ways of being and doing church. It is at this deeper level of reimagining church that I engage with in this book. My aim is to identify and assess the ecclesial assumptions of re-contextual writers and practitioners. I then propose an ecclesial framework for the re-contextual church movement that, I argue, provides the stability and flexibility needed for innovative expressions of church to be faithful to Jesus and accessible to their context. My plan is as follows:

Part 1: A Church in Transition explores the reasons why authors and practitioners are re-examining church (Chapter 1: Re-Thinking Church). I address the history and key features of the re-contextual movement and identify re-contextual proponents' underlying ecclesiology (Chapter 2: Re-Contextual Church). I conclude with methodological reflection (Chapter 3: Ecclesiology as Embodied Dialogue), arguing that ecclesiology should be conceived of as embodied dialogue, not abstract idealizing.

Part 2: Flexible Church explores the criticisms directed towards Social Trinitarianism, which is a core component of many re-contextual thinkers' ecclesiology (Chapter 4: The Church and the Social Trinity). Ironically, Social Trinitarianism is weakest on precisely those points that re-contextual thinkers seek to highlight most emphatically. In contrast to Social Trinitarianism, I outline an ecclesiology based on the body of Christ metaphor in the New Testament (Chapter 5: The Body of Christ is the Church). My goal is to demonstrate that a Trinitarian ecclesiology based on the body of Christ metaphor can overcome the inadequacies of Social Trinitarianism, adding substance and stability to the re-contextual movement, while facilitating much needed flexibility (Chapter 6: The Church as a Suspension Bridge Characterized by Gift-Exchange).

Notes

1 G. Marti and G. Ganiel, *The Deconstructed Church: Understanding Emerging Christianity*, Oxford: OUP, 2014, 35–7.

2 Paul Unsworth, 'Kahaila', YouTube website (www.youtube.com/watch?v=TomQ-TOmA2I, last modified 16.11.12); Kahaila, 'About Us', Kahaila website (http://kahaila.com/about-us).

3 G. Lings (ed.), *Messy Church Theology*, Abingdon: BRF, 2013, 127–30.

4 See, for example, the writings of Stuart and Sian Murray Williams, Michael Moynagh, Pete Ward, Craig van Gelder, Dwight Zscheile, Michael Frost, Alan Hirsch, Doug Gay, Kevin Corcoran, Robert Webber, Dan Kimball, John Finney, John Drane, Lucy Moore, Graham Cray, Ian Mobsby, Stephen Croft, Eddie Gibbs, Ian Coffey, Jim Belcher, Andrew Jones, James Thwaites, Tony Jones and Phyllis Tickle.

PART I

A Church in Transition

I

Re-Thinking Church

In obedience to the commission that Jesus gave to his disciples the Church's vocation is to proclaim the good news afresh in each generation. As disciples of our Risen Lord we are called to be loyal to the inheritance of faith which we have received and open to God's Spirit so that we can be constantly renewed and reformed for the task entrusted to us.[1]

The title 'Fresh Expressions of Church' is derived from the Church of England's commitment to 'proclaim the good news afresh in each generation'. For the authors of the *Mission-Shaped Church* report (hereafter *Mission-Shaped Church*), and re-contextual thinkers across a range of denominations, statistics indicating church decline suggest that the 'afresh' has grown stale. Moynagh notes that there was a 30% decrease in church attendance in England in the 20 years leading up to the millennium. The decline has since slowed, but is still marked among traditional denominations, with membership of Methodist churches decreasing by 33% between 2005 and 2017, Anglican churches by nearly 25%, and Baptist churches by 15%.[2]

The diminishment is starkest among the younger generations. In the decade between 2005 and 2015, church attendance among the under 30s decreased by 25%. Extend back to 1980, and the figure exceeds 60%, from over 2 million Sunday attendees in 1980 to less than 800,000 in 2015. Conversely, over the same time period (1980 to 2015), church attendance among the over 65s increased by 20%.[3] This decline in child church involvement is particularly significant given the role that childhood church attendance plays in adult churchgoing; over 90% of regular adult churchgoers went to church as children. Most newcomers to church are returning to a childhood faith or church experience. As Walker notes the diminishment in child attendance is thus a 'time bomb' for church decline as there become fewer adults with a faith to return to. Without churches enhancing their ability to attract children and those with no previous church experience, church attendance will diminish apace. Concurrently, the average age of the UK church will carry on increasing.[4]

Despite churchgoers being in the minority, the 2001 Census reveals that seven out of ten people consider themselves 'Christian'. As Fox notes, though, national surveys consistently show that around 15% of self-identifying Christians do not believe in God. For many, being 'Christian' means holding to an ill-defined collection of morals and principles, only some of which are based on the Bible. 'Cultural Christianity' is thus still present in England but the UK's post-Christendom context means that those who, in yesteryear, might have been nominal churchgoers are now less likely to be involved in church. Therefore, the figures indicating church decline reflect, in part, the dropping away of nominal believers leaving a more devoted, but smaller, core. Significantly, however, two-thirds of people pray, a quarter doing so weekly, suggesting that spiritual openness is prevalent. Moreover, 6% of UK adults who are not regularly involved in church are open to attending. Therefore, although increasing numbers are not involved with church in any form, there are ways that churches can engage effectively in a culture that is more open to God than is often supposed.[5]

Re-contextual authors note that current generations are as interested in faith as those in previous eras, if not more so – although the challenges and barriers to accepting Christianity's tenets are different. However, they contend that the church has not adapted adequately to recent cultural changes, making it increasingly detached from people's everyday lives. The alienness of church culture and language to those not brought up in the church hinders people's reception of the gospel message. This inertia and irrelevance is exacerbated by the over-assimilation of the church into culture in the past, specifically modernity and Christendom. This assimilation, they argue, has dented the health and impact of the church in the present. Re-contextual proponents thus have a twofold goal; they urge the Western church to re-embed itself in its Christ-centred foundations while innovatively embodying this message in its contemporary context.[6]

Notable anomalies to the overarching picture of decline demonstrate that church diminishment is far from inevitable. Attendance at Fresh Expressions churches increased fourfold between 2005 and 2015, and nearly two-thirds of newcomers were previously unchurched or dechurched. Messy Church saw numbers double between 2012 and 2017. Other church expressions have also seen marked growth. Two-thirds of denominations have grown, with the fastest-growing 19 denominations increasing their membership by over 50% between 2012 and 2017. Immigration has been a significant factor, but a focus on evangelism and revitalization has also proved effective for church groups such as Vineyard and Hillsong. Church growth has been especially high in London, particularly among black, Asian, ethnic minority communities, and new churches. In addition, the church is more popular among certain demographic groupings than others, namely the older generations, females, professionals, and those of black ethnicity in contrast to the younger generations, males, and lower-skilled workers.[7]

The overall picture of the church in the contemporary world is complex. Among an overall trend of decline, areas of the church are seeing notable growth. However, the challenge to engage the younger generations remains strong. To best respond to this complexity, re-contextual authors argue, the church must be flexible and innovative in its engagement with different groups.

Notes

1 Justin Cantuar and Sentamu Ebor, 'In Each Generation: A Programme for Reform and Renwal, GS 1976, January 2015', *Church of England* website (https://churchofengland.org/media/2140062/gs%201976%20-%20a%20note%20from%20the%20archbishops%20giving%20an%20overview%20of%20the%20task%20groups.pdf). This call to 'proclaim the good news afresh' is also contained in the preface to the Declaration of Assent.

2 M. Moynagh, *Changing World, Changing Church*, London; Grand Rapids, MI: Monarch, 2001, 10 citing figures for 1979 to 1998 from P. Brierley, *The Tide is Running Out*, London: Christian Research, 2000, 27; cf. 12; P. Brierley (ed.), *UK Church Statistics 2005–2015*, Tonbridge: ADBC, 2011 and *UK Church Statistics No.3 2018 Edition*, Tonbridge: ADBC, 2018; J. Walker, *Testing Fresh Expressions*, Abingdon: Routledge, 2016 (2014), 7 and 42.

3 Although the population of England aged during this period, the shift in church attendance is disproportionate (Brierley, 2018). Going back further still, the percentage of the UK child population attending Sunday school dropped dramatically from 55% in 1900 to 4% in 2000 (G. Cray [ed.], *Mission-Shaped Church*, London: Church House, 2004, 41 drawing on statistics from P. Brierley [ed.], *UK Christian Handbook, Religious Trends* No. 2, 2000/01 *Millennium Edition*, London: Christian Research, 1999).

4 Walker cites the Northern Ireland Social Attitudes (NISA) and British Social Attitudes (BSA) surveys to show that, in 1991, 91–95% of weekly adult churchgoers had gone to church weekly as children (Walker, *Testing*, 111). He notes that the 2001 International Congregational Life Survey (ICLS) supports this strong correlation between child and adult church attendance (Walker, *Testing*, 112). In addition, more recent BSA data (1998 and 2008), shows a decrease in the percentage of adult churchgoers who went to church weekly as a child, but more than 90% went at least occasionally as a child. He concludes that 2008 results show that 'any attendance, not just regular attendance, as a child of 11 or 12 is a significant factor in later adult churchgoing' (Walker, *Testing*, 114–19).

5 K. Fox, *Watching the English*, rev. ed. London: Hodder & Stoughton, 2014 (2004), 487–91. The nominal 15% in the 2001 Census probably accounts for the lower percentage of UK adults (53%) who affiliated themselves with Christianity in Tearfund's research; the phrasing of the Tearfund researchers' question, 'Do you regard yourself as *belonging* to any particular religion?' was intentionally designed to exclude those willing to tick 'Christianity' in response to a question asking their religion, but reluctant to see themselves as 'belonging' to the Christian faith (J. Ashworth et al., *Churchgoing in the UK*, London: Tearfund, 2007).

6 Drane argues that, with perverse irony, contemporary generations often see the church as not spiritual enough (J. Drane, *The McDonaldization of the Church*, London: Darton, Longman and Todd, 2001, e.g. 54, 71). See also, for example, J. Thwaites, *The Church Beyond The Congregation*, Carlisle: Paternoster, 1999, 5; Walker, *Testing*, 7; M. Frost and A. Hirsch, *ReJesus*, Peabody, MA: Hendrickson, 2009, 5–6.

7 'Unchurched' describes those who have never been involved in a church and 'dechurched' those who were previously part of a church but subsequently moved away from church involvement. For the relevant statistics see Brierley, 2018; Brierley, 2005–2015 and D. Goodhew, 'The Death and Resurrection of Christianity in Contemporary Britain', in D. Goodhew (ed.), *Church Growth in Britain: 1980 to the Present*, Farnham: Ashgate, 2012, 253–7; Ashworth, *Tearfund*.

2

Re-Contextual Church

The desire to be faithful to the ancient Christian message and accessible to particular contexts is defined by the missiological term 'contextualization'. All churches are contextual – no churches transcend culture. The label '*re*-contextual church' is thus an apt umbrella term for those who, in literature and/or practice, are readdressing the nature and role of church in response to cultural change.[1] Since re-contextual authors are responding to church decline and what they perceive as the church's over-assimilation into yesteryear, it is a protest movement. That said, the movement is better defined in relation to what it is for than what it is against. To this end, I offer the following definition: *re-contextual church is primarily a Western, free church, ecumenical, Trinitarian, missional, holistic, emergent movement/mindset/conversation endeavouring to incarnate the kingdom into a postmodern, post-Christendom, consumerist, technologized, globalized, individualized, networked culture.* I explain and justify this definition below.

The adoption of the umbrella label is not to brush over marked differences between various authors and practitioners. However, these variations result from divergent perspectives on a shared question: how should the Western church respond to its changing context? Individual countries within the West have their own peculiar context and culture. The focus of this book is the UK milieu, particularly England, but with attention to the insights of re-contextual thinkers from elsewhere too, particularly the USA and Australia.

Within the UK, several authors have contributed to the re-contextual conversation. Doug Gay has examined emerging ecclesiology. John Drane has produced books investigating church in changing culture. Graham Cray chaired the Church of England's *Mission-Shaped Church* report and has published works exploring Fresh Expressions. Steven Croft, Ian Mobsby and George Lings have contributed within the Fresh Expressions subset of the conversation. Lings, for example, has focused on empirical research and trend-spotting, particularly through the Church Army's *Encounters of the Edge* publications. Lucy Moore has contributed to the discussion through launching Messy Church, a prevalent subset within Fresh Expressions. Jonny Baker has pioneered within the UK alternative worship stream and Jason Clark has contributed in connection with liturgy and discipleship in an emerging context. At the far end of the post-modern and deconstructive spectrum, Pete Rollins has been influential.

The three UK authors who have contributed most extensively to the re-contextual conversation, and over the longest timespan, are Michael Moynagh, Stuart Murray Williams, and Pete Ward.[2] Michael Moynagh is the Director of Network Development and Consultant on Theology and Practice for Fresh Expressions and has produced comprehensive theological and practical treatises for birthing fresh expressions of church in his *Church in Life* and *Church for Every Context*, alongside an accessible manual and compilation of stories in *Being Church, Doing Life*. His earlier contributions *emergingchurch.intro* and *Changing World, Changing Mission* have also been influential. In many ways, Moynagh's work spear-heads the Fresh Expressions discussion.

Stuart Murray Williams has written extensively from within the Baptist denomination and Anabaptist Network on the changing church scene within the UK, particularly in light of the post-1960s Christendom to post-Christendom shift – albeit the roots of Christendom's decline date back much earlier. His main contributions are *Post-Christendom*, *Church After Christendom*, *Changing Mission*, and *Multi-Voiced Church*, the last of which he co-authored with his wife Sian Murray Williams.

Pete Ward is Chair of the Ecclesiology and Ethnography Network at Durham University and has a background in youth ministry within the Anglican Church. He has written extensively on church and culture, in particular the connection between youth culture, popular music and the evangelical movement in his books *God at the Mall*, *Growing Up Evangelical* and *Selling Worship*. Further, within *Liquid Church* and *Participation and Mediation*, he has promoted 'liquid church' as a more fluid and flexible mode of church appropriate to contemporary Western culture. He has also contributed empirical research in *Mass Culture* and *Explorations in Ecclesiology and Ethnography*. Most recently, he has highlighted incongruity between the Western evangelical church's espoused understanding of the gospel and its lived expression in his 2017 publication *Liquid Ecclesiology*. Such incongruity, he argues, has arisen because of the Western church's lack of self-awareness as to the impact that culture has on theology, and the intertwined connection between the two.

I engage with a range of voices in this chapter but, because of their significance, the writings of Ward, Moynagh, and Murray Williams will be prominent in my evaluation of the re-contextual movement and its underlying ecclesiology.

'Primarily'

I include 'primarily' within the definition to acknowledge the re-contextual movement's diversity. 'Re-contextual church' is not a bounded-set word, like 'pregnant' (which someone is or is not), nor a denomination or affiliation that groups belong to or not (one of the movement's characteristics is that it is cross-denominational). Rather, re-contextual church is a centre-set term, consisting of a (disputed) core of values and characteristics that different groups may affirm and display to varying degrees. These are as follows. Re-contextual proponents are primarily Western. They primarily assume free-church ecclesiology, but are influenced by other church traditions (the Anglican influence on Fresh Expressions makes this subset exceptional, but even here free-church ecclesiology is influential). Mission largely drives the discussion, particularly the contention that Western mission has been hindered by uncritical and ineffective contextualization. It is agreed that the church should pursue more holistic modes of faith, church and mission, although there is discord regarding the nature and implications of this proposed holism. Re-contextual church is primarily a grassroots movement that has emerged organically (the more formal structures of Fresh Expressions makes it exceptional, but emergent characteristics are evident here too). The recent resurgence of Trinitarian scholarship has influenced re-contextual thinkers' conceptions of both mission and ecclesiology, contributing to the movement/mindset/conversation's aim to incarnate the kingdom into the various contexts in which Western Christians live and work. Re-contextual thinkers identify this changed context as postmodern, post-Christendom, consumerist, technologized, globalized, individualized and networked.

Descriptors such as 'fresh expressions' and 'emerging', which I incorporate within the term 're-contextual', are often contrasted with 'inherited' to distinguish established modes of church from those that are experimental and innovative. Inherited thinking and practice influences re-contextual practitioners, however, and inherited churches can be infused with re-contextual sensibilities. *Inherited* versus *new/fresh/emerging* are thus not mutually exclusive entities; rather all churches are to some degree both inherited and emerging.[3] Indeed, Anderson asserts that about 98% of people's behaviour is rooted in one tradition or another: 'Those who operate at the 99% level are considered to be the old-fashioned traditionalists, and those who operate at the 97% level are called avant-garde nontraditionalists. It is mostly a matter of degree.'[4] Therefore, while comparing *re-contextual* to *inherited* is helpful for analysis, these terms are best conceived as different mindsets rather than a discrete set of churches in one corner versus a constrasting set in another. Moreover, just as re-contextual expressions might not demonstrate all the characteristics

I have outlined, neither will these characteristics be wholly absent from inherited churches.

'Western'

Tickle contends that Western culture has shifted notably every 500 years, with political, economic, cultural and technological factors intertwining with religious developments. The Western world, she argues, is at the start of another such cycle and every area is affected.[5] Moynagh concurs, noting that in the last 50 years the West has experienced a cultural blizzard. The prevalence of *post-* within cultural depicters indicates that this is a period of transition; culture is not what it once was but neither is it clear where it is heading.[6]

The re-contextual church has arisen in this mutating milieu, with particular people, events and movements contributing to its birth. These include: the rise of Pentecostalism and the Charismatic movement, especially Wimber's influence; the development of the Social Gospel; the house-church movement; renewed interest in so-called Celtic spirituality and monasticism and, related to this, the founding of Taizé; the start of the third-place phenomenon (places such as cafés and sports clubs that provide a space between home and work and into which, it is argued, the church should be incarnated); the development of Liberation Theology; the 1960s rise of the New Age movement and the *spiritual but not religious* mantra; the 1970s launch of Christian music festivals; Vatican II; the ecumenical movement; missiological developments prompted by decolonization, particularly the work of Newbigin and Bosch; the 1970 to 1990s church-planting movement; the 1980s to 1990s painful rise and fall of the Nine O'Clock Service; the 1990s growth of the emerging church in the USA and alternative worship groups in the UK; Webber's promotion of 'ancient-future' (the need to revisit the past in a contemporary setting); the Trinitarian ecclesiology of Moltmann and Volf; McLaren's writings; N. T. Wright's theologizing, particularly his eschatology; and Fresh Expressions' 2004 publication *Mission-Shaped Church*.[7]

This historical sketch is not exhaustive; for instance the movement has international resonances. Overall, though, the re-contextual church is a primarily Western phenomenon provoked by an interrelated assortment of cultural change and the response to this shift by various individuals and Christian/church groups.

'Free Church'

> Today's global developments seem to imply that Protestant Christendom of the future will exhibit largely a Free Christian form. Although the episcopal churches will probably not surrender their own hierarchical structures, they, too, will increasingly have to integrate these Free Church elements into the mainstream of their own lives both theologically and practically.[8]

The free church movement traces back to the Anabaptists, who were part of the sixteenth-century Radical Reformation. Its most distinctive features are congregationalism, an emphasis on believers' unmediated access to God, the priesthood of all believers, and the identity of the church as a prophetic counterculture, separate from the state. The re-contextual church's underlying assumptions and explicit assertions regarding what church is, how it should be structured, and the role of the sacraments accord with these distinctives. For example, re-contextual proponents generally accord with the free church conception of the church as primarily the local congregation, without the necessity of formal connection to episcopacy. Fresh Expressions is exceptional in this regard, but the connection between Fresh Expressions and episcopacy is much debated. Moynagh, for instance, refers to ordination positively, but questions whether all church planters must be ordained. Empirical evidence indicates that others within Fresh Expressions are also unsure of the need for ordination. Among those affirming ordained leadership, there is a desire to facilitate the ordination of leaders who emerge organically within a community, resonating with the free church ethos wherein the group itself, through the Spirit's leading, appoints and validates its leaders.[9]

The re-contextual movement also aligns with the free church emphasis on unmediated access to God through his Spirit and Word aside from ordained ministers, the sacraments and liturgy. Jones notes the informal approach to Communion among emerging church groups, wherein various people preside (not necessarily the leaders). Fresh Expressions is again exceptional in that some proponents assert that the Eucharist, with ordained presidency, is part of the church's *esse*. Others, however, decry the institutionalization of previously organic lay communities into existing ecclesial patterns. Moynagh maintains that practices, including the Eucharist, are not essential for a group of Christians to be called a church. Ward affirms the classical 'marks' of the church but does not appear to regard ordination as a prerequisite for Eucharistic presidency. The corresponding free church focus on the priesthood of all believers is also reflected in the re-contextual conversation, with empowering the 'laity' for works of service in the church and wider world a key concern.

This partly stems from a distrust of authoritarian structures within wider culture, but theological conviction remains a primary motivation.[10]

The promotion of new monasticism to help incarnational missionaries avoid both irrelevance and syncretism (particularly in Fresh Expressions) resonates with the free church emphasis on church as a countercultural community. Further, Gelder traces the seeds of contemporary missiology, which has impacted the re-contextual discussion, to free church ecclesiology, particularly the separation of church and state.[11]

The correlation between the re-contextual movement and free church ecclesiology is unsurprising given that many of its proponents lie within the free church tradition.[12] However, the Anglican and Methodist-initiated (now ecumenical) Fresh Expressions movement also displays free church features. This is not to deny that Fresh Expressions is authentically Anglican. It is its free church tendencies, however, that have provoked most criticism from Anglican opponents.[13] Moreover, though some prominent re-contextual authors are Anglican, Ward and Moynagh, these authors accord with the free church inclination among re-contextual thinkers.

'Ecumenical'

The re-contextual discussion has been influenced by Roman Catholicism, Anglo-Catholicism and Eastern Orthodoxy. Engagement with these older traditions has been selective, with certain aspects incorporated into the movement's free church framework. Fresh Expressions is exceptional, wherein there is concern for how ancient practices can be maintained within Anglican ecclesial forms and government. Elsewhere the re-contextual discussion has drawn from Roman and Anglican Catholicism's sacramental and liturgical resources while 'unbundling' these practices from their episcopal origins. Further, the movement has drawn on Eastern Orthodoxy's Trinitarian focus, theology of divinization and emphasis on mystery, while transplanting these from their original hierarchical structures and incorporating them into a more egalitarian framework. The monastic traditions, through the rise of new monasticism, have also impacted the re-contextual movement. As Mobsby notes, though, new monasticism exhibits both continuity and discontinuity with historical monasticism.[14]

Various factors contribute to this interest in older Christian traditions. The first is illustrated by Gay's story about a Catholic boy who, on a trip to the local Presbyterian church, walks into the minimalist structure, looks around and asks in surprise, 'When were you robbed?' Gay traces this perceived loss to the Reformation and, while acknowledging that the Reformers' minimalism was originally a strong aesthetic statement, remarks that their purging both enhanced and depleted the Protestant churches that followed. Protestant churches became just ears and lungs; the eyes, noses, hands, and feet were sidelined. The re-contextual project aims to redress the balance by digging into the older traditions to regain a more corporeal mode of faith. This retrieval has been aided by Vatican II, which impacted Protestants alongside Catholics. Following Vatican II, low-church Protestants saw Roman Catholic liturgical traditions as less threatening and alien than they had previously been perceived.[15] The modernity to postmodernity shift has contributed to an ecumenical desire to transcend old dualisms between church streams. Moreover, borrowing certain components (liturgy) while rejecting others (hierarchical leadership and eucharistic presidency) has been facilitated by postmodernity's pick 'n' mix approach. Reflection on consumerism's impact has also contributed to the retrieval, with the recovery of ancient practices perceived as combating solipsism.[16]

This engagement with older traditions has not gone unchallenged. Murray Williams expresses concern that the retrieval is superficial, with some aspects of the church's heritage glorified and others overlooked or demonized. He maintains that believers must familiarize themselves more broadly with their heritage, while accepting that they will have more affinity with some parts than others and that unhealthy aspects of the church's history should be disavowed. Clark supports the retrieval but is concerned that ancient traditions are being commodified by the consumerist tendency to remove practices and symbols from their original framework and relocate them into a construct of a person's own choosing, distorting their meaning. Moreover, it is difficult to draw from history while also acknowledging its strangeness and re-contextual thinkers may at times be guilty of reading the present into the past.[17]

Gay agrees that the re-contextual retrieval is selective but, drawing on Matthew 13.52, asserts that the traditions of more established churches can, in some sense, be approached as a huge dressing-up box. The church is an 'assimilative tradition', which the Spirit is constantly reforming, so adaptations made in the present can correct old mistakes. Retrieving resources contributes to this tradition and can deepen ecumenical relations. Moreover, missiological insights should prompt humility regarding worship praxis; embedment in culture disallows any claim to be 'the one true church'.[18]

The re-contextual church also enhances ecumenism by its cross-denominational nature. Fresh Expressions' partners include the Church of England, Church of Scotland, United Reformed Church, Methodist Church, Baptist Union, Salvation Army, and Youth with a Mission (YWAM). The movement promotes a 'mixed economy', whereby inherited and new expressions of church are encouraged to work together.[19] Messy

Church has spread even wider. Launched in 2004 in one Anglican church, by 2013 it had spread into all the main denominations and 14 countries.[20]

'Trinitarian'

> If I am right, and I believe that in this area I may be, the Holy Trinity is beckoning the Emerging Church to model a way of being a spiritual community that reflects the very nature of the Trinitarian Godhead. The Holy Spirit is drawing those seeking missional and contemporary expressions of church for our postmodern consumerist context, to experiment with forms of church drawing on a perichoretic model.[21]

There is a lack of clarity and consensus within re-contextual ecclesiology.[22] The ecclesial reflection that has occurred is predominantly based on relational views of the Trinity, particularly the Social Trinitarianism of Volf, Moltmann and Gunton.[23] Social Trinitarianism is a relatively new and much disputed concept. Holmes cannot trace the term's origin but notes its prevalence since the 1980s. Sexton argues that Moltmann probably initiated the movement when he pitted his social doctrine against psychological models, arguing that the Trinity is best conceived as a fellowship of people, not a solitary individual. Within Social Trinitarianism, the Trinity is seen to exhibit an ideal communal life serving as a model for human collectivity, with implications for human identity, ethics, church and politics. The Trinity's unity, God's oneness, is conceptualized via *perichoresis*, which denotes the mutual indwelling and interpenetration of the persons.[24]

Volf's Social Trinitarianism derives from his criticism of free church ecclesiology, which he believes is insufficiently Trinitarian. Instead of the Trinity, he argues, free church ecclesiology is founded on Christology, in contrast to Eastern Orthodoxy and Western Catholicism. Volf finds deficiencies in both Catholic and Orthodox Trinitarianism, however, criticizing a prioritizing of the one substance over the three persons in Catholic ecclesiology and the asymmetrical relations in the Eastern view, both of which lead to hierarchical structures that Volf finds unsatisfactory. Following Moltmann, Volf posits a Trinitarian ecclesiology built on an egalitarian conception of the Orthodox notion of *perichoresis*. The church, Volf maintains, is to reflect in its communal relationships the mutual giving and receiving that exists within the Trinity.[25]

Accordingly, re-contextual proponents have adopted Social Trinitarianism to promote egalitarian conceptions of church. Jones' pursuit of 'flat church' epitomizes this pursuit. Jones warns that the emerging church movement lacks the necessary depth of theological reflection to be both sustained and developed. He contends that critical engagement with Molt-mann's relational ecclesiology could provide the intellectual resources necessary for this development. He concludes that Moltmann's vision for a church that is formed by and reflects the *perichoretic* love of the Trinity provides a robust foundation for egalitarian communities of love and mutuality.[26]

Other re-contextual authors emphasize the church's participation in the Trinity's life. Ward's foundational ecclesial concept is Paul's 'in Christ' motif in its Trinitarian setting. The church is formed as believers are brought into the Trinitarian communion through their union with Christ. For Ward, *perichoresis* connotes a divine dance, within which the dancers do not just move around each other but within and through each other. The Holy Spirit incorporates believers into this dance such that the church becomes a visible echo of Trinity's relations. Prioritizing participation in the life of the 'liquid Trinity', through believers' connection to Christ, grants the flexibility for new ways of being church beyond institutionally-bound traditions by recognizing that believers are 'in Christ' both when they worship and celebrate together *and* when what they do and say in the wider world is directed by Christ's Spirit and in accord with his character and life. The church's mission involves participation in God's self-sending, through the Son and Holy Spirit, into the world.[27]

Similarly, Moynagh draws on Gunton's writings to highlight the mutual interdependence and interrelationship within the Godhead, main-taining that this does not mean that the Trinity is a model that the church copies but a life that the church participates in. That said, Moynagh's ecclesiology incorporates modelling as well as participation. He argues that the church is constituted by its participation in the Trinity's 'peri-choretic dance' and the mutual giving and receiving within the church's life is to reflect the Trinity's relations. Moynagh's Trinitarian conception of the church provides the foundation for his relational view of church, wherein the church's essential nature consists of four sets of relationship: the church's relationship with God (up); believers' relationships with each other (in); the church's relationship with the wider world (out), and the local church's connection with the wider church (of).[28] These relation-ships, he argues, are rooted in the church's call to reflect God's life in its own:

The [church's] relationship with God is modelled on the Father's giving to the Son (Matt. 28.18) and the Son's obedience to the Father (John 8.28–9). The relationship with the world is participation in God's mission through the Spirit. Fellowship within the gathering reflects the mutual love of the divine persons.[29]

The language of *Mission-Shaped Church* shares this relational framework, rooting the four relational trajectories in the four marks of the church conveyed through the Nicene Creed: the church is one (in), holy (up), catholic (of), and apostolic (out). A Trinitarian foundation is implicit, particularly in relation to the 'in' component; the report asserts that relationships within the church are to model the oneness and diversity of the persons of the Trinity.[30]

Murray Williams takes it as read that God is not an individual but a 'team'. He maintains that Western theology has not paid sufficient attention to the relational nature of God's being until recently and explores the implications of this for the church; ministry models based on the individual pastor or leader, for example, are not just unwise and ineffective but fail to reflect God's modus operandi and *esse*. Frost also contends that the interaction between the Trinitarian persons provides a model for the Christian community, noting that believers participate in the Trinity as co-heirs with Christ.[31]

The influence of relational views of the Trinity within re-contextual authors' ecclesial reflections is matched by empirical research evidencing the contribution of Social Trinitarianism to re-contextual communities. Based on their qualitative research into the ideas and practices of leaders and attendees of emerging churches, mainly in the USA, Marti and Ganiel maintain that 'Emerging Christians think of God as a community, seeing their lives with others as reflecting the nature of God.'[32] In the UK, Peter Holmes has documented the influence of Social Trinitarianism on the Christian community to which he belongs. He observes that the community's belief in a relational Trinity has led, for instance, to the introduction of programmes that have no ulterior goal than to develop relationships. Not every meeting, he argues, needs to be for discipleship or teaching or evangelism. Rather building community is an end in itself, and a vital one if the church is to take seriously its call to reflect Trinitarian relationships in its own interpersonal connections.[33]

Alongside drawing on Social Trinitarianism, re-contextual authors express dissatisfaction with certain aspects of this concept. Jones maintains that Moltmann's ecclesiology is overly idealistic and anthropologically naive. Ward is critical of idealized conceptions of church resulting from a Social Trinitarian ecclesial foundation. Moynagh criticizes Volf for relegating mission to the church's periphery. He complains that the Trinity's inner communion, and thus the church's internal life, tends to be prioritized over God's self-giving missionary activity, and thus the church's mission. He argues that, *contra* Volf, since self-giving, and thus mission, is at the heart of the Trinity, mission is central to the church's life too; when the church gives itself in mission, it participates in God's self-giving. Volf himself notes limitations in viewing the Trinity as a model for church. God is not a human community and the exact nature of God as Trinity remains a mystery that can only be partially grasped. Therefore, conceptions of the Trinity can only be applied analogously to the church.[34]

Despite these caveats and concerns, Social Trinitarianism is central to the ecclesial reflection undertaken by re-contextual thinkers. The ecclesiology that I promote in Part 2 of this book is a direct response to this component of re-contextual ecclesiology. As I elucidate in Chapter 5, Social Trinitarianism is a problematic foundation on which to build.

'Missional'

Re-contextual proponents complain that ecclesiology and missiology have been unhelpfully separated and seek to reconnect the two. As recently as 40 or 50 years ago, church was seen as an irrelevance and distraction to the task of evangelism by organizations such as Young Life, Youth for Christ, and UCCF, whose aim was to present a relevant gospel not a relevant church (whereas now it is increasingly acknowledged that to communicate the former you must cultivate the latter). Re-contextual thinkers argue that Christendom and modernity prompted this disconnection. Murray Williams asserts that, under Christendom, the church and Western world were viewed as synonymous. Mission only occurred outside Christendom's geographical borders and became the role of specialists, separating mission from church. More ominously, he observes, mission sometimes involved violence and coercion. Christendom also led to an over-focus on church members, which is still a problem today. Moynagh agrees, claiming that the church became over-capitalized, clergy-dominated and acquired too many buildings, which take time and resources to maintain, leaving people tired and disillusioned. Despite claiming to exist for the benefit of non-members, the church has dedicated most of its resources to maintaining itself. Why, Moynagh asks, would those outside the church feel welcome?[35]

Ward maintains that modernity affected this detachment of mission from church. Churches assimilated into modernity often reflect the values of modernist social clubs, wherein members put their time and effort into keeping the club going, pay little regard to non-members and, through this, find a place of security and significance. He also blames the impact of Christian youth work. Fear of dark influences within the wider world led evangelicals to create a separate subculture, drawing on certain contemporary youth culture forms, like popular music and festivals, but Christianizing these to make them 'safe'. This alternative subculture separates Christian teenagers from their faith-sabotaging non-Christian peers, with outreach consisting of brief forays to encourage non-Christians to join the Christian haven. But even in outreach, he laments, fear leads inherited churches to espouse evangelistic ideals and then reject the very young people they claim to want to reach. Ward concludes that, reversing Jesus' parable of the lost sheep, rather than leave the 99 to look for the one, the church puts most of its efforts into maintaining the one (the proportion of the population involved in church) and ignores the 99 who are lost. The result is one pampered sheep, who comes to church meetings, while no impact is made on the wider world.[36]

Re-contextual authors and practitioners seek to reconnect the church with its mission. Mission, they contend, should be at the heart of ecclesiology, not the periphery. The influence of missiologists such as Bosch and Newbigin is notable in this regard. Bosch notes that the word 'mission' originally referred to the Father's sending of the Son, and the Father and Son's sending of the Spirit. In the sixteenth century, its meaning shifted and mission was characterized by faith propagation, founding new churches, and conversion. Since the 1950s, missiologists have sought to re-root the concept of mission in God's being and acts. The Latin term *missio Dei* (mission of God) is now commonly used to denote mission as the church's participation in God's self-sending. *Mission-Shaped Church*'s theological rationale for 'missionary church', for example, begins with an exploration of *missio Dei* and the church's role within this. Frost explores the practical implications of the *missio Dei* paradigm, criticizing the church for hoping that, if it concentrates on building an internally orientated community, characterized by mutual encouragement and support, mission will flow naturally from that community. This, he argues, is the wrong way around. Rather, when believers unite in mission, community follows. When believers focus on themselves, mission gets overlooked, and the quality of the community is diminished.[37]

Missiology has also impacted the re-contextual movement through the notion of centre-set church. The centre-set model aims to maintain the Christian distinctives of the church group, while making entry easy for non- or new-believers, by encouraging people to move towards the centre, which is Christ. There are no boundaries per se, so everyone is welcome. More established Christians, particularly church leaders, do their best to live faithfully to their Christian calling, setting an example others can emulate. Discipline is not absent but is implemented relationally, with the person's relationship to Christ always in view. A person who visits a weekly gathering and/or has not professed faith in Christ would be treated differently to someone who has been a professing Christian for a while and/or has a leadership role.[38]

The re-contextual church is thus missional. However, the exact nature of the church's mission is disputed, particularly the role and validity of evangelism. Some are reticent to recruit others. For others, the problem is the word 'evangelism', not the concept. McLaren argues that in his US context the word 'evangelism' carries associations with the pressure created by street evangelists and the inauthenticity of tele-evangelists.[39] Clapp argues that, because of the influence of modernity, traditional evangelism (and apologetics) is construed as 'intellectual combat, rational debate, dialectical duelling'.[40] Finney notes, contrarily, that it has strong associations with stadium evangelism, which many see as unthinking, aggressive, fundamentalist and crude.[41] Moynagh affirms the centrality of evangelism but notes that there has been a shift from decision-based to process-based evangelism within Western Christianity. He cites Warren's observation that the 'evangelistic appeal' has changed from 'I want you to get up out of your seats and come forward now' to 'we invite you to join a group that will be exploring the Christian faith over the coming weeks'.[42] The Fresh Expressions movement also emphasizes evangelism, affirming that the Five Marks of Mission are: proclaiming the good news of the kingdom; teaching, baptizing and nurturing new believers; loving service; bringing justice; and creation care.[43]

Another area of contention within the re-contextual movement's missional focus is the Homogenous Unit Principle. I address this topic below in relation to the re-contextual church's focus on incarnational ministry.

'Holistic'

Clark notes that in his early low-church experience, liturgical practices were seen as irrelevant at best and 'religious', therefore inauthentic, at worst. Conversely, liturgical worship has been central to the evangelistic growth and spiritual formation of his current church community.[44] Re-contextual authors see this anti-sacramentalism as a symptom of the church's assimilation into modernity, which led to over elevating the cerebral and sidelining the physical. In contrast, the re-contextual movement seeks to recapture the holistic worldview of the Bible. The ancient traditions of liturgy, sacraments and spiritual disciplines are central to this. Habits, especially spiritual disciplines, are essential for character formation, thus discipleship. The sacraments embed Christians deeper in God's story and can rescue them from over-activism. Short-term catechisms embed these practices in believers' lives, helping them to sustain their Christian faith in a consumer society.[45]

Ward argues that, alongside distrust of sacramentalism, modernity's elevation of rationality has influenced the church's communication and conception of the gospel, which has been reduced to a series of dogmatic assertions. While effective in facilitating conversion, reducing the gospel to easy-to-memorize statements has diminished the gospel's centrality in whole-life discipleship. Ward calls the church to re-immerse itself in Scripture's grand narrative, particularly the Gospel accounts of Jesus' life, death and resurrection, to recover the fullness of the gospel, which, he stresses, is ultimately constituted by a person, Jesus, not a doctrinal assertion.[46] In line with Ward's concerns, McKnight seeks to reunite the concepts of kingdom and salvation, which he believes have been unhealthily separated. McKnight also highlights the importance of the Bible's grand narrative, urging believers to read individual sections in light of Scripture as a whole.[47]

Re-contextual proponents pursue greater holism through the elimination of false dichotomies that they believe are symptomatic of modernist church culture. They wish to connect discipleship and mission more firmly, and mission and worship. Mobsby asserts that new monasticism facilitates this connection, since it demonstrates a concern for social engagement alongside the desire to be a countercultural community rooted in contemplative spirituality.[48] Frost complains that, when believers are reminded that their main calling is worship, the first thing that comes to mind is singing songs of praise at a corporate gathering. While this is an expression of worship, in Romans 12.1 Paul defines worship as whole-life dedication to God. Therefore, mission must not be isolated from worship, but seen as an expression of worship: 'when I act charitably toward someone, I give glory to God. When I share with someone about my friendship with Jesus, I am worshipping God.'[49]

Re-contextual thinkers promote a more holistic view of identity than the modernist-dualistic conceptions that they see in Western churches, specifically the elevation of abstract intellectualism over concrete experience. Ward highlights the tendency to prioritize cerebral theologizing over lived experience, and assume that the former (ideas) always forms the latter (practice). In contrast, his holistic conception of personhood prompts reflection on the relationship between form and content (humans are embodied so cannot comprehend abstract propositions that are disconnected from tangible life experiences). This has implications for 'third-place' gatherings and Christian practices; venue and form influence the message conveyed. Ward also maintains that theology must be less abstract and more connected to spirituality and practice. Moynagh argues that engaging with Christian practices can be an important first step on an unchurched person's faith journey, promoting the evangelistic model behave–belong–believe alongside the more established belong–believe–behave.[50]

In their desire to eradicate dualisms, re-contextual thinkers raise the issue of God's transcendence and immanence. Many seek to eradicate any duality between the sacred and profane and thereby accentuate God's immanence. Thwaites, for instance, urges the abolition of Greek-influenced dualisms through re-rooting the Christian faith in Hebrew holism. He seeks to reunite work and church, which he believes have been divided by the material and spiritual split that Greek philosophy promoted. Rather than see church in terms of meetings, buildings and programmes, Christians must recapture the vision of the church as God's people dispersed into every sphere of society. Moynagh suggests that highlighting Christianity's immanent aspects, such as its wisdom in relationships, work and finance, without minimizing the transcendent, could help the church to engage with contemporary people. Conversely, Mobsby maintains that contemporary culture is characterized by a search for the transcendent and urges the church to re-explore God's transcendence.[51]

Alongside dispute as to which has been most neglected, God's transcendence or immanence, there is discord within other aspects of the re-contextual church's pursuit of holistic faith. Murray Williams criticizes Thwaites for overlooking the church's role as a countercultural community and accuses him of promoting a Christendom worldview, wherein the church seeks to Christianize society, in contrast to Jesus' mustard-seed approach. Clark values engagement with ancient traditions but warns against a consumerist commodification of these traditions' symbols and practices. The increased emphasis on the kingdom facilitates holistic faith, but some re-contextual streams have been criticized for narrowing their conceptions of the kingdom by underplaying the centrality of Jesus' death and resurrection. In addition, rather than emphasizing the importance of orthopraxy alongside orthodoxy (the aim being right behaviour *and* right beliefs), some imply that restoring the former (orthopraxy) necessarily usurps the latter (orthodoxy). Lastly, tension is created between some re-contextual proponents' desire to be non-religious and the simultaneous aim to reignite ancient (religious) traditions.[52]

Despite this discord, re-contextual thinkers desire to see Western Christians proclaim and embody a more holistic faith, in contrast to what they perceive as modernist tendencies towards reductionism and false dichotomies.

'Emergent'

Moynagh explores Lichtenstein and Plowman's 'emergence' model of change, derived from complexity studies, to explain the re-contextual church's development. Lichtenstein and Plowman define emergence as: the unintended changes that occur within and beyond an organization when organizational members interact, exchange information and act without central coordination. Jones delineates emergence as change induced by 'bottom-up' interaction, rather than hierarchical 'top-down'

communication. In Lichtenstein and Plowman's model, however, interaction between organizational levels is key, regardless of whether the
process is initiated top-down or bottom-up. Indeed, they note, the process
of change will be curtailed unless the organization's leaders support it.[53]

There are four stages within emergence: *dis-equilibrium*, wherein the
current system is disrupted through an opportunity, threat or crisis from
within or outside the system; *amplification*, whereby relatively small
contributions have a magnified impact as a result of the dis-equilibrium;
recombination/self-organization, wherein the system reaches its limits so
is forced to collapse or reorganize – the latter occurring when the agents
restructure to improve the system; *stabilizing feedback*, whereby the
changes are managed without spiralling out of control.[54]

Moynagh maintains that the emergence model's four stages are
exhibited in the re-contextual church's development. First, there was
dis-equilibrium within the Western church through a growing *dis-ease*
with church, particularly in the 1990s–2000s, wherein the emerging
church conversation was influential. Re-contextual proponents often cite
statistics demonstrating church decline and/or observe an unnecessary
and unhealthy disconnection between church and culture.[55] Concurrently,
new experimental expressions of church arose, such as alternative worship
groups and youth congregations. Second, amplification occurred through
the multiplication of networks (such as Urban Expressions), the establishment of the Fresh Expressions team, the spreading of stories (for instance
through the *Encounters on the Edge* series), and key publications (such
as *Mission-Shaped Church*). Third, re-organization may occur through
the ethos of the mixed economy (wherein inherited and fresh expressions
of church co-exist), regional and local cooperation, and the emergence
of a tent-synagogue-temple model, which differs from the 1990s cell–
congregation–celebration model in that it demonstrates greater fluidity,
a more organic structure, and the different levels overlap.[56] Fourth,
stabilization could come through the adaptation of fresh expressions and
other re-contextual groups to both existing denominations (to ensure they
maintain a family resemblance) and their immediate context (to ensure
they are accessible to this context).

Moynagh omits Lichtenstein and Plowman's observation that leaders
and members who reflect critically on the changes that are occurring are
essential for the reorganizational task. The quantity of literature produced and the interaction between different authors, however, has been
central to the re-contextual movement's development. Moreover, Lichtenstein and Plowman argue that leaders enable emergence when they act
as role models, accepting 'tags' that identify them with the changes that
are occurring. This is evident within the re-contextual movement. Tickle
overstates her case by nominating McLaren as the 'Martin Luther' of the

emerging church, for instance, but his influence has been notable. Tickle also notes the impact of Gibbs' critical engagement. Moreover, Rowan Williams has contributed to Fresh Expressions' growth and acceptance.[57]

Interpreting the re-contextual church's development in light of complexity theory does not negate the Spirit's role in leading and guiding the movement. Moynagh draws on Murphy's account of the Spirit's involvement at different levels of reality to promote an understanding of God's guidance that accords with emergence principles. Other re-contextual thinkers emphasize that God is at work in and through the movement. There is an emphasis on *listening to the Spirit* and *discerning what God is doing and joining him*. Within this, the influence of the Pentecostal and Charismatic movements, and John Wimber in particular, is significant. Western churches pursue a more intimate and invasive relationship with the Spirit as a result of these movements.[58]

Gay describes the re-contextual church as 'grassroots', but 'emergent' is a more accurate descriptor.[59] Emergent conveys the conversation's grassroots nature while acknowledging the influence of particular individuals. The movement's emergent nature explains the difficulty in identifying the re-contextual church's key characteristics and why the descriptor 'primarily' is essential – the traits identified are not equally apparent in every segment of the movement. Moreover, it explains why the re-contextual church is simultaneously a movement, conversation and mindset.

'Movement/Conversation/Mindset'

The re-contextual church is not a denomination, geographical location, or discrete set of churches. Re-contextual thinkers deny that they are promoting a new blueprint for church. Instead, they are united by a desire to see Western churches engage more positively, critically and intentionally with their context. Their proposals accord with this aim. Moynagh contends that, rather than 'make it up as they go along', founders of re-contextual churches should draw on others' good practice alongside maintaining flexibility and spontaneity. Others utilize the analogies of planting and seed to express their assertion that new expressions of church need a genetic core that is manifest in different forms depending on the expression's context. Overall, re-contextual thinkers challenge Western Christians to think critically about church planting and growth from the basis of biblical and theological principles, rather than impose a model that has worked well elsewhere.[60]

Since principles unite re-contextual thinkers, the movement is best described as a shared mindset or common heartbeat. This shared mindset is prototypically depicted by the definition afforded in this chapter.[61] As Lakoff notes, however, categorizing is not as simple as specifying shared properties. Human beings are embodied and inculturated, so experience and imagination affect categorization. For instance, people can identify good and bad examples within the same category – a robin is perceived as a better example of a bird than a penguin, which cannot fly.[62] Subjectivity is thus inevitable in any attempt to categorize church expressions – to identify how 're-contextual' they are. A church involved in social justice but reticent about evangelism, for example, would be viewed as more or less 'missional' depending on one's understanding of this term, specifically how central evangelism or social justice are. The ability to categorize is essential for human functioning and academic evaluation, however. Therefore, the subjectivity involved in defining the re-contextual movement does not invalidate the attempt.

Alongside the similarities of a shared mindset, the movement has been formed through conversation. This conversation revolves around contextualization, ecumenism, the Trinity, mission, holism, incarnational ministry, the kingdom, postmodernity, post-Christendom, globalization, network-culture, technology, individualism and consumerism, within which key questions regarding the nature of church, theological method, personal identity and epistemology have been raised. The movement's conversational nature is evident in the interaction between different authors. Moreover, much of the literature produced is co-authored or collections of essays.[63]

The re-contextual church is thus a movement, united by a shared mindset, that has developed through conversation about theology and praxis. I aim to further this conversation by proposing an ecclesiology for the movement that is biblically informed and contextually appropriate.

'Incarnate'

Re-contextual thinkers believe that the church has failed to adapt adequately to recent cultural shifts. Moynagh maintains, for instance, that contra the emphasis on customization within contemporary culture – the specific tailoring of products and services to meet the needs and expectations of particular individuals – the church displays one-size-fits-all thinking. Ward agrees, complaining that the inherited church's monochromic mentality has resulted in a bland and inoffensive diet of middle-of-the-road music and safe spirituality. To be more accessible to those not currently involved in church, Moynagh argues, the church must demonstrate greater variety by contextualizing into individual subcultures and networks; the church must 'go-to-them'.[64] Thus its form should vary according to context. Moreover, expressions of church could meet in 'third-place' venues, such as coffee shops and pubs, to help unchurched people feel more comfortable than they might in traditional church buildings.[65]

Re-contextual advocates turn to the incarnation to support their plea for more specific contextualization.[66] Often, re-contextual authors refer to 'incarnational' as a missional concept without definition, indicating the prevalence of this mode of thinking. When explored, incarnational is usually defined as a call for abiding inculturation based on Jesus' birth into a specific culture.[67] *Mission-Shaped Church* contends:

> The incarnation of God in Christ is unique. Only God can take human nature for our salvation. God in Christ entered the world, taking on a specific cultural identity. The revelation of God for all cultures was embodied in one particular culture. If cultural solidarity with the Palestinian communities of his day was a necessary aspect of Christ's mission, the same principle applies to us.[68]

Moynagh maintains that the church corresponds to Jesus' life and ministry when it: identifies with its specific context; serves this context through modelling the kingdom in community; dies to its own cultural presuppositions and preferences to form a church expression that is appropriate for its context; and infiltrates all spheres of life as an (imperfect) anticipation (sign, instrument and first-fruit) of the ascended Christ's future filling of all things. He distinguishes incarnational ministry ('go and stay') from attractional ('you come to us') and engaged (in which believers 'go into their communities in loving service, often hoping that the people they serve will be drawn into church on Sunday').[69] Using Jesus' incarnation as a model of mission is not, however, without its critics.[70] This is therefore a topic that I explore in more depth in the second part of this book.

The call to 'go-to-them' has resulted in a demographic-specific focus. This focus has been influenced by the missiologist Donald McGavran and his promotion of the Homogenous Unit Principle, which is summarized by his contention that people 'like to become Christians without crossing racial, linguistic, or class barriers'.[71] Demographic-specific churches are seen as more effective than diverse groups at introducing the Christian faith to those with no prior church experience. For example, regarding one particularly effective church, Hunter notes,

> I asked several of the … leaders, 'How do you reach so many people, when most of the other urban neighbourhood churches in your area struggle to survive?' … [they answered] 'You do it here like on any other mission field in the world. Indigenous Christianity engages the

population you want to reach. That means using language they understand, and adapting to their cultural style in all the ways you can.'[72]

Unnecessary cultural barriers hinder people's reception to the Christian
faith; people 'resist becoming Christians because they "don't want to
become like church people" – which they believe is a prerequisite for
becoming a Christian'.[73]

Despite the apparent effectiveness of a demographic-specific approach,
the notion of homogeneous mission is contentious. Moynagh notes that,
for some, this strategy is a 'missional no-go'. Davison and Milbank, for
example, refer to the early church's uniqueness in breaking down walls
of segregation between Jew and Gentile, slave and free, male and female.
They argue that tailoring church to one subculture or age group rebuilds
the walls that early Christianity removed and undermines the reconcili-
atory power of the gospel.[74] Murray Williams affirms such objections. He
agrees that demographic-specific churches undermine the gospel's power
to break down cultural, gender and ethnic barriers, affirming, rather than
challenging, societal fragmentation. Furthermore, discipleship is stunted
when people are only in fellowship with those like them. However, Murray
Williams wryly notes that those objecting to culture- or age-specific
expressions of church usually belong to homogeneous churches themselves through default rather than design. 'All welcome' is the strapline
but, he complains, most inherited churches represent a narrow proportion of society and unintentionally ostracize those who do not fit. Many
working-class believers feel uncomfortable in middle-class church culture
and postmoderns wrestle with the inherited church's modernity.[75]

Murray Williams and Moynagh propose a solution that they believe
facilitates the missional advantages of a culturally-specific approach
while ensuring that the reconciliation that lies at the heart of the gospel
is not undermined: focused-and-connected church. Churches can be
homogeneous, by focusing on a particular subculture, but heterogeneous,
by connecting with the wider church. For instance, demographic-specific
churches could join with other local churches for mission and discipleship.
Similarly, Cray argues that a 'mixed economy' partnership, connecting
fresh expressions of church to their inherited counterparts, can ensure
diversity in unity, rather than greater fragmentation.[76]

The 'go-to-them' approach raises the conundrum that one person's
contextualization is another's heresy and one person's gospel-faithfulness
is another's cultural blindness. While promoting a contextual approach,
re-contextual thinkers recognize that churches can over-assimilate into
their wider culture. Indeed, they criticize the Western church for uncritically imbibing modernist, consumerist and Christendom mindsets.[77]
Rowan Williams notes that to contextualize effectively a dual translation

is required: of the gospel into the context and the context into the gospel; 'to translate the good news afresh, it [the church] seeks at the same time to "translate" the world around, to re-locate it in the context of God's new creation'.[78] It is not the context per se that should set a local church's agenda, but rather the transformation that Christ seeks to bring to that place.[79]

Moynagh thus explores the 'limits' of contextualization; what guides the church as it seeks to be faithful to Jesus and accessible to its context? Moynagh maintains that the limits of contextualization are the four interlocking relationships that constitute the church's essence. These are: the church's relationship with God (up); the relationships between those within the local church community (in); the church's relationship with the wider world (out); and the church's relationship with the historical and universal church (of). Local churches will be accessible to, but not assimilated into, their context when they: engage with God through prayer and Scripture; sharpen and challenge each other within their own community; observe God's work within wider culture and assess their message's impact; and learn from their contemporaries in other churches and historical forbears.[80]

In addition, Moynagh draws on Stephen Bevans' six models of contextualization, arguing that all six are needed since they limit and counterbalance each other.[81] Bevans' first model is the 'translation model'. This is similar to a 'kernel-and-husk' approach, wherein the husk of the gospel, the language and illustrations used, can be contextualized, but the unchanging kernel of the gospel's core, usually understood as propositional truths, must be preserved. However, since the core of the gospel is a person, Moynagh seeks to put Jesus at the centre rather than propositions about him. Propositions are important – through communicating truths about Jesus, they help believers to walk with the real Christ, not one of their imaginations – but a helpful proposition in one context can be confusing and unhelpful in another. As Newbigin asserts, even a statement such as 'Jesus is Lord' is dependent on how a culture views the concept 'lord'.[82] Moreover, highlighting the shame involved in Jesus' crucifixion in a Japanese context is more important than explaining Western notions of penal substitution, for example. The translation model is most relevant in evangelism, Moynagh maintains, since it challenges churches to consider the gospel content of their message. Its weakness is that it implies that Jesus must be taken to a new context, whereas he will already be at work there through his Spirit.

Second, the 'anthropological model' assumes that God is at work in a new context. Therefore believers should learn from the culture how to present the gospel within it. This model encourages re-contextual churches to examine their context, looking for what God is already doing and how they can join him. However, Moynagh maintains that taking this model in isolation from the others would be too optimistic and overlook each context's fallenness.

Third, the 'praxis model' consists of a cycle of action and reflection. Moynagh argues that this model is particularly helpful when new contextual churches are being launched since, at each stage, the team should reflect on their experience before taking the next step. However, reflection on past experience must go hand-in-hand with an openness to outside input and new ways of thinking and doing.

Fourth, the 'subjective (or transcendental) model' focuses on the individual's subjective experience of faith. Moynagh maintains that this model encourages each individual to reflect on the authenticity of their own relationship with Jesus, rather than rely on their leader or church founder's faith. However, taking the model on its own is overly relativistic. Are all experiences of faith equally valid? If not, how can the validity of different experiences of faith be determined?

The fifth model is the 'conversation model' (or 'synthetic model'), which seeks to synthesize the previous four models and learn from people in different contexts. A re-contextual church can benefit from conversations with more inherited and traditional churches, for instance, and learn from their practices and beliefs. However, at times, he notes, it is necessary to choose between different perspectives rather than assume that they can sit happily together.

Lastly, the 'countercultural model' emphasizes that every context needs to be challenged by the gospel's healing and liberating power. This model is particularly pertinent for disciple-making, since discipleship must challenge cultural norms when they contravene kingdom values. However, in isolation from the other models, this model overlooks the positive features of each context.

Moynagh concludes that by utilizing these models and the framework of the church's four interconnected relationships (up, in, out and of), the church will be able to adapt appropriately to its context while maintaining its distinctive Christian identity.

'The Kingdom'

Re-contextual proponents strive to see the kingdom invade the here and now. Moreover, they maintain that the church's nature and role must be understood in reference to the kingdom. However, as Moynagh notes, different authors envisage the relationship between the church and kingdom in different ways. At one end of the spectrum, Moynagh observes, is the 'church-shaped kingdom' view that was common in the Christendom era, particularly the nineteenth and early twentieth centuries. In this view, the church is God's agent in extending the kingdom and so mission consists of extending the church. Moynagh argues that a 'church-shaped kingdom' conception reduces mission to evangelism and overlooks the Spirit's presence outside the church. Some accuse *Mission-Shaped Church* of presenting the church's relationship with the kingdom in this way. Moynagh argues that the book overlooks the church's ability to receive gifts from God from the wider world, which can happen when external groups make the church aware of social and ecological issues, for example. McKnight promotes an equation of church and kingdom, arguing that when both concepts are properly located in their 'now' and 'not yet' eschatological framework, the differences between them dissolve.[83]

The other extreme Moynagh identifies is 'world-shaped kingdom', which was popular in the 1960s and 1970s, especially in the World Council of Churches. A 'world-shaped kingdom' approach focuses on the Spirit's kingdom-bringing presence outside the church; the church must simply recognize the kingdom's growth and help others notice its presence. This view is reflected in Loisy's provocative complaint that 'Jesus proclaimed the kingdom of God, and what came was the Church.'[84] In rejecting a 'church-shaped kingdom' approach, Moynagh warns, some emerging church proponents have moved too far towards the 'world-shaped kingdom' extreme. This warning is echoed by Shogren, who argues that the emerging church's kingdom-focus, at least in the stream that McLaren figureheads, exhibits an over-realized eschatology, a reduction of the kingdom to a this-worldly socio-political reality, a denial of in/out boundaries, and a refusal to speak of an end-time judgement. Indeed, some re-contextual authors' emphasis on the kingdom's existence outside the church pushes towards universalism. Rollins, for example, argues that in their engagement with other religions, Christians should endeavour to learn, not teach. Such a view is problematic, Moynagh maintains; the church has a unique relationship with Jesus that the wider world does not have. The church is to not just embrace the kingdom's presence when it finds it, but prophetically denounce its absence and point to salvation in Christ its king.[85]

The third possibility Moynagh identifies is 'kingdom-shaped church'. In this view, the church is seen as a sign, foretaste and instrument of the kingdom, while being alert to Spirit-brought kingdom traces outside the church. As a foretaste of the kingdom, through its Spirit-empowered and Jesus-centred life, the church pre-empts the eventual reconciliation of creation to God and thus mediates the future to the world, but it does so imperfectly. As Zizioulas asserts, the church has 'its roots in the future and its branches in the present'.[86] Therefore, although the church shares similarities with the world and can learn from it, it has a distinctive contribution to offer – Jesus and the reconciliation, forgiveness, new life and restoration that he brings. The Spirit is active in the world but, as Christ's body, the church has a unique connection to Jesus that the world does not have. Moynagh contends that this last view warns against the two extremes of either neglecting the church to focus on the kingdom – which overlooks the church's distinct role in constituting, representing and extending the kingdom – or overlooking the kingdom's presence in the world.[87]

Other re-contextual proponents affirm the church's uniqueness while encouraging believers to join God's work in the world. Ward maintains that the church has an active role in mediating Christ's presence. In a parents-and-tots group, for instance, the message of Jesus can flow both inside and out from the group through each person's network of relationships. Ward also contends that, though the development of faith beyond the Christian community may well be limited, the church must identify and engage with what the Spirit is doing in popular culture. The church should be alert to the theological flow in song lyrics, film plots, advertising, and so on. For instance, Iris DeMent's *Lifeline* album contains stripped-down renditions of old American gospel songs and hymns. Despite DeMent's sleeve-note assertion that she is not religious, Ward notes that she has found a haven in the lyrics and musicality of these old hymns. Those listening may also experience a lifeline of sorts; why can these lyrics not mediate divine encounter just because they are sung outside the Christian community? For other re-contextual proponents too, recognition of God's work outside the church prompts an emphasis on listening to the Spirit and thus the slogan: seeing what God is doing and joining him.[88]

Re-contextual proponents agree that, as a *sign, instrument* and *foretaste* of the kingdom, the church is called to bring the kingdom into the present. They also agree that the church does so imperfectly. Accordingly, re-contextual thinkers rail against idealistic, abstracted blueprints of church that deny the weaknesses and complexities of real ecclesial life. Ward complains that too often theoretical models of the ideal church are elevated while the church's historical reality is overlooked. This historical reality, he notes, is always imperfect and provisional, in need of reflective evaluation and correction. In its imperfection, however, Christ's presence through the Spirit is manifested in the church's life.[89]

'Postmodern'

Although the re-contextual movement is a response to cultural change, its proponents do not simply desire to make Christianity more accessible in its new context. They believe that influences such as modernity, consumerism and Christendom have distorted the Western church, which therefore needs refounding. They seek to embed the Western church more deeply in its biblical, Christ-centred foundations and embody this message in their specific context. Ward, for instance, is critical of what he refers to as 'solid church': church inculturated into 'solid modernity'. Solid modernity is Bauman's term for the rational, production-focused, fixed, organized culture that displaced the medieval feudal system and which is epitomized by the car company Ford. Solid church internalized modern values, Ward argues, with problematic results. For example, reflecting the principles of a tightly managed production line, within solid church, attendance at church services is the main indicator of faithfulness – the congregation is king. Size indicates success and thus church planting increases influence and 'market share'. Solid modernity (especially its product standardization) also explains solid church's one-size-fits-all mentality, which inhibits the church's ability to contextualize into different subcultures. Moreover, Ward complains, solid church reflects the values of modernist social clubs, wherein members put their time and effort into keeping the club going, pay little regard to non-members and, through this, find a place of security and significance.[90]

Ward concedes that solid church needed to adapt to modernity to be relevant to its context. However, he complains that modernist churches have reacted uncritically and defensively to cultural changes rather than thoughtfully and positively. Since geographical churches are no longer the hubs of community life, and because the changes have induced insecurity, solid churches have unwittingly remoulded into heritage sites, refuges, and nostalgic communities, none of which are well placed to influence society beyond their barricaded doors. He urges the church to change critically and intentionally to its new context, rather than unwittingly. For Ward, changing critically, and thus effectively, requires appropriate inculturation into what he, following Bauman, refers to as liquid modernity.[91]

Liquid modernity (or postmodernity) developed in the 1960s and 1970s, although its roots trace back to the early 1900s.[92] Ward posits Sweet's definition:

> If the Modern Era was a rage for order, regulation, stability, singularity, and fixity, the Postmodern Era is a rage for chaos, uncertainty, otherness, openness, multiplicity and change. Postmodern surfaces are not landscapes but wavescapes, with the waters always changing and the surfaces never the same. The sea knows no boundaries.[93]

Although many, like Ward, see postmodernity as central to the cultural shift that has occurred, a number believe that it has been overemphasized. Corcoran argues that cultural factors such as globalization, connectivity, technology, decentralization, the information explosion, and interdependence are more significant than their philosophical postmodern cohorts. Drane questions whether the quest to understand postmodernity has been successful, or even useful. Murray Williams suggests that, although postmodernity is often hailed as the largest philosophical shift since the Enlightenment, the post-Christendom shift is more missiologically significant. Tickle affirms the impact of the postmodern philosophers Lyotard, Foucault, Wittgenstein and Derrida, but asserts that the term 'postmodern' has been rendered almost useless by the 'collective tendency to use it as a dumping bin for all those incongruities and disparate shifts we could not quite bring ourselves to analyze'. Sweet et al. agree that cultural postmodernity precedes its philosophical component.[94]

Despite their reticence towards postmodernity as a label, re-contextual thinkers highlight the cultural changes that are often collated under this term. These include a preference for: narrative above proposition; paradox, mystery and holism over dichotomy, simplism and dualism; embodied experience over abstract rationalism; orthopraxy over orthodoxy; organic, egalitarian spontaneity above fixed, hierarchical institutionalism. Postmodernity is also characterized by scepticism, pessimism, relativism, playfulness, the loss of confidence in objectivity, and a distrust of metanarratives (which it believes are oppressive, even though, ironically, postmodernity is governed by unacknowledged metanarratives of its own).[95] Central to these changes lies a critique of modernist epistemology, wherein modernism's objective 'I' gives way to the fact that there are many subjective 'I's', whose understanding is therefore relativized.[96] Corcoran notes that this leads either to epistemic humility or antirealism. Philosophical realism contends that things exist apart from people's conception of them. Antirealism asserts that things are created by a person's language and lack an ontological existence of their own. A softer form of antirealism is social-constructive antirealism, which acknowledges that things have an objective reality but denies that it is possible to know them as they are aside from each individual's perception of them. Re-contextual thinkers range from social-constructive antirealists such as Rollins, who are the minority, to those, such as Corcoran, who observe that it is unnecessary to adopt antirealism to acknowledge that human beings are finite and constrained by their context and limitations. Corcoran notes that the notion of epistemic humility, which he promotes, is present within the Christian doctrine of God as the creator and human beings as mere creatures.[97]

Re-contextual thinkers criticize its critics for reducing the movement to McLaren and postmodern epistemology.[98] This may contribute to some authors' reluctance to use the term 'postmodern' – not to deny that many view postmodernity as an ill-defined and overused label. Moreover, the cultural changes have not arisen from philosophical thinking alone, even primarily. Rather the rise in technology, consumerism and globalization are decisive factors. That said, despite the assertions of many that post-modernity is passé, there is as yet no agreed terminological successor.

'Post-Christendom'

Post-Christendom is also a cultural shift that re-contextual thinkers engage with. Murray Williams argues that, while the two are intricately connected, post-Christendom should be neither subsumed under postmodernity nor equated with it. Indeed, he argues that the Christendom-post-Christendom shift is more missiologically significant than its modernity-postmodernity counterpart. Gibbs traces the diminishment of Christendom to the First World War, but the seeds of its demise were unwittingly sown through the Reformation in that, though the Reformers did not intentionally oppose Christendom, their reform resulted in fragmentation. Dissident Anabaptists, who rejected the Christendom system, were also influential. Postmodernity has also contributed to Christendom's decline; the postmodern distrust of metanarratives casts doubt over the church's authoritative claims. Despite its diminishment, aspects of Christendom still remain, such as the influence of Christianity on British laws, the Queen's position as Supreme Governor of the Church of England, and the maintaining of bishops in the House of Lords. Nevertheless, re-contextual advocates agree that Western society is now post-Christendom, which they generally perceive as a good thing, and they urge the church to adapt accordingly.[99]

The changes that re-contextual thinkers propose are often seen as reversing the negative effects of Christendom, which are presented as manifold. Frost claims that when Emperor Constantine adopted Christianity as the imperial religion, the church changed from a marginalized, persecuted, subversive, dynamic, spiritual and revolutionary community to a static institution. Murray Williams maintains that the Christendom shift represented a triumph of the state over Christianity and resulted in: forcible conversion; crusades; discrepancies between the prescribed beliefs Christians were instructed to have and their actual beliefs; syncretism with pagan festivals, rituals and beliefs; the exclusion (at least marginalization) of other religions; nominalism; totalitarianism, wherein dissenting views were not tolerated; the shift from participating to spectating in church; the decline in morality as doctrine usurped ethics (belief became more important than behaviour); the elevation of the Old Testament above the New Testament; the meshing of church and state; an altered view of baptism; a diminishing emphasis on mission; controlling, hierarchical leadership and a lay–priestly divide; the reduction of God's kingdom to something 'coterminous with the state church or relegated to the future';

a distortion of the cross, which went from being a sign of self-sacrifice and love to imperial power; and an emphasis on Jesus' divinity to the expense of his humanity, such that worshipping Jesus was detached from following him.[100]

Frost and Hirsch are similarly denunciatory; they decry the centrality of buildings, hierarchical leadership, over-elevation of the pastor–teacher role, and over-institutionalization of Christendom churches. Hirsch also criticizes what he perceives as an unhealthy pursuit of safety and security within Christendom. Gelder contrasts what he calls the 'Christendom maintenance model' with the missional paradigm that he promotes. Moynagh urges the church to follow Jesus into every crevice of society, influencing the world subversively, rather than follow the Christendom way of gaining power and influence. Mobsby laments the hierarchical and centralized power structures of Christendom churches, asserting that this model does not accord with the biblical notion of church.[101]

Not all re-contextual thinkers are as critical of Christendom. Sudworth warns that the post-Christendom shift poses a threat to the church's ability to engage in public worship.[102] Re-contextual thinkers' evaluation of Christendom is thus not beyond critique. Murray Williams' negative stance towards Augustine, for example, invites further scrutiny and Randall protests that Murray Williams overlooks the wider UK free church trad-ition, as if only Anabaptists sought to influence society from the margins.[103] Overall, though, re-contextual authors see post-Christendom as an oppor-tunity to exploit more than a loss to lament.

'Consumerist'

Intricately connected to modernity and postmodernity is the paradoxical, globalizing, meaning-generating, desire-based, reality-shifting, inequality-enhancing, economic and cultural phenomena 'consumerism'. Miles notes that consumerism is hard to define but that it consists of a way of life, a philosophy, even a religion, rather than just economic behaviour, which re-contextual proponents affirm.[104] Sine suggests that the West's primary metanarrative, at least in affluent suburbs, is a 'story born of the Enlightenment, which defines the good life as ever expanding levels of individual consumer choice and the endless quest for more'.[105]

Miles asserts that consumerism developed following the Second World War and is intricately connected with Fordism: 'the ideas and principles of the American industrialist Henry Ford, who is generally accredited as the pioneer of the modern mass-production system, notably in the guise of the car assembly line'.[106] More recently, he claims, the size-orientated homogeneity, uniformity and predictability of Fordism have given way to the scope-focused heterogeneity, diversity and flexibility of post-Fordism. This Fordism to post-Fordism shift has been linked to the modernity to postmodernity move and accords with re-contextual thinkers' criticism of modernist church culture for its focus on size, one-size-fits-all ethos, and predictability. In contrast, re-contextual churches promote wide scope (communities of Christians that infiltrate every crevice of society), diversity (church expressions that are pertinent to their context), and risk-taking experimentalism.[107] Thus *unhealthy assimilation into consumerist culture* is a complaint made both by re-contextual thinkers against their inherited church counterparts and vice versa.[108]

Despite claims to the contrary, re-contextual proponents do not encourage the church to adopt consumerism uncritically but rather affirm those aspects that they see as compatible with biblical revelation, while criticizing those that they perceive as incompatible. They want the church to be accessible to those enmeshed within a consumerist culture without diluting the demands of discipleship.[109] Some, however, are more negative towards consumerism than others. Clark contends that consumerism separates belief from practice and its 'perverted liturgy', by which he presumably means the associated habits and worldview consumerism forms, has led to faith and church being privatized. Consumerism has also prompted blueprint ecclesiologies that are discarded when the hoped-for results fail to materialize. Instead of trying to build an ideal church, he warns, Christians should endeavour to build a deep church that is rooted in the past and engaged in the present. Clark also suggests that churches that meet in third places, such as cafés or pubs, are pandering to consumerism. The church building is the best third place, he claims, being one of the few places set apart from both consumerist markets and the politically defined state.[110]

Consumerism's adverse consequences, Clark contends, originate from the redirection of people's desires away from God and towards things. This 'misplaced, misdirected desire reveals our deepest longings for transcendence, justice, and self-transformation', but when people do not allow God to meet this desire they become 'superficial, picking and choosing beliefs, shaping them around ... [their] ... particular practices'.[111] Some thus believe that the recent revival of ancient forms reflects a consumerist tendency to pillage traditions for their symbolic content and then repackage them without their original meaning. Others believe that new monasticism, for example, offers a countercultural remedy to consumerism – although proponents of new monasticism warn against watering down the tradition. Cray argues that, in contrast to the corroding of commitment, individualism, counterfeit spirituality, and un-Christlike character formation that consumerism brings, new monasticism can provide the accountability, habits and commitment to enable healthy spiritual formation. Moreover, in contrast to the passive consumption of consumerism, new monastic communities involve interdependence, with everyone having an important role to play.[112]

Mission-Shaped Church is more positive than Clark about the opportunities consumerism affords. The authors urge the church to be accessible to those living within this culture; the church should be *in* consumer culture but not *of* consumerism. People's identity is based not on what they produce but on what they consume and society's central value has shifted from progress to choice. Therefore, one-size-no-longer-fits-all. Some people may not be able to attend church on Sunday.[113] In addition:

> No one kind of worship can attract, much less hold, a major proportion of the varied population of this country. The Church will be able to reconnect with both society and individuals through a pattern of diversity and unity, rooted in the triune, endlessly creative, life of God. It is a pattern that looks ahead to the diversity, brought from all corners of the earth, that will be celebrated in God's eschatological reality.[114]

This view of consumerism contributes to *Mission-Shaped Church*'s endorsement of a demographic-specific approach to church. *Mission-Shaped Church* is also more positive about third-place expressions of church, arguing that the table fellowship within café church, for example, is based on Jesus' ministry. It notes, however, that there are relatively few expressions of church in secular venues. The notion of third-place is also supported by Rollins, who asserts that it is easier for people to discuss their lives honestly and openly in cafés and pubs than in church buildings due to the connotations of each location.[115] Overall, there is a consensus among re-contextual thinkers that consumerism is a pervasive feature of contemporary Western culture and an issue that churches cannot ignore.

'Technologized'

Connected to the Fordist rise of consumerism and the post-Fordist shift is the development of new technology, which had provided both opportunities and challenges. Mobsby contends that the combination of consumerism and information technology has prompted a new group of spiritual seekers, who seek spirituality within the hyper-real – 'an experience of transcendence over and above the real'. These seekers increasingly look for spirituality outside organized religions, including Christianity.[116] Gelder argues that technology has affected locality. People now live in both spatial and virtual spheres, which has led to the deterritorialization of culture; people's identities have become unmoored from the localities and historical norms that identity used to be embedded in. People can reinforce their desired identity through engaging online with those who share their assumptions and worldview, leading to self-reinforcing tribalism. Moreover, the Internet provides free and secret access to pornography and a potentially damaging overload of information. The image-reality disjunction and blurring of personal boundaries that can result from applications such as Facebook have also provoked concern.[117]

Others highlight the opportunities that new technology brings. Tickle and Gay compare the influence of technology on today's church with the printing press' impact on the Reformation. New technology, Gay argues, has facilitated: *content creation*, wherein believers create their own worship resources, alongside utilizing those produced in the wider church body; *meaning generation*, inasmuch as the fusion of modern technology and ancient traditions creates new meaning, it does not just repackage the old; and *new expressions of catholicity*, through online sharing of resources and ideas. Moynagh is also positive about the possibilities technological developments afford. The church, he contends, should inhabit the 'space of flows' – connective technology, such as social media, mobile phones, and so on. He maintains that, although people question the legitimacy of online worshipping communities, virtual relationships can be as meaningful as those formed offline. He is even willing to explore how Communion could be taken in this context. Sweet argues that social networking sites can enhance people's connections with others. He also notes that the Internet provides a unique opportunity to share the Christian message, but questions how well this platform is used.[118]

Since new technology generates both opportunities and threats, re-contextual thinkers pursue informed engagement that avoids uncritical embracement, on the one hand, or knee-jerk rejection, on the other. For instance, they note that local church communities offer a remedy to the isolation and identity-fragmentation that social media exacerbates, while recognizing the value of Christians participating in online social webs. As Gelder observes:

> The question, who is my neighbor? is now much more complex. It is not enough merely to focus on an immediate geographic neighborhood. If one does, one will likely discover that the neighbors' tightest relational networks may span hundreds or thousands of miles. Building relationships with neighbors and participating in their lives and living space must engage virtual, as well as physical, forms of community.[119]

In addition, both re-contextual proponents and critics note that medium matters. Critics make this assertion to promote inherited forms of church, arguing that altering the medium away from traditional modes distorts the message. Re-contextual thinkers counter that such criticisms are blind to the effect that traditional forms have had on the Christian message. Sudworth provocatively contends, if 'form and content are inextricably intertwined, what does the form of the inherited Church tell us about the content of … [its] … gospel? Cynics could be forgiven for answering that this gospel is white, middle-class, middle-aged, literate, introverted and male!' Nevertheless, re-contextual thinkers are aware that, as Christians experiment with technology, they must do so critically, examining the inextricable connection between medium and message.[120]

'Globalized'

Consumerism, new technology, and unprecedented migration have contributed to globalization, which has further integrated and disintegrated the global community. Regarding integration, Sine notes that 'the young all over the planet are wearing the same jeans, drinking the same soda and watching the same MTV'.[121] Sweet asserts that:

> For the first time in human history, the world is forging an awareness of our existence as a single entity, a *Unum Humanum*. The people of Planet Earth are having the same experience at the same time around the same events and the same people creating a planetary consciousness. Each person with a screen now has the whole world at his or her fingertips. No wonder globalization has been called 'the most ambitious collective experiment ever undertaken by the human race.'[122]

Regarding disintegration, Sweet notes a connection between globalization and increasing tribalism. Gelder observes that, alongside mixing and fusing cultures, globalization highlights cultural variance, creating boundaries based on difference rather than locality.[123]

Alongside the influence of missiology, Eastern Orthodoxy, Western Catholicism, and Latin American Liberation Theology, globalization's impact on the re-contextual movement is evident in the interconnection between the UK movement and its corresponding global (mainly US and Australian) counterparts. Moreover, the plurality of cultures within one locality is cited in support of demographic-specific expressions of church.[124] Re-contextual critics, however, and some within the movement, argue that the church should seek to overcome, through local mixed-culture communities, the fragmentation that often accompanies cultural plurality.[125] Re-contextual proponents identify further positive and negative consequences to globalization. Positively, it can facilitate the sharing of good practice and encourage local Christian communities to consider ways in which they can connect with the global church. Its detriments include environmental damage and economic exploitation. These negative features should compel the church to go 'glocal' – to root itself in its particular locality while demonstrating a concern for global issues.[126]

'Individualized'

Postmodernity has prompted a shift in people's sense of identity; personal identity in postmodernity is more fluid and subjective (nay problematic) than in preceding eras. As economies have developed, Moynagh argues, materialist (or survival) values, such as sustenance, physical security, shelter and so on, have been usurped by post-materialistic (or self-expression) values, leading to changing attitudes towards work, religion, child-rearing, sexual ethics and so forth. In contrast to the dutiful self of yesteryear, the expressive (or post-materialistic) self now dominates society and church; human teleology is understood not in relation to external (or objective) duties, roles and obligations, but as the fulfilment of individual (subjective) desires and experiences. This is not a superficial change, Moynagh notes; rather, human purpose has been realigned: a person's goal is to live authentically out of who they are, so long as they do not hurt anyone, rather than conform to societal, religious, political or generational models or expectations.[127]

Moynagh draws on Taylor to support his contentions. Taylor observes that, although modernity was individualistic, Western culture has individuated further over recent years. In particular, there is an unprecedented prevalence of expressive individualism. Consumerism has contributed to this, but to blame the shift entirely on egoism and hedonism, Taylor contends, misses the point. The main cause is a shift in how 'the good' is perceived. For the first time in history, individual human flourishing has become an ultimate goal in and of itself without the need for allegiance to something beyond this flourishing. Therefore, instead of *inauthentic* conformity to externally prescribed expectations and roles, individual human beings are to live *authentically*, according to their own desires and feelings. Living authentically requires each individual to know who they are so that this authentic self can be released, giving rise to the seemingly contradictory mantras that one must *find, make* and *be* oneself. [128]

Ward explores how this change in personal identity has influenced the Western church with particular reference to sung worship and, connectedly, believers' lived experience of the gospel (or 'operant theology'). He contends that, influenced by modernity, formulations of 'the gospel' consisting of rationalized doctrinal assertions, such as *the cross as a bridge* tract and Four Spiritual Laws, have dominated evangelism. While failing to express the full breadth of the gospel, these simplified presentations have been effective in facilitating conversion. However, Ward contends that this 'espoused theology' of gospel presentations fades into the background in believers' lived expression of the gospel, their operant theology. In contrast to espoused gospel formulations, which focus on forgiveness from sin, believers' operant theology mirrors the contemporary shift in personal identity; in practice, believers focus on subjective personal experience, particularly individual encounter with God, rather than objective propositional statements. Western Christians are drawn to the notion that God has a plan for each individual life and interpret this concept in line with society's shift towards self-enhancement and self-fulfilment.[129]

This move towards a more expressive and experiential conception of faith is reflected in sung worship. Ward observes that, over the last 50 to 60 years, the style and content of worship songs has changed from 'objective' accounts of biblical themes and events, and 'subjective' hymns (focusing on the implications of these themes and events for the worshipper), to 'reflexive' songs, which focus predominantly on the experience of worship itself (with abstract metaphors replacing explicit gospel and biblical content). Encounter with God is the main aim. The adoption and adaptation of the popular music genre by Christian songwriters has contributed to this shift (as exemplified by John Wimber). Form affects content, Ward observes; it is not coincidental that contemporary worship songs often mirror the intimate language of popular music.[130]

Within wider culture, society's shift towards self-expression correlates with a more open desire for spirituality and intimate community. This is seen in the increasing popularity of the New Age movement and the rise of the *spiritual but not religious* mantra. 'Spiritual' (nowadays) refers to an individual's subjective experience of a higher power. The term is juxtaposed with 'religious', which is perceived as institutionally prescribed rules, rituals and dogma that hinder authentic spirituality rather than enhance it. Heelas and Woodhead argue that religious groups that have adapted to this shift, by catering for personalized spiritualities and focusing less on 'oughts', have fared better (in terms of numbers of adherents) than those emphasizing external authority. Marti and Ganiel contend that part of Emerging Christianity's appeal is its accommodation of individuated spiritual paths.[131]

Re-contextual thinkers are wary of over-individualization but recognize that the recent identity shift is an issue that the church must address. Ward, for example, is concerned by the disjunction between the church's espoused (proclaimed) and operant (lived) presentations of the gospel and the overemphasis on reflexive worship songs at the expense of more objective lyrics. He urges the church to expand its conception of the gospel by encompassing the whole of Scripture and refocusing its attention on Christ's life, death and resurrection as recorded in the Gospels. He also implores the church to redress the balance in sung worship to include songs about Jesus alongside those intended to facilitate encounter with him. Ward warns that an overemphasis on experience diminishes believers' ability to encounter God in the mundaneness and challenges of everyday life and mission. Believers end up feeling like run-down batteries needing regular top-ups at experiential worship events. Moreover, darker emotions get sidelined, even though the biblical tradition of lament models faith in suffering and pain. However, while Ward seeks to bring correction, his complaint is not that culture has affected the church per se, but that the church is so often oblivious to this influence. Engaging critically with cultural changes, he argues, enables the church to adapt appropriately while remaining faithful to Christ.[132]

Moynagh urges the church to create freedom for exploration without undermining the central tenets of the Christian faith. Drane criticizes the inherited church for failing to connect with young people's identity search and asserts that visionaries who will step out of the church's current paradigms are needed if a generation of hedonist seekers is to be reached. Gelder contends that, in the midst of people's ontological insecurity, the church needs to offer an alternative perspective on humanity's nature and role, asserting that Christian communities can play a vital role in identity formation. Re-contextual thinkers thus engage with the individualization of society both positively, identifying the opportunities that it affords, and negatively, criticizing the shift's more damaging effects.[133]

'Networked'

Mission-Shaped Church maintains that the importance of location is becoming increasingly subordinated to the rise of networks. People's friendships are more likely to be based around their work network, or common interest, than locality. *Mission-Shaped Church* concludes that, since society is connected through networks, the church should follow suit; neighbourhood and network-based churches, working in collaboration, are needed if every segment of society is to be reached. Moynagh concurs, asserting that churches grow by expanding into networks, which requires contextualization into a network's subculture.[134]

Ward proffers a more radical proposal. Rather than construing the church as primarily a congregation (a gathering of people meeting at a fixed place and time), the church should be seen as a network (a series of relationships and communications) – a 'liquid church'. Church consists of relationships; it is not an institution per se. Informal fellowship with other Christians, through which believers experience Christ, *is* church. Worship and meeting together are important, he notes, as is organization and structure, but they could be decentred. The emphasis should be on *living as Christ's body in the world*, with gatherings arising more informally as the result of a Spirit-filled relational network.[135]

Others are wary of such a fluid approach. Murray Williams recalls his research into organic expressions of church, which he labelled 'deconstructed church'. Before long, though, these churches had deconstructed themselves away. Moynagh agrees with Ward that the church should pursue shared leadership, communication-rich networks rather than top-down, communication-poor hierarchies. However, he, like Murray Williams, notes that liquid churches tend to evaporate into gas. Without a fixed meeting time, relationships become too transient and gatherings too infrequent to build a healthy church community. *Mission-Shaped Church* warns that the shift towards networked communities has brought a corresponding decrease in people's commitment. The church must adapt to changes in societal structure, but challenge decreasing levels of dedication. In addition, networks can connect but also fragment, include but also exclude. Some people are in several networks but others are not in any. For instance, those living in poverty can end up excluded due to a lack of transportation and technological resources.[136]

Ward agrees that structure is important, but argues that no particular structure is, or ever has been, the chief constituent of church. The nature and quality of a network's communication flows and processes are more integral to its success than its structure. Therefore the church's primary focus should be on believers' relationships and activities, not the weekly gathering. Structures should be flexible, he argues, to serve these relationships, not detract from them. Moreover, instead of the church gathering being the location in which everyone ministers, Christians must recognize that the church emerges as every believer ministers in their own context and a network of communication and relationship is formed between them. For too long, Ward complains, the focus has been on what Christians do while they are in the church group, instead of encouraging Christians to serve Christ in every sphere of life. The church has adopted the mantra *the church is the body of Christ* (the institutional church constitutes Christ's body) at the expense of the greater truism that *the body of Christ is the church* (believers serving Christ in every area of their lives constitute the church). Reversing the traditional order shifts the focus from the gathered congregation to the dispersed body of Christ, highlighting the church's responsibility to make Jesus known in every sphere of life.[137]

Moving the Movement Forwards

Given the global import of the re-contextual movement and its emergent nature, its definition must be nuanced. Re-contextual church is a centre-set term, wherein its core distinctives are paradigmatically identified as Western, free church, ecumenical, Trinitarian, missional, holistic, emergent, incarnational, kingdom-focused, and located within a postmodern, post-Christendom, consumerist, globalized, technologized, individualized and networked culture. The emergent nature of the movement, which is not a denomination or discrete set of churches, means that it is aptly described as simultaneously a movement, conversation and mindset. These features are not restricted to the re-contextual church; on the contrary the movement's Trinitarian focus has been influenced by Eastern Orthodoxy, for example. Rather, the re-contextual church is identified by the particular combination of the characteristics listed, alongside the specific conception of them as outlined in the subsections above – such as egalitarian Trinitarianism and a missional emphasis on joining God's work. Most notably, re-contextual practitioners and authors share the overarching goal of re-contextualizing the Western church into a markedly changed context.

One of the strengths of the re-contextual movement is that it has been largely driven and moulded by practitioners (it is grassroots/emergent). As Moynagh notes in the introduction to his 2017 publication *Church in Life*, 'Those of us who write about new ecclesial communities are little more than extras in a drama dominated by the leaders of these communities and the people involved in them.'[138] The re-contextual movement exhibits *lived* theology – theology rooted in the challenges and realities of everyday Christian life and service. The prevalence of practitioners' voices mitigates against the disconnection that can occur between formal theology (as derived within academia) and practice. Not that theology derived on the field is immune from contradiction and inconsistency. Ward observes a disconnection between espoused (spoken) and operant (lived) theology within the Western evangelical church's proclamation of the gospel, perpetuated by a dearth of theological reflection on the embodied and encultured nature of faith.[139] This disconnection between the Western church's spoken and lived expression of the gospel has arisen in the context of the church's practical experience. However, attention to the practitioner's voice helps the re-contextual church avoid aloof abstraction; the movement maintains a pragmatic realism that keeps it closely connected to the challenges and complexities of everyday life and ministry.

A negative corollary to the prevalence of the practitioner's voice is a lack of consensus and clarity within the movement's ecclesiology: the nature and role of the church. Jones' endeavour to promote a relational ecclesiology for the emerging church based on Moltmann's Trinitarian reflections was prompted by his concern that the movement's ecclesial practice was not supported by adequate theological reflection. He notes that every reform movement that has lasted the test of time has combined its renewed practice with robust theologizing. Walker affirms a lack of robustness when he argues, of *Mission-Shaped Church*, that in this one book a variety of definitions of church are proposed, which are in places conflicting. For instance, due to the book's multi-authorship, it is unclear whether a café church gathering *is* church, because it is seen as church by those who attend, or *not* church, because the Eucharist is not held. Walker maintains that the relational approach advocated by those such as Moynagh (up, in, out, of) fails to provide the required clarity since synods, missionary societies, and Bible studies also exhibit these marks.[140]

The re-contextual movement's ecclesiology is united in assuming key aspects of free church ecclesiology. In addition, the movement seeks to connect missiology and ecclesiology more closely; a missional orientation is central to re-contextual authors' conceptions of church. In addition, key voices within the movement base their ecclesiology on the work of Social Trinitarians.[141] However, although there are thus common features, the movement's ecclesiology would benefit from greater perspicuity and robustness.

Alongside ecclesiology, there are other unresolved issues and questions that investigation into the re-contextual movement has raised. Regarding the church's relationship with God, has God's immanence been overlooked in favour of his transcendence or vice versa? How could right balance be restored and maintained? Regarding human identity, how might the church best respond to the fragmentation and reimagining of personal identity, the longing for community, and the increased openness to spirituality within contemporary culture, alongside people's reluctance to look for these things in the church? To what extent can online forums mediate community and church? What is the relationship between medium and message, especially as regards the use of technology?

Questions also arise in relation to the internal structure and essence of the church. To what extent should the church be viewed as an institution? What is the role of structures? How can Spirit-brought order and Spirit-inspired spontaneity be held in a healthy tension? The relationship between the church and culture has also come to the fore. There is a tension in the movement between those emphasizing the church's calling to infiltrate all aspects of society and those highlighting the church's unique identity as a countercultural community. How might both be held together? Moreover, what is the relationship between missiology and ecclesiology? How might the answer to this question affect the identity, form, vision and priorities of the church? What are the limits for contextualization and what is the most appropriate methodology? Is 'incarnational' a legitimate missional strategy? How should the church respond to consumerism? To what extent are third-place church and demographic-specific expressions valid and helpful proposals?

Questions are also raised regarding the contemporary church's engagement with inherited traditions. How are contemporary churches to discern which aspects of church tradition should be maintained, even reclaimed, and which should be abandoned or reformed? Within this, how can a pick 'n' mix approach be avoided? What overarching framework could guide the church's engagement with its past? Are ordination and sacrament essential components of church? Moreover, there is an apparent inconsistency within the movement regarding the desire to be non-religious *and* draw from the older, religious, traditions. How might this be resolved?

Lastly, an investigation into the movement raises the question of the relationship between the church and the kingdom. To what extent is the kingdom present in the church and in the world now? To what extent is the kingdom a future reality? What are the practical implications of the church's answers to these questions? In addition, how can the church move away from idealistic blueprint ecclesiologies towards an ecclesiology that incorporates the church's current imperfect state? How can the church help people to engage with the darker emotions and experiences of life, instead of upholding an overly triumphalistic stance?

These unresolved issues can be grouped into seven interconnected areas: the nature of God and his relationship with the church; human identity and spirituality; the church's internal relations and structures; the connection between church and culture; the relationship between the contemporary church and church tradition; the church and the kingdom; and the church's current imperfect state. In the second part of this book, I shall explore these seven areas while engaging critically with the movement's underlying ecclesiology. The movement's current ecclesial base has been significantly influenced by Social Trinitarianism. However, social models of the Trinity have received a great deal of criticism suggesting that Social Trinitarianism is an inadequate foundation on which to build. Therefore, I shall argue that the seven areas raised by the conversation are best addressed from an alternative foundation. As I demonstrate in Part 2, an ecclesiology based on Paul's body of Christ metaphor overcomes the weaknesses of Social Trinitarianism and provides stability for the re-contextual movement while facilitating flexibility.

Notes

1 Moynagh defines contextualization as 'the attempt to be church in ways that are both faithful to Jesus and appropriate to the people the church serve' (M. Moynagh, *Church for Every Context*, London: SCM, 2012, 151). Dan Kimball, for example, defines the emerging church as 'those who notice culture is changing and are not afraid to do deep ecclesiological thinking' (D. Kimball, 'The Emerging Church and Missional Theology', in R. Webber [ed.], *Listening to the Beliefs of Emerging Churches: Five Perspectives*, Grand Rapids, MI: Zondervan, 2007, 81–105, 84).

2 Moynagh's most significant works addressing re-contextual church span from 2001–2017, Murray Williams' span from 2004–2012, and Ward's range from 1996–2017.

3 S. Murray, *Post-Christendom*, Carlisle; Waynesboro, VA: Paternoster, 2004, 255 and *Church After Christendom*, Milton Keynes: Paternoster, 2004, 112.

4 L. Anderson, *Church for the 21st Century*, Grand Rapids, MI: Bethany House, 1992, 146 as cited by Murray, *Christendom*, 112.

5 The Reformation (AD 1500); Great Schism (AD 1000); Roman Empire's decline (AD 500); and the Great Transformation (AD 1) (P. Tickle, *Emergence Christianity*, Grand Rapids, MI: Baker, 2012, 17–28).

6 Moynagh, *Context*, 151; S. Murray, *Changing Mission*, London: Churches Together in Britain and Ireland, 2006, 33; e.g. postmodern, post-Christendom, post-industrial, post-secular, post-colonial, post-evangelical, post-liberal, post-denominational, etc.

7 For further reading see Tickle, *Emergence*, 47–102; Moynagh, *Context*, 28–71; D. Gay, *Remixing the Church*, London: SCM, 2011, 19–47; P. Ward, *Selling Worship*, Milton Keynes: Paternoster, 2005, 98–101; Murray, *Changing*, 117–20; C. V. Gelder and D. J. Zscheile, *The Missional Church in Perspective*, Grand Rapids, MI: Baker Academic, 2011, 35–9; E. Gibbs and R. K. Bolger, *Emerging Churches*, London: SPCK, 2006, 53; R. Ellis and C. Seaton, *New Celts*, Eastbourne: Kingsway, 1998.

8 V. M. Kärkkäinen, *An Introduction to Ecclesiology*, Downers Grove, IL: IVP, 2002, 59.

9 Regarding the distinctives of free-church ecclesiology see Kärkkäinen, *Introduction*, 59–67; E. Zimmerman, 'Church and Empire: Free-Church Ecclesiology in a Global Era', *Political Theology* 10.3 (2009) 471–95; E. Ferguson, 'The "Congregationalism" of the Early Church', in D. H. Williams (ed.), *The Free Church and the Early Church*, Grand Rapids, MI/Cambridge: Eerdmans, 2002, 129–40; and F. H. Littell, 'The Historical Free Church Defined', *Brethren Life and Thought* 50.3–4 (2005) 51–65. Moynagh argues that being ordained may draw a person away from founding the church where they are but notes that there are increasing opportunities for ordination training to occur in situ or part-time (Moynagh, *Context*, 229–34). See also Cray, *Mission*, 131; I. Mobsby, *Emerging and Fresh Expressions of Church*, London: Moot Community, 2006, 79–80.

10 A. H. Jones, *The Church is Flat*, Minneapolis, MN: JoPa, 2011, 14, 101; Moynagh, *Context*, 106–15; P. Ward, *Liquid Church*, Peabody, MA: Hendrickson; Carlisle: Paternoster, 2002, 66–71 and *Participation and Mediation*, London: SCM, 2008, 121–34; Gay, *Remixing*, 75–9; E. Gibbs and I. Coffey, *Church Next*, Leicester: IVP, 2001, 88–9; Gibbs, *Emerging*, 155. Regarding the role of the sacraments in Fresh Expressions see S. Croft, 'Persuading Gamaliel: Helping the Anglo-Catholic Tradition Engage with Fresh Expressions of Church', in S. Croft and I. Mobsby

(eds) *Fresh Expressions in the Sacramental Tradition*, Norwich: Canterbury, 2009, 36–51.

11 Zimmerman, 'Free-Church', 474; G. Cray et al. (eds), *New Monasticism as Fresh Expressions of Church*, Norwich: Canterbury, 2010; Gelder, *Missional*, 19.

12 E.g. Michael Frost, Alan Hirsch, Stuart Murray Williams, James Thwaites, and the current author.

13 For example, Gittoes et al. criticize *MSC* for giving 'scant attention to the sacramental aspects of the Church's life' and argue that there has not yet been a 'thoroughgoing theological critique of the consequences of Fresh Expressions for …[Anglican] … ecclesiology' (J. Gittoes et al., 'Introduction: An Invitation to Conversation: Mission and the Church', in J. Gittoes et al. (eds), *Generous Ecclesiology*, London: SCM, 2013, 1–33, 2 and 4). See also A. Davison and A. Milbank, *For the Parish*, London: SCM, 2010.

14 Mobsby, *Authentically*, 76; Gay, *Remixing*, 48–71; cf. Moynagh, *Context*, 353–4; Ward, *Participation*, 185; I. Mobsby, 'The Importance of New Monasticism as a Model for Building Ecclesial Communities out of Contextual Mission', in G. Cray et al. (eds), *New Monasticism as Fresh Expressions of Church*, Norwich: Canterbury, 2010, 12–18; cf. Murray, *Changing*, 117–20.

15 Gay, *Remixing*, 1–18. Hastings argues that the 'Protestant world was Catholicized quite as much as the Catholic world was Protestantized' (A. Hastings, *A History of English Christianity 1920–2000*, London: SCM, 2001 [1986, 1987, 1991], xviii).

16 J. Clark, 'The Renewal of Liturgy in the Emerging Church', in K. Corcoran (ed.), *Church in the Present Tense: A Candid Look at What's Emerging*, Grand Rapids, MI: Brazos, 2011, 75–6. On the influence of the modernity to postmodernity shift see P. S. Franklin, 'John Wesley in Conversation with the Emerging Church', *AsTJ* 63.1 (2008) 75–93; Gay, *Remixing*, 19–20 and 50–1.

17 Murray, *Post-Christendom*, 210–12; J. Clark, 'Consumer Liturgies and Their Corrosive Effects on Christian Identity', in K. Corcoran (ed.), *Church in the Present Tense: A Candid Look at What's Emerging*, Grand Rapids, MI: Brazos, 2011, 44 drawing on V. J. Miller, *Consuming Religion*, New York: Continuum, 2003. Mobsby, for example, reads history through a contemporary egalitarian lens when he maintains that both old and new monasticism exhibit a 'strong sense of shared decision-making and leadership' (I. Mobsby, *God Unknown*, Norwich: Canterbury, 2012, 86). Regarding the past's strangeness, see R. Williams, *Why Study the Past?*, London: Darton, Longman and Todd, 2005, 11.

18 Gay, *Remixing*, 51, 67, 74–5, 93. Gay gives women's ordination as an example where an overly patriarchal church tradition has been corrected by later generations. Gay draws on K. Barth, *Church Dogmatics I.1, The Doctrine of Reconciliation*, Edinburgh: T&T Clark, 684.

19 Moynagh, *Context*, 432.

20 L. Moore, 'How Does Messy Church Travel?' in G. Lings (ed.), *Messy Church Theology*, Abingdon: BRF, 2013, 52–67, citing 55; Fresh Expressions, 'Partners', *Fresh Expressions* website (www.freshexpressions.org.uk/about/partners).

21 Mobsby, *Unknown*, 74–5.

22 R. T. Michener, 'The Kingdom of God and Postmodern Ecclesiologies', *ERT* 34.2 (2010) 119–30, 120.

23 Jones, *Flat*, esp. 178–80; Frost, *ReJesus*, esp. 26–33, 42–3; Gay, *Remixing*, 59–61; Ward, *Participation*, 96–9, 185; idem, *Liquid*, 49–55; Moynagh, *Context*, 435–6. Re-contextual proponents draw mainly from M. Volf, *After Our Likeness*, Grand Rapids, MI; Cambridge: Eerdmans, 1998; J. Moltmann, *The Church in the*

Power of the Spirit, trans. M. Kohl, London: SCM, 1977; C. E. Gunton, *The One, the Three and the Many*, Cambridge: CUP, 1993. It is not only re-contextual thinkers who have been influenced by Social Trinitarianism. Foord, for example, cites Trinitarian Ecclesiology as one of the main moves within contemporary Anglican ecclesiology (M. Foord, 'Recent Directions in Anglican Ecclesiology', *Chm* 115.4 [2001] 316–49).

24 K. Kilby, 'Perichoresis and Projection: Problems with Social Doctrines of the Trinity', *NB* 81 (2000) 432–45, esp. 435–8; S. R. Holmes, 'Three Versus One? Some Problems of Social Trinitarianism', *JRT* 3 (2009) 77–89, esp. 78; J. S. Sexton, 'The State of the Evangelical Trinitarian Resurgence', *JETS* 54.4 (2011) 787–805, 791.

25 Volf maintains that 'the more a church is characterized by symmetrical and decentralized distribution of power and freely affirmed interaction, the more will it correspond to the trinitarian communion' (Volf, *Likeness*, 236, cf. 196, 203–20, 234–6).

26 Jones, *Flat*, esp. 1, 145–7, 150–7, 179–80.

27 Ward, *Liquid*, esp. 5, 36–7, 54–5 and *Participation*, 103.

28 Moynagh, *Context*, 435–6. Moynagh claims to be citing Gunton, but Gunton's Trinitarianism has been criticized for omitting the notion of participation and thus Moynagh has presumably read his own thoughts into Gunton's work (Y. Ge, 'The Many and the One', PhD Thesis, Cambridge University, 2015, 12–13).

29 Moynagh, *Context*, 108.

30 Cray, *Mission*, 99.

31 S. Murray, *Church Planting: Laying Foundations*, Carlisle: Paternoster, 1998, 34; M. Frost, *Exiles*, Peabody, MA: Hendrickson, 2006, 147.

32 Marti, *Deconstructed*, 105.

33 P. R. Holmes, *Trinity in Human Community*, Milton Keynes: Paternoster, 2006. Holmes contends that the 'Social Trinity can and should be a vibrant example of what human relationships can become, especially within the Body of Christ' (Holmes, *Social*, 15; cf. 66).

34 Jones, *Flat*, 149; P. Ward, 'Blueprint Ecclesiology and the Lived', *Ecclesial Practices* 2.1 [2015] 74–90, esp. 77–80; Moynagh, *Context*, 105–6 and 108; Volf, *Likeness*, 198–9.

35 Ward, *Liquid*, 13 cf. Mobsby, *Authentically*, 7; Moynagh, *Context*, 78–80, 120; Murray, *Post-Christendom*, esp. 23–46, 79, 130, 200–3, 251.

36 Ward, *Participation*, 5; *Liquid*, 20 and *Growing Up Evangelical*, London: SPCK, 1996, esp. 1–3, 11, 20, 161–85.

37 Cray, *Mission*, 84–6; Frost, *Exiles*, 108, 111, 128; cf. Ward, *Participation*, 5, 103; *Evangelical*, esp. 1–3, 11, 20, 161–85 and *Liquid*, 20; Gay, *Remixing*, 82–4; Moynagh, *Context*, 104–8; Frost, *ReJesus*, 26–7; Gelder, *Missional*, 26–7; D. J. Bosch, *Transforming Mission*, Maryknoll, NY: Orbis, 1991, esp. 1–12, 389, 493–4.

38 M. Frost and A. Hirsch, *The Shaping of Things to Come*, Peabody, MA: Hendrickson, 2003, 206–10, who are presumably influenced by P. G. Hiebert, 'Conversion, Culture, and Cognitive Categories', *Gospel in Context* 1.4 (1978) 24–9, although Frost does not specify this. Cf. S. Law, 'Anticipating Change: Missions and Paradigm Shifts in Emergence', *AsTJ* 67.1 (2012) 4–26, 15; Murray, *Christendom*, 29.

39 Rollins, for example, maintains that Christians should not only be willing to learn from others but must also lay down their desire to teach (P. Rollins, *How [Not] to Speak of God*, London: SPCK, 2006, 54). In his empirical research into one particular 'emerging' church in the UK, Labanow concludes that although 'commu-

nicating with contemporary culture was perhaps the most strongly felt value at JV [the emerging church] ... JV had a strong distaste for evangelicalism's evangelistic techniques'. He asserts, however, that 'they still wanted to communicate "the message of Christianity" despite the fact that they were unclear about how to communicate that message and exactly what that message is if it is more than praying a prayer for salvation in the afterlife' (C. E. Labanow, *Evangelicalism and the Emerging Church*, Farnham: Ashgate, 2009, 117). See also B. McLaren, *More Ready than you Realize*, Grand Rapids, MI: Zondervan, 2002, 12; Gay, *Remixing*, 94–9.

40 R. Clapp, *A Peculiar People*, Downers Grove, IL: IVP, 1996, 12.

41 J. Finney, *Emerging Evangelism*, London: Darton, Longman and Todd, 2004, 8.

42 R. Warren, *Signs of Life: How Goes the Decade of Evangelism?*, London: Church House, 1995, 65 as cited by Moynagh, *Context*, 338.

43 G. Cray and I. Mobsby, 'Introduction', in G. Cray et al., *Fresh Expressions of Church and the Kingdom of God*, Norwich: Canterbury, 2012, xv.

44 Clark, 'Renewal', 76, 79–80.

45 E.g. Moynagh, *Context*, 346–50; Murray, *Post-Christendom*, 91; D. Kimball, *The Emerging Church*, Grand Rapids, MI: Zondervan, 2003, 82–3.

46 P. Ward, *Liquid Ecclesiology*, Leiden: Brill, 2017, 110–21, esp. 111, 123–4, 195–7.

47 McKnight argues that, in contrast to the theological knots that Christians have tied themselves into when desiring to emphasize discipleship without turning *salvation by faith* into *salvation by works*, re-contextual Christians, in re-examining the gospel, are genuinely trying to connect Jesus' kingdom emphasis with Paul's salvation and justification by faith motives (S. McKnight, 'Atonement and Gospel' and 'Scripture in the Emerging Movement' in K. Corcoran [ed.], *Church in the Present Tense*, Grand Rapids, MI: Brazos, 2011).

48 I. Mobsby, 'The Importance of New Monasticism as a Model for Building Ecclesial Communities out of Contextual Mission', in G. Cray et al. (eds), *New Monasticism as Fresh Expressions of Church*, Norwich: Canterbury, 2010, 12–18, citing 14.

49 Frost, *Exiles*, 126.

50 Ward, *Ecclesiology*, 79 and *Participation*, 21–6; 36, 75–6, 126–30; cf. Murray, *Post-Christendom*, 302; Moynagh, *Context*, 334–5.

51 Moynagh, *Context*, 86–7; Mobsby, *Unknown*, 34, 103; Thwaites, *Beyond*, 3–5; cf. Marti, *Descontructed*, 129–30.

52 See Murray, *Christendom*, 203–7 for his criticism of Thwaites. See Clark, 'Consumer' for his concerns regarding the consuming of religious traditions and symbols. On the narrowing of 'kingdom' see Morris, 'Emerging', 48–9. On orthopraxy trumping orthodoxy see Tickle, *Emergence*, 165; Frost, *Shaping*, 120–1. Others affirm the importance of both head-knowledge and praxis (e.g. Mobsby, 'Importance', 15).

53 Moynagh, *Context*, 54–71; B. B. Lichtenstein and D. A. Plowman, 'The Leadership of Emergence', *LQ* 20 (2009) 617–30. Moynagh is referring specifically to the fresh expressions movement, but his assessment applies to the broader re-contextual discussion; A. Jones, 'March 18, 2005, EmergAnt.:1 Emerging Vocabulary', *Tall Skinny Kiwi* website (http://tallskinnykiwi.typepad.com/tallskinnykiwi/2005/03/emergant_1_an_e.html).

54 Lichtenstein, 'Emergence', 620.

55 E.g. Gibbs, *Next*, 10–12; Cray, *Mission*, 13–14; Frost, *Shaping*, 3–7; M.

Moynagh, *emergingchurch.intro*, Oxford; Grand Rapids, MI: Monarch, 2004, 15–19.

56 Moynagh argues that the church has three different levels: temples, synagogues, and tents. Temples are occasions when believers connect to the whole body of Christ, such as festivals, retreats, conferences and websites. He asserts that, like Jesus, believers need to engage with this wider temple at times. Synagogues are the local church, wherein believers receive sustenance from Scripture and other church practices. Similarly, believers should attend the synagogue regularly. Tents are church-in-life: small missional and worshipping communities that serve their specific context and draw others into faith. He notes that these may well be more transient. This threefold temple-synagogue-tent model is not a reworking of the celebration-congregation-cell model that has been popular recently. Rather, he contends, it conveys greater fluidity, with tents coming and going and the boundaries between the three aspects overlapping and interlocking. For example, members of the same tent may attend different synagogues. Overall, there will be less central control and a greater emergent feel. (Moynagh, *Context*, 67–8.)

57 Lichtenstein, 'Emergence', 624–5; Tickle, *Emergence*, 101–8.

58 Moynagh, *Context*, 52–3 drawing on N. Murphy, 'Divine Action on the Natural Order: Buriden's Ass and Schrodinger's Cat', in R. J. Russell, *Complexity: Scientific Perspectives on Divine Action*, Vatican/Berkeley: Vatican Observatory and Centre for Theology and the Natural Sciences, 1995, 325–57; E. Gibbs, *Church Morph*, Grand Rapids, MI: Baker Academic, 2009, 9; Tickle, *Emergence*, 39–42, 67–70; G. Cray, 'Communities of the Kingdom', in G. Cray et al. (eds), *Fresh Expressions of Church and the Kingdom of God*, Norwich: Canterbury, 2012, 21.

59 Gay, *Remixing*, 93.

60 Moynagh, *Context*, 197–205; Cray, *Mission*, 20, 30–3; cf. Gibbs, *Next*, 11, 211–12, 230.

61 Re-contextual church is *primarily a Western, free church, ecumenical, Trinitarian, missional, holistic, emergent movement/mindset/conversation* endeavouring to *incarnate the kingdom* into *postmodern, post-Christendom, consumerist, technologized, globalized, individualized, networked* culture. Labanow's empirical research supports the contention that the movement is best depicted as a shared mindset; when studying an 'emerging' expression of church in the UK, Labanow observed that, rather than new forms, the congregation's distinctiveness was ideological (Labanow, *Emerging*, 92). Labanow writes that at the start of his research the structure and forms felt so familiar to his inherited church background that he doubted the value of his study (Labanow, *Emerging*, 91). However, over time he sensed a noticeable ideological differentiation from what he describes as 'evangelical Christianity', noting that the church's 'interpretive framework' thus became the focus of his research (Labanow, *Emerging*, 92). See also Moynagh, *emergingchurch*, 24.

62 G. Lakoff, *Women, Fire and Dangerous Things*, Chicago, IL: University of Chicago, 1987, esp. 5–8, 41.

63 E.g. Murray Williams critique of Thwaites (Murray, *Christendom*, 204–7); Moynagh's development of Frost and Hirsch's work on 'attractional' versus 'incarnational' (Moynagh, *Context*, xvi–xvii); the critique of Ward's liquid church proposals by both Murray Williams and Moynagh (Murray, *Changing*, 96; Moynagh, *emergingchurch*, 151).

64 Cray, *Mission*, 12; Moynagh, *emergingchurch*, 25; *Changing*, 19, 33 and *Context*, 77–8; Ward, *Liquid*, 19.

65 Places such as cafés and sports club are seen as a 'third-place' between home and work (Frost, *Shaping*, 74–5). MSC defines the unchurched or non-churched as 'the increasingly large proportion of society that has no history of church attendance' (Cray, *Mission*, 39).

66 E.g. Moynagh, *Context*, 182. The notion of incarnational mission is not unique to the re-contextual conversation, however. Stott, for example, advocated an incarnational approach to mission (J. Stott, *Christian Mission in the Modern World*, London: Falcon, 1977 [1975], 24–5). Moreover, Kärkkäinen outlines the Catholic notion of *the church as the continued incarnation* (Kärkkäinen, *Introduction*, 26–7).

67 E.g. Frost, *Shaping*, 35–41.

68 Cray, *Mission*, 87.

69 Moynagh, *Context*, xvii, 182–90. Moynagh here is contrasting *hit and run* style mission with actually staying somewhere for a longer period.

70 E.g. J. T. Billings, *Union with Christ*, Grand Rapids, MI: Baker Academic, 2011, 123–66.

71 D. A. McGavran, *Understanding Church Growth*, 2nd ed., Grand Rapids, MI: Eerdmans, 1980 (1970), 163. The first part of this quote is referred to by both Cray, *Mission*, 108 and Moynagh, *Context*, 168; cf. Moynagh's reference to D. A. McGavran, *Bridges of God*, London: World Dominion, 1955.

72 G. G. Hunter, *Church for the Unchurched*, Nashville, TN: Abingdon, 1996, 55.

73 Hunter, *Unchurched*, 59.

74 Davison, *Parish*, 66 as cited by Moynagh, *Context*, 169–70.

75 Murray, *Changing*, 75–6.

76 Murray, *Changing*, 75; Moynagh, *Context*, 171–80; G. Cray et al., 'Afterword', in G. Cray et al. (eds), *Fresh Expressions of Church and the Kingdom of God*, Norwich: Canterbury, 2012, 172–9, citing 175.

77 E.g. Gibbs, *Next*, 31–2, 41–54; Ward, *Liquid*, 17–21.

78 R. Williams, 'Fresh Expressions, the Cross and the Kingdom', in G. Cray et al. (eds), *Fresh Expressions of Church and the Kingdom of God*, Norwich: Canterbury, 2012, 1–11, citing 11.

79 Cray, 'Afterword', 172.

80 Moynagh, *Context*, 151, 160–1.

81 The arguments summarized below are taken from Moynagh, *Context*, 161–6. Moynagh draws on S. B. Bevans, *Models of Contextual Theology*, Rev. ed., Maryknoll, NY: Orbis, 2002.

82 L. Newbigin, *The Gospel in a Pluralist Society*, London: SPCK, 1986, 144.

83 Moynagh, *Context*, 99–101; K. Corcoran, 'Thy Kingdom Come (on Earth): An Emerging Eschatology', in K. Corcoran (ed.), *Church in the Present Tense*, Grand Rapids, MI: Brazos, 2011, 59–72; S. McKnight, *Kingdom Conspiracy*, Grand Rapids, MI: Brazos, 2014, 205. I address McKnight's arguments in more depth later in this book.

84 A. Loisy, *L'Evangile et l'Eglise*, Paris: Alphonse Picard, 1902, 111 as cited by Ward, *Liquid*, 8; cf. Moynagh, *Context*, 101–2.

85 G. S. Shogren, 'The Wicked Will Not Inherit the Kingdom of God', *TrinJ* 31.1 (2010) 95–113, 105. Shogren believes that Liberation Theology has strongly influenced emerging Christians' conception of the kingdom. See also Rollins, *How*, 54; Moynagh, *Context*, 101–2.

86 J. Zizioulas, *Being as Communion*, Crestwood, NY: Saint Valdimir's Seminary Press, 1985, 59.

87 Moynagh, *Context*, 102–4, drawing on the work of Moltmann, *Church*,

194–5 and Volf, *Likeness*, 207. N. T. Wright has also contributed to this way of conceptualizing the church's relationship with the kingdom (e.g. Gibbs, *Emerging*, 54).

88 Ward, *Participation*, e.g. 108–14, 176–9, 189–91 and *Liquid*, 44–5; cf. Cray, 'Communities', 21.

89 Ward, *Ecclesiology*, 178; *Participation*, 41 and *Liquid*, 8–10; Moynagh, *Context*, 111 drawing on N. M. Healy, *Church, World and the Christian Life*, Cambridge: CUP, 2000 and 'Communion Ecclesiology: A Cautionary Note', *Pro Ecclesia* 4.4 (1995) 442–53; cf. Cray, *Mission*, 95.

90 Ward, *Liquid*, 17–20.

91 Ward, *Liquid*, 21–30.

92 Guarino, for example, argues that 'Heidegger and Wittgenstein constitute the dual-headed Zeus from whom postmodernity springs' (T. Guarino, 'Postmodernity and Five Fundamental Theological Issues', *TS* 57 (1996) 654–89, 655); cf. C. V. Gelder, 'From the Modern to the Postmodern in the West', *Word & World* 20.1 (2000) 32–40, 35.

93 L. Sweet, *Aquachurch*, Loveland, CO: Group, 1999, 24 as cited by Ward, *Liquid*, 15.

94 K. Corcoran, 'Who's Afraid of Philosophical Realism? Taking Emergence Christianity to Task', in K. Corcoran (ed.), *Church in the Present Tense*, Grand Rapids, MI: Brazos, 2011, 3–21, esp. 9–11; Drane, *McDonaldization*, 1; Murray, *Post-Christendom*, 12–14; Tickle, *Emergence*, 129; L. Sweet et al., *A is for Abductive*, Grand Rapids, MI: Zondervan, 2003, 241.

95 Drane, *McDonaldization*, 133; Murray, *Post-Christendom*, 12–14; idem, *Changing*, 33–4, 120; Ward, *Liquid*, 14–16; Gelder, 'Postmodern', 38–9.

96 D. A. Carson, *Becoming Conversant with the Emerging Church*, Grand Rapids, MI: Zondervan, 2005, 95.

97 Corcoran, 'Realism', 3–21; P. Rollins, 'The Worldly Theology of Emerging Christians', in K. Corcoran (ed.), *Church in the Present Tense*, Grand Rapids, MI: Brazos, 2011, 23–36.

98 E.g. S. McKnight, 'Five Streams of the Emerging Church', *Christianity Today* website (www.christianitytoday.com/ct/2007/february/11.35.html?paging=off).

99 Murray, *Post-Christendom*, 9–14, 145; Gibbs, *Morph*, 26; Frost, *Shaping*, 8–9.

100 Murray, *Post-Christendom*, 60–72, 83–124; Frost, *Shaping*, 9.

101 Moynagh, *Context*, 446; Mobsby, *Unknown*, 91; Frost, *Shaping*, 9; A. Hirsch, *The Forgotten Ways*, Grand Rapids, MI: Brazos, 2006, 226; Gelder, *Missional*, 156–7.

102 R. Sudworth, 'Recovering the Difference that Makes a Difference: Fresh Ideas on an Older Theme', in G. Cray et al. (eds), *Fresh Expressions of Church and the Kingdom of God*, Norwich: Canterbury, 2012, 29–40, citing 30.

103 I. M. Randall, 'Mission in post-Christendom: Anabaptist and Free Church Perspectives', *EQ* 79.3 (2007), 227–40, 240; Murray, *Post-Christendom*, 75–82.

104 E.g. S. Miles, *Consumerism – As a Way of Life*, London: SAGE, 1998, esp. 1–4, 10–11, 147, 150, 153, 155. Miles asserts that consumerism is paradoxical inasmuch as 'on the one hand, consumerism appears to offer us as individuals all sorts of opportunities and experiences, on the other hand, as consumers we appear to be directed down certain predetermined routes of consumption, which ensure that consumerism is ultimately as constraining as it is enabling' (Miles, *Consumerism*, 147); cf. Clark, 'Consumer'.

105 T. Sine, 'Creating Communities of Celebration, Sustainability and Subversion', in G. Cray et al. (eds), *New Monasticism as Fresh Expressions of Church*, Norwich: Canterbury, 2010, 67–79, citing 70–1.

106 Miles, *Consumerism*, 7–8.

107 Miles, *Consumerism*, 9 cf. Drane, *McDonaldization*, 3–4, 35–49; Ward, *Liquid*, 2–4, 17–21, 40–8; Cray, *Missional*, 90–1.

108 For example, see Ward's assertion that the Western evangelicalism has uncritically adopted modern marketing methods and ethos in relation to worship music – although he stresses that this is not entirely detrimental (Ward, *Selling*, e.g. 1–2); cf. Davison, *Parish*, 81–4.

109 E.g. Moynagh, *Context*, xvi; Cray, *Mission*, 10.

110 Clark, 'Consumer', 39–57; cf. J. M. Hull, *Mission-Shaped Church: A Theological Response*. London: SCM, 2006, 19–20.

111 Clark, 'Consumer', 46–7.

112 V. J. Miller, *Consuming Religion*, New York: Continuum, 2003, 83–9, esp. 84; Mobsby, 'Importance', 16–17; G. Cray, 'Why is New Monasticism Important to Fresh Expressions?' in G. Cray et al. (eds), *New Monasticism as Fresh Expressions of Church*, Norwich: Canterbury, 2010, 1–11, esp. 3–5.

113 Cray, *Missional*, 9–13.

114 Cray, *Missional*, 13.

115 Cray, *Missional*, 50–1, 108–10; P. Rollins, 'Transformance Art: Reconfiguring the Social Self', in K. Corcoran (ed.), *Church in the Present Tense*, Grand Rapids, MI: Brazos, 2011, 89–102.

116 Mobsby, 'Importance', 13.

117 Gelder, *Missional*, 127; T. Chester, *Captured by a Better Vision: Living Porn-Free*, Nottingham: IVP, 2010; J. Rice, *The Church of Facebook*, Colorado Springs, CO: David C. Cook; Eastbourne: Kingsway, 2009, esp. 105, 128, 146, 197.

118 Gay, *Remixing*, 85–91; Tickle, *Emergence*, 132–3; Moynagh, *Context*, 90, 376–7; L. Sweet, *Viral*, Colorado Springs: Waterbrook, 2012, 6, 26, 114, 191.

119 Gelder, *Missional*, 129–30.

120 Sudworth, 'Recovering', 31; Davison, *Parish*, 1–27; Ward, *Participation*, 126–30.

121 Sine, 'Creating', 71; cf. G. Ritzer, *Globalization*, Chichester: Wiley & Sons, 2010, 2.

122 Sweet, *Abductive*, 138. Although here Sweet's Western focus and location cause him to overlook those in the majority world who do not have access to the Internet.

123 Sweet, *Viral*, 194; Gelder, *Missional*, 127.

124 E.g. Cray, *Missional*, 80–1, 107–9.

125 E.g. Davison, *Parish*, 64–5.

126 T. Dakin, 'What is at the Heart of a Global Perspective on the Church?' in S. Croft (ed.), *Mission-Shaped Questions*, London: Church House, 2008, 42–53, esp. 52–3; Cray, *Missional*, 4–5; Sweet, *Abductive*, 139–40; Cray, 'Communities', 27.

127 Moynagh, *Context*, 82–6; cf. Murray, *Post-Christendom*, 12–14; Murray, *Changing*, 33–4, 120.

128 Taylor phrases this as *find*, *realize* and *release* yourself (C. Taylor, *A Secular Age*, Cambridge, MA/London: Harvard University Press, 2007, 18–19, 473–89). A focus on authenticity is apparent in the UK 'emerging' church that Labanow examined. One of the key values is the perception that the church is a safe place for

people to be themselves; 'to use their favored term, JV [the emerging church] was a place where they could "be real"' (Labanow, *Emerging*, 109; cf. 81–2).

129 Ward, *Ecclesiology*, 110–21, 125–41, 187.

130 Ward, *Selling*, 1–6, 145–9, 206–7 and *Participation*, 127. Ward utilizes the hymnological categorization of L. Adey, *Hymns and the Christian Myth*, Vancouver: University of British Colombia, 1988.

131 As Heelas and Woodhead note, the 'subjective turn', wherein individual emotions and desires are emphasized and conformity to external roles and duties is downplayed, has led to the growth of individualized 'spirituality' and the diminishment of externally prescribed 'religion' (P. Heelas and L. Woodhead, *The Spiritual Revolution*, Oxford: Blackwell, 2005, 2–7, 75, 149; Drane, *McDonaldization*, 14–17; Marti, *Deconstructed*, 164. See also Bethke's spoken word 'Why I Hate Religion, But Love Jesus', which has received over 28 million views on YouTube (J. Bethke, 'Why I Hate Religion, But Love Jesus', YouTube website (www.youtube.com/watch?v=1IAhDGYlpqY)).

132 E.g. Ward, *Ecclesiology*, 129–31, 140–1.

133 Moynagh, *Context*, 87; Drane, *McDonaldization*, 64–5; Gelder, *Missional*, 122.

134 Cray, *Missional*, 4–8; Moynagh, *Context*, 422–3; cf. M. Castells, *The Rise of the Network Society*, 2nd ed., Chichester: Wiley-Blackwell, 2010 (1996), 501.

135 Ward, *Liquid*, 2–6, 41.

136 Murray, *Changing*, 96; Moynagh, *emergingchurch*, 151 and *Context*, 93; Cray, *Missional*, 5–10.

137 Ward, *Liquid*, 2, 37–55, 78–86 and *Evangelical*, 15.

138 M. Moynagh, *Church in Life*, London: SCM, 2017, xiii.

139 Ward, *Ecclesiology*, 200–10. Ward adopts Cameron et al.'s categorization to distinguish four intertwined streams within theology: formal, that produced within academia; normative, that derived from church tradition and/or officially pronounced as the formal doctrine of any one church or group of churches; espoused, that which is proclaimed; and operant, the theology that is lived and embodied (Ward, *Ecclesiology*, 95–9 drawing on Cameron et al., *Talking about God in Practice*, London: SCM, 2010, 49–56).

140 Michener, 'Kingdom', 120; Jones, *Flat*, 179; Walker, *Testing*, 29–30.

141 Jones, *Flat*, esp. 178–80; Frost, *ReJesus*, esp. 26–33, 42–3; Gay, *Remixing*, 59–61; Ward, *Participation*, 96–9, 185; idem, *Liquid*, 49–55; Moynagh, *Context*, 435–6. The key works that re-contextual proponents draw from include Volf, *Likeness*; Moltmann, *Church*; Zizioulas, *Being* and *Communion and Otherness*, London: T&T Clark, 2006; Gunton, *One*.

3

Ecclesiology as Embodied Dialogue

It may be possible to argue that ecclesiologies that have proved their significance and adaptability by their longevity tend to display a greater willingness to listen to and be truly guided by Paul's texts rather than distorting or ignoring them. As the church faces new situations and challenges, it should continue to turn to Paul in order to discern its nature, function, and shape.[1]

Healy complains that much recent ecclesial thinking is abstract and idealistic, removed from the messy reality of the historical church. The solution to theoretical ecclesiologies based on the church triumphant rather than the pilgrim church, Healy argues, is to acknowledge that ecclesiology must be prophetic and practical. Ecclesiologies that are appropriate to their context and faithful to Christ are achieved by bringing the church's context into dialogue with Scripture (and church tradition). Since church and its setting are interrelated, this process is not straightforward. Nevertheless, the goal is more obtainable if ecclesiologists make their context explicit, and unapologetically promote their ecclesiology within this context, rather than maintain the illusion of being able to transcend their cultural location to promote an ideal mode of church for all time.[2]

Therefore, the first part of this book is not simply an introduction to the ecclesiology proper of the second part. Rather, it provides an essential constituent of the ecclesiology proposed. My analysis of the re-contextual church and the reasons for its formation compose the 'explicit analysis of the ecclesiological context', which is integral to 'properly theological reflection upon the church'.[3] In the second part of this book, I propose an ecclesiology for the re-contextual church based on Paul's body of Christ metaphor. The Pauline texts must be allowed to speak for themselves through identifying the author's most likely intent. However, their distinctive contribution is best heard when the context within which they are being explored is made explicit, *contra* the modernist fallacy that one can approach Paul's texts neutrally. Therefore, rather than approaching Paul's texts with the illusion of no preconceived agenda, I bring the issues raised by the re-contextual movement unapologetically to the Pauline corpus such that an ecclesiology for the re-contextual movement is derived through dialogue between the two. These issues are: the nature of God and his relationship with the church; human identity and spirituality; the church's internal relations and structures; the connection between church and culture; the relationship between the contemporary church and church tradition; the church and the kingdom; and the church's current imperfect state.

Notes

1 N. M. Healy, 'Christian Theology: The Church', in S. Westerholm (ed.), *The Blackwell Companion to Paul*, Chichester: Wiley-Blackwell, 2011, 589–601, citing 603.

2 Healy, 'Church', 589–601 and *Church*, 25–51; cf. Ward, *Participation*, 41, 48–9; Moynagh, *Context*, 111.

3 Healy, *Church*, 39.

PART 2

Flexible Church

4

The Church and the Social Trinity

Social Trinitarianism epitomizes the contemporary tendency towards abstract idealized blueprints of church. Within social conceptions of the Trinity, the Godhead is seen to exhibit an ideal communal life serving as a model for human collectivity, in particular, the church. However, since God's self is hidden to his creatures outside the insight afforded through his interaction and revelation in history, theologians must be wary of reading too confidently from the economic Trinity, as revealed in Scripture, to the immanent Trinity, God's life *in se*. Human perceptions of God's inner life too readily compose blank canvases, onto which pre-conceived ideas about church, human personhood and community can be painted, then applied back to the church with the authoritative stamp of God's nature added in support. Social Trinitarianism is thus not without its critics. Notably, the criticism that social conceptions of the Trinity have received relates to the seven issues raised by the re-contextual conversation: the nature of God and his relationship with the church; human identity and spirituality; the church's internal relations and structures; the connection between church and culture; the relationship between the contemporary church and church tradition; the church and the kingdom; and the church's current imperfect state.[1]

First, re-contextual thinkers seek to enhance the church's relationship with the Trinity, but social models of the Trinity have been criticized for distorting classical conceptions of the Godhead. Moltmann probably initiated Social Trinitarianism when he pitted his social doctrine of the Trinity against psychological models, arguing that the Trinity is best conceived as a fellowship of people, not a solitary individual. Within this he, and other Social Trinitarians, have sought to revive the so-called Eastern view, which started with the three and then identified the one, in contrast to the 'corrupting' influence of the Western view, which started with the one and then tried to explain the three. Thus Social Trinitarians emphasize God's threeness, and the oneness of the three is explained via the notion of *perichoresis*, which denotes the mutual interpenetration of the persons. Critics argue that, in this, Social Trinitarians have altered the meaning of *perichoresis*, which originally described God's unity as one substance, by using it to depict the Trinitarian persons' togetherness. This altered conception of *perichoresis* is seen as inadequate for maintaining the Trinity's oneness. Thus presentations of the Trinity as an ideal community provoke cries of tritheism.[2]

In addition, re-contextual thinkers seek to correct a perceived distortion in the inherited church's conception of God's transcendence and immanence, while disagreeing on which of these elements requires greater emphasis. However, *perichoresis* is problematic in this regard too. If *perichoresis* within the Godhead is something his created beings imitate, the ontological gulf between creator and creation is not bridged and there is no adequate ontology to support the vertical relationship between God and creature. If creation is incorporated within the Godhead's *perichoretic* relations, God is dependent on history and his freedom is impinged. Therefore, a primary criticism of Social Trinitarianism is that its construal of God's transcendence and immanence is misguided, leading to a God who is either dependent on creation (impinging his freedom) or too removed.[3]

Second, re-contextual thinkers seek to root the church in a more robust view of human personhood. Social Trinitarians explore the members of the Trinity's personhood to throw light on contemporary human personhood, particularly its relationality. However, critics argue that such attempts involve projecting modernist notions of personhood onto the Trinity, then reading these conceptions back onto human beings with the authority that an argument from the divine nature affords. Further, re-contextual thinkers pursue a more holistic mode of faith. Due to its inadequate conception of God's transcendence and immanence, however, Social Trinitarianism leads to either overly dualistic or monistic conceptions of personhood, so appears an inadequate foundation for this pursuit.[4]

Third, re-contextual thinkers criticize the inherited church's internal structures; they think that the church is too hierarchical. Some Social Trinitarians have produced egalitarian conceptions of church but others, namely Zizioulas, draw on relational views of the Godhead to support hierarchical models. These applications of Social Trinitarianism to the church are thus accused of sequestering Trinitarian theology to rubber-stamp proponents' predetermined proposals, suggesting that Social Trinitarianism provides a deficient basis for re-contextual concerns.[5]

Fourth, re-contextual thinkers argue that mission is part of the church's essential nature and urge the church to prioritize it. Social models of the Trinity usually apply *perichoresis* horizontally, such that the Trinitarian relations provide a model for believers' communal lives. This leads to a preoccupation with the church's internal life; mission is overlooked. Conversely, when *perichoresis* is applied vertically, God is seen to permeate creation interdependently (*panentheism*), which leads to universalism. Neither downplaying mission or universalism are conducive to re-contextual aims.[6]

Fifth, re-contextual thinkers seek to refound the church on its founder, Jesus, and they urge believers to draw from church tradition, albeit not uncritically. However, Social Trinitarianism is faulted for overlooking Christ's centrality and distorting inherited orthodoxy. Reviving so-called Eastern conceptions of the Trinity is adjudged a misreading of history.[7]

Sixth, the re-contextual church desires to reconfigure the church's relationship with the kingdom, pursuing eschatological impetus and direction. The eschatology promoted within some strands of Social Trinitarianism, however, is criticized for presenting God as dependent on history. Moreover, God's work outside the church is emphasized in a way that undermines the church's unique nature and role.[8]

Seventh, the re-contextual movement is critical of idealistic blueprint models of church and warns against triumphalism and a failure to give space to negative emotions. Ironically, however, in seeing the Godhead as a model for community, Social Trinitarianism is deemed overly idealistic by its critics.[9]

I do not aim to add to these appraisals. Rather, I contend that a Trinitarian ecclesiology derived from the body of Christ texts, and in line with (not in contravention of) classical Trinitarian conceptions (particularly God's otherness), avoids such criticisms and adds substance and stability to the re-contextual movement. What constitutes classical Trinitarianism is a moot point. The controversy relates to the relationship between God's actions and revelation in history (the economic Trinity) and his life *in se* (the immanent Trinity). In this regard, an ecclesiology based on the body of Christ texts has a marked methodological advantage over Social Trinitarianism; it is less dependent on abstraction. Social models of the Trinity are predominantly derived from engagement with the Gospels, whereupon the economic relationships between Jesus, the Father and the Spirit are abstracted into the Trinity's life *in se*. Within this, Holmes warns, Social Trinitarians pay insufficient heed to the Chalcedonian formulations and therefore risk collapsing the immanent Trinity into the economic Trinity.[10] In contrast, the body of Christ texts outline the church's relationship to the economic Trinity, avoiding the speculation involved in abstracting from the economic Trinity onto the immanent Trinity and then back onto the church. The question of the relationship between the immanent and economic Trinity cannot be dodged completely, however, thus some points must be made.

Classical Trinitarianism affirms that who God is towards creation he is in himself. The economic Trinity is the immanent Trinity – although *contra* Rahner this statement must not be reversed. What is debatable is the extent to which human beings can comprehend how this is so. Within this debate, the classical emphasis on God's otherness is crucial; the consequences of overlooking this facet of God's being have marked implications for the doctrine of God. Despite the classical emphasis on the unknowability of God's essence, God's life *in se* has become a strong focus in Trinitarian discussions. To understand why this is so, one must revisit Kilby's contention that Social Trinitarianism involves a projection of modernist notions of personhood onto the Trinity. Kilby highlights how contemporary understandings of human personhood have influenced Social Trinitarians' presentation of the relationships between the three persons of the Trinity. What Kilby overlooks, however, is the extent to which modern notions of human identity have impacted Social Trinitarians' conception of God as a single entity.[11]

On this latter point, Taylor's propositions regarding contemporary culture's 'inward turn' prove illuminating. Tracing its development through the apostle Paul and Augustine, while noting the pre-eminent influence of Descartes, Taylor observes that contemporary views of human identity emphasize interiority over exteriority. Subjective, individualized, internal emotions, desires and characteristics have usurped external markers (such as family lineage, job role, nationality and so on) as the defining features of personal identity. Contemporary notions of personhood can be summed up in three seemingly contradictory mantras: find yourself, be yourself, and make yourself. Authentic human identity is formed by looking into the inner depths of oneself (find yourself) and living in accord with the inner self that is found (be yourself). This inner self is shaped by life experiences and personal interactions, which one has some control over (make yourself). This inward turn is not neutral, however, but marked with mistrust as to the darkness that might be found there. In addition, there is the suspicion of hypocrisy and inauthenticity in relation to those who seem not to act in accord with who they really are.[12]

The renewed (unparalleled) interest in God's inner life coincides with this inward turn in relation to human identity. Within Social Trinitarianism and (therefore) the re-contextual conversation, tracing God's attributes to his life *in se* is paramount (God must be himself and human beings must find him so). If God is relational towards creation, he must be relational in himself; thus God is better depicted as a community than an individual. If God is missional, since mission is a movement towards an other, there must be such movements in God's essential being; thus the persons of the Trinity must be distinct enough that such movements can be seen. Indeed, to ensure continuity between God's inner and outer life, some streams of Social Trinitarianism even make God's essential being dependent on his actions in history (God making himself?). Continuity between who God is in himself and who he is in relationship to creation must be preserved. However, overlooking God's otherness leads to over-speculation as to how this might be so, creating seemingly unresolvable conundrums. How can God be missional *in se* without tying God indissolubly to his creation thus undermining his freedom? How can God be depicted as a community without succumbing to tritheism?[13]

Rather than unwittingly apply the inward turn to God, one must note that God's life *in se* is not corrupted by sin and need not be approached with the suspicion that marks human beings' own journeys inwards; one need not doubt that, unless it can be proved otherwise, God's actions in history might somehow be at odds with who he is. Maintaining God's otherness reconciles who God is *in se* with his actions in history without undermining his freedom by affirming that, while God's actions are consistent with his being, the finite human mind is unable to grasp how this is so. Rather than build a Trinitarian conception of church on abstract speculation into God's interior life, ecclesiology should be founded on what is revealed in Scripture about how God, as Father, Son and Spirit, relates to the church. The body of Christ metaphor provides a lens through which Paul's view on this matter can be seen, indicating its potential to provide a surer foundation for re-contextual thought than Social Trinitarianism can afford.

Notes

1 Ward, 'Blueprint', 74–90; Kilby, 'Problems', 435–8.

2 J. Moltmann, *The Trinity and the Kingdom of God*, London: SCM, 1981, esp. 157; K. Tanner, *Christ the Key*, Cambridge: CUP, 2010, 210–1; cf. S. Coakley, '"Persons" in the "Social" Doctrine of the Trinity: A Critique of Current Analytic Discussion', in S. T. Davis et al. (eds), *The Trinity*, Oxford: OUP, 1999, 123–44; Sexton, 'Resurgence', 791; Holmes, 'Social', 77–89; Kilby, 'Problems', 434–5.

3 P. D. Molnar, *Divine Freedom and the Doctrine of the Immanent Trinity*, Edinburgh; New York: T&T Clark, 2002, 197–233, esp. 220 (criticizing Moltmann); cf. A. J. Torrance, *Persons in Communion*, Edinburgh: T&T Clark, 1996, 311, 317 and Ge, 'One', 13–14.

4 Molnar, *Freedom*, 220 (critiquing Moltmann); Coakley, 'Persons', 123; Kilby, 'Problems', 433–44. I explain in Chapter 7 ('In') how conceptions of God's transcendence and immanence affect notions of personhood. Moltmann explicitly promotes panentheism (J. Moltmann, *God in Creation*, trans. M. Kohl, Minneapolis, MN: Fortress, 1993, 98, 103).

5 Zizioulas, *Being* versus Volf, *Likeness*. Kilby argues that because the three-in-oneness of the Trinity is essentially a mystery, contemporary applications rely on projecting preconceived notions onto the Trinity in order to have something concrete and engaging enough to apply (Kilby, 'Problems', 442–3); cf. Ward, *Liquid*, 14–16; Holmes, 'Social', 82–4. Moreover, ironically, Trinitarianism 'is not often – to say the least – historically associated with an egalitarian politics and respect for diversity within the community. Trinitarian thinking arose in tandem with Christian support for an increasingly centralized Roman Empire, once Christianity became the state religion under Constantine' (Tanner, *Key*, 209).

6 J. Moltmann, *The Coming of God*, trans. M. Kohl, London: SCM, 1996, 254–5; T. Chester, *Mission and the Coming of God*, Milton Keynes: Paternoster, 2006,

73; cf. Ge, 'One', 13; S. Pickard, *Seeking the Church*, London: SCM, 2012, 107–8; J. G. Flett, *The Witness of God*, Grand Rapids, MI: Eerdmans, 2010, 206–7.

7 Molnar criticizes Moltmann's Christology as redefining both the incarnation and Christ's lordship (Molnar, *Freedom*, 227–8). Holmes deems ST to be at odds with Trinitarian orthodoxy (Holmes, 'Social', 85–6); cf. Holmes, *Trinity*, xv, 2.

8 E.g. Holmes argues that scholars such as Pannenberg and Moltmann see God's being as, in some way, fulfilled only at the eschaton (Holmes, *Trinity*, 19 referring to W. Pannenberg, *Systematic Theology*, Vol. 1, trans. G. W. Bromiley: Edinburgh: T&T Clark, 1991, 328–31; J. Moltmann, *The Crucified God*, 2nd ed., trans. R. A. Wilson and J. Bowden, London: SCM, 2001 [1972, 1974]; idem, *Trinity*, 52–6, 161). See also P. C. Wagner, 'Mission and Hope: Some Missiological Implications of the Theology of Jürgen Moltmann', *Missiology* 2.4 (1974) 455–74.

9 Tanner contends, for instance, 'Direct translation of the trinity into a social program is problematic because, unlike the peaceful and perfectly loving mutuality of the trinity, human society is full of suffering, conflict, and sin. Turned into a recommendation for social relations, the trinity seems unrealistic, hopelessly naïve, and, for that reason, perhaps even politically dangerous' (Tanner, *Key*, 228).

10 Holmes, 'Social', 88.

11 Coakley, 'Persons', 123; Kilby, 'Problems', 441–2; Holmes, 'Social', 88; Molnar, *Freedom*, 313; K. Rahner, *The Trinity*, trans. Herder and Herder, London: Burns and Oates, 1986, esp. 21–3.

12 C. Taylor, *Sources of Self*, Cambridge: Harvard University Press, 1989, 36 and *Secular*, 18, 474–89.

13 For example, Collins argues that 'many fear that Moltmann's insistence on the crucifixion and resurrection as an inner-trinitarian event (with a rupture in the divine life and the Father "ceasing" to be Father) may be confusing the intra-divine life with the story of salvation to the point of "imprisoning" God in the world's becoming' (G. O'Collins, 'The Holy Trinity: The State of the Questions', in S. T. Davis et al. (eds), *The Trinity*, Oxford: OUP, 1999, 1–25, citing 4).

5

The Body of Christ is the Church

The Body of Christ Metaphor

My claim that the body of Christ metaphor can provide a more stable and substantial ecclesial basis for re-contextual thinkers leads to the question, why the body of Christ? Why not one of the other images that Paul uses to depict the church? Indeed, why Pauline ecclesiology as opposed to Petrine or Johannine? Healy maintains that believers' socio-cultural context must be taken into consideration when constructing an ecclesiology, including decisions about which model to focus on.[1] I contend that the body of Christ metaphor is particularly apt for the re-contextual movement, as evidenced through the following.

First, there is accord between the cultural context into which Paul first introduced the body of Christ metaphor and the context of the re-contextual church. Out of the four epistles containing the metaphor, 1 Corinthians was penned first. Therefore Paul introduced the metaphor to those whose faith was being distorted by the culture of first-century Corinth which, Thiselton argues, resonates with contemporary Western culture as regards the West's: consumerist culture; 'postmodern' ethos; emphasis on social construction; preoccupation with individual autonomy; pursuit of success; elevation of substanceless audience-pleasing rhetoric; and a desire for relativistic 'local' theology. It follows that, as the body of Christ image was pertinent to the Corinthian church, it will have aptness for today's church.[2]

Second, through Paul's adoption and adaptation of the body metaphor (which was a common image that ancient writers used to depict the state), he models the contextual approach that re-contextual church thinkers aspire to. Addressing this motif provides insight into Paul's approach to contextualization and what factors both guide and limit this.

Third, unity in diversity is a marked feature of the body of Christ motif. Unity and diversity are important facets within re-contextual thinkers' aim to see the church contextualized into different subcultures and yet maintain the unity of the one church of Christ, as exemplified by Moynagh's promotion of 'focused-and-connected' church. I argue below that diversity in gift-giving within local communities (1 Cor. 12.12–31) has implications for gift-giving between local communities too.

Fourth, the body of Christ metaphor addresses the most contentious areas within the re-contextual discussion. The metaphor's emphasis on diversity appears to challenge the promotion of homogenous expressions of church. The body of Christ refers to both the Eucharist and the church, indicating its pertinence to debates regarding the sacraments. Moreover, is the re-contextual movement's emphasis on looking out (in mission) challenged by a motif that some scholars argue is exclusively concerned with looking in (the church's internal relations)? Selecting a model that addresses the most controversial areas means that these issues cannot be glossed over.

Fifth, re-contextual thinkers include the body of Christ metaphor in their ecclesiology but it is not at the fore of their ecclesial thinking. Ward reverses the order from the church (as an institution) is the body of Christ to the body of Christ (believers in their everyday work and lives) is the church. He describes the body of Christ metaphor as Paul's dominant ecclesial image but subsumes this image under Paul's 'in Christ' motif. For Ward, the church is defined a priori by its incorporation into the 'liquid Trinity' through its union with Christ, and this provides the basis for his fluid conception of church.[3] While Paul's 'in Christ' and 'body of Christ' motifs are intricately connected, theoretical contentions derived from the former (in Christ) should not overshadow the practical implications that can be drawn from the latter (body of Christ), particularly in relation to church structure. An ecclesiology based on the body of Christ image progresses the re-contextual conversation by bringing a motif to the fore-ground that currently lies in the background.

Lastly, this motif aligns with re-contextual thinkers' pursuit of a Trinitarian ecclesiology. The body of Christ image outlines the different members of the Trinity's roles within the church. Although it is the body of *Christ*, the Holy Spirit plays as prominent a role as Christ. The Father's role is also indispensable. The body of Christ image thus reveals Paul's view of the church's relationship to Christ, the Spirit and the Father. An ecclesiology based on this motif thus progresses re-contextual thinkers' Trinitarian reflections.[4]

Referring to *the* body of Christ motif assumes that the relevant texts present a single metaphor, which is much disputed. The body of Christ metaphor is utilized in four New Testament books (1 Corinthians, Romans, Ephesians and Colossians) in a range of contexts and to a variety of ends.[5] Perriman thus denies that Paul had a set, preformed notion of what he meant by the body of Christ. He argues that each instantiation of the motif must be interpreted in light of its literary context, especially the argumentation of the passage that it is located in. Minear agrees that the body of Christ metaphor cannot be sharply delineated – attempts to do so fail to account for the variety and flexibility of Paul's thought. In particular, the use of the metaphor in Colossians and Ephesians is often contrasted with the motif's utilization in Romans and 1 Corinthians. Hübner notes that Christ is identified with the body in 1 Corinthians 12.12 but, in Colossians 1.18, he is the head. Lohse argues that this shift arises because, in Colossians and Ephesians, the body of Christ image is derived from Hellenistic notions of the cosmic body instead of the Stoic tradition that is evident in 1 Corinthians and Romans.[6]

However, the differences are not as marked as these scholars maintain. For instance, within Stoicism, the cosmos was analogous to the human body; there was thus no difficulty in depicting a cosmic entity (the cosmos in Stoicism/universal church for Paul) *and* a local entity (the state/local church) as *sōma* (body); it was commonplace to compare the macrocosmic and microcosmic. Expanding the body of Christ metaphor to universal dimensions in Colossians and Ephesians is a precedented development; indeed, Lee notes that Paul uses the body of Christ image in 1 Corinthians to refer to the universal body of Christ (12.13) and the local Christian community (12.27). Further, reference to Christ as the head of the body does not contradict the identification of him with the body in 1 Corinthians 12.12 and 27; rather the body of Christ metaphor, both with and without the specification of Christ as the head, depicts the church's organic union with Christ. The designation 'head' emphasizes Christ's lordship over his church but, when this specification is missing, the church and Christ are not amalgamated. Conversely, Christ's headship does not diminish the notion of organic union conveyed through the presentation of the church as Christ's body (for example, Eph. 4.15–16). The head–body metaphor differs from the body motif only in emphasis; both express the church's union with Christ, while not merging the two.[7]

Moreover, as Minear contends, every New Testament image sheds a unique shade of light on the one underlying reality of the church that lies behind them all. This reality is not static, as if the church should only ever adopt one ideal structure or form. Rather it is relational; it regards God's work in and through the Christian community in the Son and through the Spirit. Since one (relational) reality lies behind the different images used within the New Testament to depict the church, surely one (relational) reality lies behind the body of Christ metaphor but, in different instances, different aspects of this reality are highlighted. In the sections that follow, the context and emphasis of the different texts will be considered. However, I maintain that the notion of incorporation into Christ is present in all occurrences.[8]

Minear warns that no one New Testament image can or should be allowed to dominate the rest. The various images point to a singular reality that underlies them all – the redemptive work of God, Jesus and the Spirit.[9] Focusing on the body of Christ metaphor is not intended to relegate other New Testament models to secondary status; I examine one image to see what progress is made. The aptness of addressing the re-contextual church discussion through the lens of the body of Christ image must be demonstrated but, as Wright argues, 'the real proof of the pudding is in the eating'.[10] The fruitfulness of my endeavour is best assessed by its outcome.

Flexible Church

The outcome is a series of dialectical tensions that the church must maintain in order to adapt flexibly to its context while faithfully preserving its Christian identity. These tensions relate to the four interlocking relationships that re-contextual proponents see as constituting the church's essence: the church's relationship with God (up), the relationships between believers (in), the relationship between the church and the wider world (out), and the relationship between individual local communities and the broader church body of which they are a part (of). These four dimensions do not, however, adequately summarize either re-contextual thinkers' view of church or Paul's body of Christ metaphor. The re-contextual movement's focus on God's initiative, for instance in the mantra 'see what God is doing and join him', is misrepresented by 'up' as this trajectory implies that the onus is on the church's pursuit of God, not the other way around. The emphasis on God's initiative and sustaining power within the body of Christ texts also indicates that 'up' alone is inaccurate and inadequate. Rather, the vertical relational component is better depicted as both 'down', emphasizing God's initiative, and 'up', highlighting the church's response.

In addition, re-contextual thinkers' emphasis on the church's eschatological nature, which accords with the eschatological emphasis within the body of Christ metaphor, prompts the addition of a fifth trajectory, 'towards'.[11] Moreover, re-contextual thinkers highlight the imperfect state of the church's current eschatological existence. This 'not yet' component of the now/not yet eschatological tension that permeates the New Testament, including Paul's texts, is a marked feature of the body of Christ image. Therefore, alongside 'towards', the preposition 'between' highlights that the church's location between two eras has implications for the church's current existence that must not be ignored. Therefore, 'down', 'towards', and 'between' are added to 'up', 'in', 'out', and 'of' to emphasize God's initiative and sustaining power and the now/not yet nature of the church's current eschatological state. These components have been separated for analysis, but this distinction is not absolute. Each dimension impacts and interlocks with the others.[12]

Each of these relational trajectories (down, up, in, out, of, towards and between) contains a tension that the church should seek to maintain. These tensions are not paradoxes per se, but the two sides appear sufficiently contradictory that pulling on one risks distorting the other. Presenting an ecclesiology in the form of tensions is apt; Mazarr argues that paradox is one of the defining features of the current age.[13] More importantly, these tensions are inherent within the body of Christ metaphor; highlighting them is not deferring to the current mood. In pursuing God in the midst of paradoxes and tensions, believers experience God to be more awe-inspiring than they had previously realized. Further, their struggles to relate to God in the midst of these tensions often lead to new levels of intimacy with him.[14] In addition, tensions can stabilize. In contrast to the inflexible solid church that Ward criticizes and the liquid church he promotes, which Murray and Moynagh warn may evaporate into gas, an ecclesiology founded on tensions promotes a flexible mode of church, one which can re-contextualize into different forms depending on its context while maintaining its distinctive identity.

The tensions posited here are best examined through the heuristical conundrum of the 'One', 'Many', and 'One and Many'. Conceptualizing the 'One and Many' relationship is one of philosophy's most ancient challenges. I utilize this notion because it exemplifies the need for dialectical tensions to be upheld; the 'One' and 'Many' collapse into each other if the 'One and Many' tension is not maintained (if 'One' is prioritized over 'Many' or vice versa).[15] Both sides of each tension must be maintained, rather than a central road forged between two extremes. In addition, the tension between the 'One' and 'Many' relates to the issue of unity and diversity that is central to body of Christ metaphor.

In order to convey most effectively the flexibility and stability that the tensions afford, I have coined a metaphor: the church as a suspension bridge characterized by gift-exchange. Just as the tensions within a suspension bridge provide the bridge with the strength and elasticity that it needs to withstand both the load that goes across it and external environmental factors, so too maintaining the tensions conveyed within the body of Christ metaphor provides the church with the solidity and flexibility that it needs to remain true to its calling while adapting to its changing context. The dialectical tensions that are explored below and which, when combined into the framework of the suspension bridge metaphor, form the substance of the ecclesiology promoted are as follows: God's transcendence and immanence (down); the church as spiritual and religious (up); the church as an institution and a network (in); the church as cultural (inculturated) and countercultural (out); the church as inherited and innovative (of); and the eschatological now/not yet tension in which the church is located (towards). In addition, the notions of suffering and conflict that result from the church's current eschatological existence are also explored (between). The language of dialectical tension is vital because the tensions promoted offer stability to re-contextual ecclesiology not to the extent that a middle path is walked between two extremes, but to the degree that the tug of both ends is felt.

The Suspension Bridge Metaphor

The flexibility of a suspension bridge's component parts is vital to the bridge's stability and strength, making this image an illuminating metaphor through which to explore the tensions within the body of Christ metaphor. Indeed, the suspension bridge metaphor I have coined is the clearest and most compelling way to convey the ecclesiology that I promote in this book. However, the suspension bridge metaphor does not simply present predetermined findings; rather this metaphor is a third dialogue partner, of sorts, in that reflection on a suspension bridge's components has shaped my application of the body of Christ metaphor to the re-contextual discussion. For instance, the centrality of the main cable in upholding the bridge resonates with the church's complete dependence on the gracious initiating and sustaining power of God, in Christ and through the Spirit; the church's dependence on God is the category under which everything else must be nested. The devastating effect of resonance brings to mind the way in which too close accord between the church and its surroundings diminishes the church's unique identity and its impact in the world. The massive anchors that hold a suspension bridge firm prompts reflection on the church's anchorage in Christ's life, death, resurrection and ascension, in the past, and his return, in the future. The role of compression towers in counteracting the bridge's tension recalls the compression that the church experiences through its existence within the now/not yet eschatological tension. This prompts an examination into the inevitable presence of both conflict and suffering while the church exists between two ages.

Metaphors generate meaning; thus the innovative power of the suspension bridge image accords with how metaphors work. Soskice defines a metaphor as 'that figure of speech whereby we speak about one thing in terms which are seen to be suggestive of another'.[16] Specifically, a 'tenor' (the nature of the church) is spoken of in terms of a 'vehicle' (a suspension bridge). Metaphors are produced through the interaction between tenor and vehicle to say something that literal speech cannot, *contra* those who view metaphors as merely flamboyant substitutions for literal speech. A metaphor is produced by a semantic clash. It is not the clash per se but rather its resolution that brings new meaning. Therefore, metaphors both depict reality and shape reality by altering a person's perception of, and so reaction to, this reality.[17]

Introducing a metaphor based on the body of Christ image affects how the body metaphor is interpreted and applied. One cannot assume, however, that the contemporary reader understands the body image exactly as Paul's original recipients did. Hesselgrave notes that, insofar as contexts change, theology must adapt or, by ceasing to adapt, find that its meaning has changed de facto.[18] The body of Christ metaphor was a striking image when Paul first coined it. It is now so embedded in the church's self-consciousness that a new image is needed to recreate the dissonance that it originally provoked and jolt believers into examining the metaphor afresh.

Gift-Exchange

Within a suspension bridge, the stability that the tensions afford is not an end in itself. A suspension bridge's stability is to facilitate movement and exchange: the movement of people and vehicles across it and, for example, the exchange of goods, which are transported from one region to another. So too, within the church as a suspension bridge metaphor, the tensions identified uphold a platform for that which lies at the heart of the body of Christ metaphor: gift-exchange. This is evident in the relationships between believers, regarding which the body of Christ metaphor explicitly concerns the use of gifts (Rom. 12.3–8; 1 Cor. 12.12–31; Eph. 4.11–16). However, the notion of gift is also central to the other relational trajectories.

Regarding 'down', a reassessment of God's transcendence and immanence elucidates his nature as gift-giver. In relation to 'up', the church's nature as spiritual and religious enables it to participate in gift-exchange with God, wherein even the church's ability to give to God is itself a gift from him. Regarding 'in', gift-exchange is best facilitated within the Christian community when the church maintains a tension between its existence as an informal network and formal institution. As regards 'out', the church must maintain a tension between being inculturated (cultural) and countercultural in order to be accessible to its context while not losing its distinctive identity. Accessibility and distinctiveness are essential if the church is to participate in gift-exchange with the wider world. In relation to 'of', the church will best receive the gift of the past, and be a gift to the church of the future, when it thinks critically about what it means to be inherited and innovative in every context. Regarding 'towards', the church best equips itself to pursue the gift of the future when it maintains the tension between the 'now' and 'not yet' of the kingdom. In terms of 'between', the church is called to explore the role of suffering and conflict in facilitating gift-exchange.

Notes

1 Healy, *Church*, 39.

2 Thiselton acknowledges the cultural and historical differences but argues that, if postmodernism and consumerism are viewed as mindsets rather than historical cultural phases, there are parallels between the Corinthian church's context and contemporary Western culture (A. C. Thiselton, 'The Significance of Recent Research on 1 Corinthians for Hermeneutical Appropriation of this Epistle Today', *Neot* 40.2 [2006] 320–52; cf. G. D. Fee, *The First Epistle to the Corinthians*, Grand Rapids, MI: Eerdmans, 1987, 10–1; B. Winter, *After Paul Left Corinth*, Grand Rapids, MI; Cambridge: Eerdmans, 2001, 4–7).

3 S. and S. Murray Williams, *Multi-Voiced Church*, Milton Keynes: Paternoster, 2012, e.g. 18–20; Ward, *Liquid*, 5, 33–9, 54.

4 To speak of Paul as Trinitarian would be anachronistic but his portrayal of Christ, the Spirit, and 'God' (the Father) does shed light on contemporary Trinitarian reflections. See P. S. Minear, *Images of the Church in the New Testament*, Louisville, KY: Westminster John Knox, 2004, esp. 189–90, 217.

5 In this book, I engage with the motif as it occurs in the following passages Romans 12.3–8; 1 Corinthians 6.12–20; 10.14–22; 11.23–26; and 12.12–31; Colossians 1.15–20; 1.24–29; 2.16–23; and 3.12–17; and Ephesians 1.22–23; 2.14–18; 2.19–22; 3.1–7; 4.11–16; and 5.21–32.

6 A. Perriman, 'Church and Body in 1 Corinthians', PhD Thesis, Brunel University, 1998; Minear, *Images*, 228; H. Hübner, *An Philemon, An die Kolosser, An die Epheser*, Tübingen: Mohr, 1997, 61; E. Lohse and H. Koester, *Colossians and Philemon*, Philadelphia, PA: Fortress, 1971, 55.

7 M. V. Lee, *Paul, the Stoics, and the Body of Christ*, Cambridge: CUP, 2006, 47, 135–6; G. W. Dawes, *The Body in Question*, Leiden: Brill, 1998, 236.

8 Minear, *Images*, 185–8, 221–8.

9 Minear, *Images*, 221–2.

10 N. T. Wright, *The New Testament and the People of God*, London: SPCK, 1992, 32.

11 Within the wider re-contextual movement, Jones is most explicit about the need for a towards trajectory (although he does not use this term) when he proposes a relational ecclesiology that incorporates the 'relationship of the church to Christ' (up), the 'relationship of the human beings who belong to the church' (in), the 'relationship of the Christian church to the other religions and belief systems of the world' (out), the 'relationship of the church of the present to the church of the past' (of), and the 'relationship of the church of the present to the eschatological church of the future' (towards) (Jones, *Flat*, 160).

12 When addressing the issue of personhood in Ephesians, Turner separates his discussion on personhood into vertical (with God) and horizontal (with others) components. He notes, however, that though such a heuristic strategy is convenient, 'such a distinction is not merely artificial, but in danger of missing the point' (M. Turner, 'Approaching "Personhood" in the New Testament, with special reference

to Ephesians', *EQ* 77.3 [2005] 211–33, citing 226). Similar sentiments must be echoed here.

13 M. J. Mazarr, *Global Trends 2005*, New York: St Martin's, 1999, 10.

14 K. Kandiah, *Paradoxology*, London: Hodder and Stoughton, 2014, 2, 217–21, 306–7.

15 Gunton, *One*, 18, 213.

16 J. M. Soskice, *Metaphor and Religious Language*, Oxford: Clarendon, 1985, 15, 45–8.

17 P. Ricoeur, *The Rule of Metaphor*, trans. R. Czerny, K. McLaughlin and J. Costello, London; New York: Routledge, 2004 (1977), 24–6, 254; Soskice, *Metaphor*, 13, 24, 31, 45–8. Metaphors are described as 'dead metaphors' when a clash is no longer felt.

18 D. J. Hesselgrave and E. Rommen, *Contextualization*, Grand Rapids, MI: Baker, 1989, 178.

6

The Church as a Suspension Bridge Characterized by Gift-Exchange

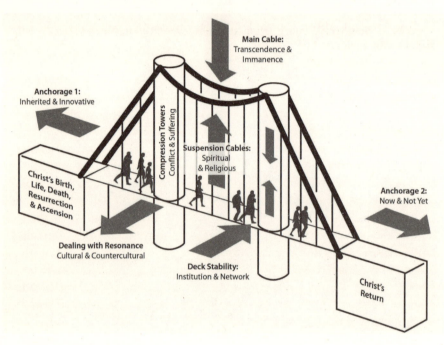

Figure 1: The Church as a Suspension Bridge Characterized by Gift-Exchange

How are bridge stresses and forces addressed in actual bridge designs? One important requirement is flexibility. Bridges are designed to move up and down and side to side in response to changes in loads, temperatures, conditions, wind, and other factors.[1]

The tension within a suspension bridge, in contrast to overly rigid structures, grants the stability and flexibility that the bridge needs to stand firm against external pressures. Similarly, in the church, the acknowledgement and maintenance of tension provides the church with the stability it needs to be faithful to Christ and the flexibility it requires to be innovative and accessible in each new context. A suspension bridge thus provides a pertinent metaphor for the church in the contemporary world. Moreover, reflection on the constituent parts of a suspension bridge sheds light on each of the tensions that are conveyed within the body of Christ texts. These components are: a main cable that bears most of the tension that holds the bridge up; vertical cables that attach the deck to the main cable; the deck; two anchorages at either end of the bridge that fasten it to the earth; and compression towers to counteract the tension in the rest of the structure (see Figure 1). I incorporate reflection on these constituent parts within my assessment of the body of Christ texts.

Down (Main Cable): God's Transcendence and Immanence – Exploring God as Gift-Giver

Re-contextual thinkers urge the church to re-explore its relationship with the Trinity and readdress its conception of God's transcendence and immanence. Proponents of social models of the Trinity have influenced the movement in this regard. However, Social Trinitarianism has been deemed to have a misguided construal of God's transcendence and immanence, leading to a God who is too removed from creation or dependent on it such that his freedom is impinged. Regarding the first of these errors (too removed), Gunton's Trinitarianism has been criticized for focusing on the horizontal relationships within the Godhead and, by analogy, human relations, overlooking the vertical relationship between humanity and God and thus disconnecting God from his creation. Regarding the second (too connected), Moltmann's panentheism is seen as contradicting divine freedom by making the creator dependent on creation, overlooking God's otherness. These two extremes result from the role of *perichoresis* within social models of the Trinity. If applied analogically (God is an ideal *perichoretic* communion that human communities should model), *perichoresis* does not adequately convey God's connection to creation. If applied to creation and God, this vertical *perichoresis* leads to panentheism – interdependent interpenetration between God and creation, which risks amalgamating the two. Gunton is seen to fall foul in the first of these, and Moltmann the second.[2] In contrast, as I argue below, a Trinitarian ecclesiology based on the body of Christ texts is able to avoid both errors by providing a framework that both preserves God's freedom while acknowledging his intimate involvement in creation.

A suspension bridge is upheld by its main cable. So too God, in his transcendence and immanence, upholds the church (see Figure 2). God's transcendence and immanence were manifest before the Christ-event; they are a major theme in the Old Testament. However, the tension between them is reconceived within the body of Christ motif in light of Christ's actions in history and subsequent sending of the Spirit. Just as a suspension

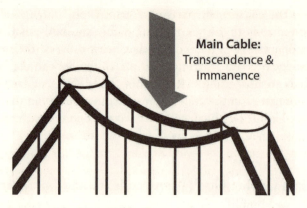

Figure 2: The Main Cable: Transcendence and Immanence

bridge's main cable is fastened to solid, unmoveable anchors, so too the divine transcendence-immanence tension, as conveyed through the body of Christ metaphor, is anchored to the Christ-event – Christ's life, death, resurrection and ascension, on the one side, and his future return, on the other.[3]

I noted that I would use the heuristic lens of 'one', 'many', and 'one and many' to ensure that the dialectical tensions I identify are conveyed as tensions, not a middle path between two extremes. Below, I maintain that the oneness of God as transcendent over creation ('one') is in tension with God's revelation, in Christ and through the Spirit, in the church as Christ's body in different ways ('many'). This dialectical tension is maintained within the body of Christ metaphor not through pitting God's transcendence against his immanence, as dualistic conceptions tend to do (see below), but through recognizing that God's transcendence enables his immanence ('one and many'). Proper conception of this transcendence-immanence dialectic enables one to say that the church, as Christ's body, is brought into an undeserved and unequal relationship of reciprocal gift-exchange with God while, simultaneously, being completely dependent on God; the ability to engage in gift-giving with God is itself a gift from God.

Transcendent ('One')

Grenz and Olson assert:

> Because the Bible presents God as both beyond the world and present to the world, theologians in every era are confronted with the challenge of articulating the Christian understanding of the nature of God in a manner that balances, affirms and holds in creative tension the twin truths of divine transcendence and the divine immanence.[4]

Where the balance is wrong, one cannot simply 'pull harder' on the opposite side of the tension. Rather, the foundation must be relaid. Given the imbalances that Grenz and Olson observe within Western theology over the last century, it is unsurprising that it is an area re-contextual thinkers believe needs readdressing.[5] Refounding this transcendent-immanent tension is thus an essential step in progressing the re-contextual conversation. It is also fitting considering the context into which the body of Christ passages were penned.

The first recipients of the body of Christ metaphor had an inaccurate construal of God's transcendence and immanence. Concerning 1 Corinthians, it is disputed whether the root cause of the problems that Paul addresses is social, philosophical, epistemological, or spiritual. Overarching these facets, however, is the paradoxical problem that the Corinthian Christians see God as simultaneously too distant and too close – too close in that their overconfidence in their own knowledge and wisdom leads Paul to remind them, 'now we see through a mirror opaquely, but then face to face' (1 Cor. 13.12a). The Corinthian believers had an overly perfected notion of their own knowledge, spirituality, and thus access to God (1 Cor. 4.8–10), regardless of whether this came from an over-realized eschatology or a lack of eschatology. Conversely, in relation to ethical and social conduct, they see God as too distant, as indicated by 1 Corinthians 3.16 and 12.27a – 'don't you know that you are God's temple and God's Spirit dwells in you?' (3.16) and 'you are Christ's body' (12.27a).[6]

The contexts of Colossians and Ephesians are less agreed but both epistles suggest that the recipients are tempted to trust in, or have an unhealthy respect for, spiritual powers and mediators, rather than Christ (Eph. 1.19–22; 6.10–17; Col. 2.18). Arnold explains this 'power-motif' in Ephesians through his contention that Ephesus was a centre for magical practices and the primary location of the cult of Artemis (Diana). Arnold distinguishes magic from religion by noting that in 'religion one prays and requests from the gods; in magic one commands the gods and therefore expects guaranteed results'.[7] Fundamental to magical practices was the belief in an intangible spirit world lying behind almost every tangible component of life. The aim of the magician or magical practice was to manipulate these spirits either for the benefit of the person seeking out the service or, in the case of curses, to harm an adversary. Arnold has been criticized for overemphasizing this particular component of the original recipients' context, and Ephesians may not have been written for believers in Ephesus.[8] However, magical practices and the Artemis cult spread across eastern Asia. The notion that Ephesians was particularly directed towards those living in the midst of this syncrenistic magic-obsessed world thus has strong support.[9]

In Colossians Paul warns his readers not to be taken captive by vain philosophy and empty deceit according to human tradition and the spiritual powers of the universe (Col. 2.8) as promoted by those who insist on the worship of angels (2.18) and have not held fast to the head (2.19). Regarding these verses, Dunn criticizes the popular notion that Paul is rebuffing the 'Colossian heresy'. He argues that Paul is simply warning against certain traditions and philosophies in Colossae that may have appealed to the Colossian believers. Hooker also maintains that Paul has in view the temptations and pressures that arise from the recipients' pagan environment and background, rather than an explicit false teaching. Moo, in contrast, contends that the tightness of Paul's argumentation indicates that a specific movement is in sight, even if the movement's promoters won people over by smug superiority rather than proselytizing.[10] Regardless of whether Paul has in mind a heretical movement or pagan beliefs and practices within the recipients' milieu, his concerns regard syncretism (2.8–23) and engagement in magical practices, including worshipping angels (2.18), maintaining magical traditions (2.8), asceticism, and the observance of festival days (2.16, 21). The Colossian believers (or former believers (2.19)) were tempted to maintain these rituals and practices because of their fear of evil spiritual powers.[11]

The influence of magic upon believers may appear to relate to God's power, not his transcendence and immanence. However, the believers' fear of and focus on spiritual powers and mediators suggests that Greek notions of transcendence and immanence had affected them. Within Greek philosophy, as Tanner notes, the more transcendent God is, the less involved he is with the earthly world around him; he is separated from the world by distance and mediators are required to bridge the gap. Ironically, though, seeing God's transcendence as his removal from creation rests on applying the 'rules' of creation to God, wherein separation and distance go hand-in-hand. In dualistic accounts of divinity, God is elevated above the world by the incorporation of a whole realm of mediators because he is seen in worldly terms, wherein he can only be separated by distance. Therefore, what appears to elevate him (his distance from creation) actually relegates him (distance only separates him from creation if he is subject to creation's rules). Thus, the problem with the recipients of Ephesians and Colossians is not just that they fail to see Christ as *above* all other powers; their faulty view of God's transcendence means that they cannot see that Christ is, in fact, *beyond* these powers – the powers' existence is dependent on him (Col. 1.16–17).[12]

Christ's transcendent supremacy beyond creation is indicated by the radical development of Wisdom and Logos language within Colossians 1.15–20.[13]

He is the image of the invisible God, the firstborn of all creation, for in him all things have been created, things in heaven and on earth, visible and invisible, whether thrones or powers, rulers or authorities, everything was made in him and through him. He is above all things and in him all things join together, and he is the head of the body, the church. He is the origin of all things, the first born from the dead, so that he might take first place in everything. Because in him all the fullness of God was pleased to dwell, and through him to reconcile to himself all things, whether things on earth or in heaven, making peace through the blood of his cross. (Col. 1.15–20)

Wisdom and Logos allusions appear here through Christ's mediatory role in creation (1.16), which resonates with Wisdom's role in Proverbs 8.22–31, and the ascription to Christ of the titles 'firstborn' and 'image'. The Genesis creation story is also alluded to, highlighting this passage's re-creation theme. Wisdom and Logos speak of God's immanence while safeguarding his transcendence through being personifications. Christ, however, is not merely a personification but the embodiment of God (1.19–20). In this passage, Paul therefore builds on Old Testament themes to convey the redefinition of Jewish monotheism that occurred as the early Christians included Jesus in their conception of God. All human beings have been made in God's image (Gen. 1.26) but Christ is uniquely God's image in that, *contra* human beings, the 'second person of the trinity is divine in and of itself and not simply in virtue of being the image of the first person'.[14] Christ's oneness with God is established by identifying him with the transcendent one: beyond and involved in creation. Christ's transcendence beyond the world does not distance him from creation, however, but enables his immanence.[15]

Immanent ('Many')

Through presenting Christ's transcendence in terms of his otherness beyond creation, Paul provides an ontological foundation for Christ's involvement in the world. This connection between Christ and creation is expressed through the concept of participation, which in Christian theology conveys creation's dependence on God's initiating and sustaining presence. Colossians 1.15–20 (cf. Eph. 1.22–23), for example, indicates that creation participates in Christ in a 'weak' sense; all life is derived from and upheld by God in Christ. *Contra* wider creation's weak participation in God, the church experiences 'strong' participation in the divine life through its incorporation into Christ as his body. Rather than the panen-theism and disconnection that accompanies social models of the Trinity, the concept of participation accounts for God's immanence within his creation while maintaining his transcendent freedom.[16]

Concerning the church's connection to Christ, scholars disagree on whether the image of the church as Christ's body is literal or 'mere' metaphor. However, this disagreement is based on the belittling of metaphor's literary power and the false assumption that a metaphor cannot refer to something real. Robinson, for example, maintains a literal interpretation because he incorrectly thinks that, if taken metaphorically, the body of Christ image is incapable of conveying the ontological union with Christ that he rightly sees as the overarching sense of the motif. A literal meaning is not viable, since the church is not literally Christ's body (it does not constitute his bodily cells), so a metaphorical sense is envisioned. Designating 'the body of Christ' a metaphor does not mean that notions of ontological union are not present. On the contrary, although the metaphor appears in a variety of contexts, and therefore the focus of application varies, the underlying reality is the same: the organic union of believers with Christ through the Spirit that brings them into relationship with the Father (for example, 1 Cor. 12.13; Rom. 8.15).[17]

For example, although the political overtones of 'body' in 1 Corinthians 12.12–31 suggest that Paul viewed the church as a political entity of sorts, these political overtones are subverted and subsumed under the specific identification of the body as Christ's and, through reference to the incorporating role of the Spirit (1 Cor. 12.13), the organic unity that this metaphorical identification conveys.[18] The addition of 'head' in Ephesians and Colossians emphasizes Christ's apartness from his body but, where the metaphor appears without 'head', care is taken to convey Christ's intimacy with his body while never amalgamating the two. Moreover, within the head–body metaphor, notions of Christ's authority are placed in an overarching context in which organic union between body and head is firmly in view (especially Eph. 5.23–32). In Ephesians 4.15–16, for example, the reference to growth into Christ, the head, and the image of a body being joined together by its connecting ligaments make the notion of organic union explicit.

The body of Christ image should be understood metaphorically and mystically – mystically in the sense of 'having a divine or sacred significance that surpasses natural human apprehension'.[19] The reality that the metaphor points to is a mystical ontological reality: the union of the church with Christ and, in Christ, the church's participation in God.[20] Viewing participation in Christ as the primary referent of the image is supported by the connection between this metaphor and Paul's 'in Christ' motif. Thompson argues that this metaphor develops and extends the 'in Christ' motif.[21] More specifically, the body of Christ metaphor is Paul's 'in Christ' motif as applied to the church. Incorporation into Christ enables the church's participation within the divine life. As Tanner contends:

Jesus Christ is more than a paradigm ... he has become for us the very means ... By the power of the Holy Spirit, the first person of the trinity sends the second person into the world so as to be incarnate in human flesh, one with the humanity of Jesus. That same power of the Spirit comes to us through the glorified humanity of Christ in order to attach us to him, make us one with him, in all the intensity of faith, hope, and love ... living off God, so to speak ... in something like the way an unborn baby lives off the life of its mother.[22]

Christ's identity as the fullness of the 'one' God made flesh (Col. 1.19–22) provides the basis for the believers' experience of this transcendent fullness (Col. 2.9–10; Eph. 3.16–19) through their organic union with him; God 'is not distant from us or aloof to our existence, rather, he is in fact closer to us than we are to ourselves'.[23] Each believer's experience of God will be to some degree unique. Therefore, as each believer articulates and outworks their experience of God, God's revelation takes 'many' forms.

Transcendent and Immanent ('One and Many')

There is no greater challenge to Greek notions of transcendence as God's distance from creation than Christ's incarnation.[24] In conceptualizing divine transcendence and immanence in Christ it must be noted that God's immanence is possible because he is 'other' (transcendent). Since God is 'other' the rules of creation do not apply; as the creator, God's transcendence enables his immanent involvement in his creation. Although Christ is fully human, his divine identity means that he is not just part of creation, rather God created all things 'in' him. Christ is supreme over every other spiritual or earthly power not simply because he is greater than them, but because they owe their existence to him. He is not just more powerful than any created being; he is beyond creation, while remaining intimately involved in it. Therefore, although Christ is interpreted through Old Testament images and figures, his activity and nature, as depicted in Colossians 1.15–20, is unprecedented.[25] As Barth contends, it is often imagined that God

must only be absolute in contrast to all that is relative, exalted in contrast to all that is lowly, active in contrast to all suffering, inviolable in contrast to all temptation, transcendent in contrast to all immanence, and therefore divine in contrast to everything human, in short that He can and must be only the 'Wholly Other.' But such beliefs are shown to be quite untenable, and corrupt and pagan, by the fact that God does in fact be and do this in Jesus Christ.[26]

This makes Christ greater than was thought, not lesser. Paul declares that God, in Christ and through the Spirit, is both more powerful and transcendent *and* more intimate and immanent than his readers have currently grasped (cf. Eph. 1.15–23). God's transcendence provides the basis for the chief motif through which his relationship with humanity is best conceived: God as gift-giver.[27] Indeed, the primary gift that Christ gives to the church is himself (Eph. 5.23–32), which is a gift that brings reconciliation with the Father (Eph. 2.16) and is manifest through the Spirit (Eph. 4.7–16).

Alongside Christ's self-giving to the church, the church is presented as a gift to Christ. In Ephesians 5.23–32 Paul draws on Old Testament bridal imagery (Ezek. 16.8–14; 36.25–27) to outline Christ's desire to cleanse his church, setting her apart for himself, 'just as a young and dazzlingly beautiful bride, in all her finery, is presented to the groom' (cf. Rev. 21.2).[28] So too, elsewhere in Ephesians, the church is depicted as both the inheritor of God's gifts (Eph. 1.14) and, as God's inheritance (Eph. 1.18), a gift to God. The church and God are not equal givers, however. Rather, God takes the initiative both for his own giving and that of the church; the church responds to and through grace (cf. Eph. 2.8–10; 4.7). In self-giving love, however, Christ enables his relationship with the church to cause him delight (Eph. 5.26–27).

The notion that God enters into an unequal but reciprocal relationship with the church, in Christ and through the Spirit, is not something that the Western church has readily embraced. Rather, as Barclay argues, Western Christianity's conception of God's grace has been affected by Derrida's assertion that a 'gift is only a gift if it requires and gets no return'.[29] Following suit, modern theologians have conceived of 'pure grace' as that which expects and demands nothing in return. Such a view, Barclay maintains, is an imposition. Paul would have held a pre-modern (specifically pre-Derrida) understanding of gift giving, within which reciprocity was essential for the formation and maintenance of relationships. In most societies refusing to give or receive is tantamount to severing (or refusing to form) a relationship. People match gifts with counter-gifts because the gift is inseparable from the giver. For Paul, it is not a lack of reciprocity that makes the Christ-gift so unique; reciprocity is assumed such that Paul finds 'no difficulty in speaking of obedience as the state of those who live "under grace" (Rom. 6.12–23)'.[30] Rather, it is the incongruous (undeserved) nature of God's grace in Christ that makes it so unprecedented.[31]

Barclay maintains that exploring how believers are able to obey (give in return) risks overloading Paul's theology of grace with matters that lie beyond its scope. However, the incongruous nature of God's gift of Christ and the Spirit casts doubt on this assertion. Barclay rightly notes that although 'Paul can swing to and fro in descriptions of agency' (1 Cor.

15.10), he does not 'complicate every statement of believer agency ("love your neighbour – or rather, not you, but the Spirit who loves in you")'.[32] However, while not eliminating human agency, or amalgamating the Spirit and the believer such that the former absorbs the latter, the qualifiers 'in Christ' and 'by the Spirit' indicate that, for Paul, the church is only capable of being God's inheritance since it is first an inheritor. Believers receive their righteousness from Christ and the Spirit (Rom. 8.3–4). However, the church's purity is not yet perfected. Rather, the church's identity is simultaneously assured (the believers are Christ's body) and under construction (they 'are to become what they already are').[33] Thus God's grace is permanently incongruous since, although in Christ and through the Spirit believers are transformed, they never become worthy of the gifts they have received (for example, 1 Cor. 12.7).

Highlighting God's initiative in enabling the church to give to him may seem to support Derrida's unilateral notion of gift-giving after all. However, as Tanner notes, if God's transcendence is properly understood as otherness, the relationship between the human creature and God contravenes the usual rules of 'active' and 'passive'. Between creatures, one is either active or passive (and cannot concurrently be both). However, the dependency of finite creatures on an infinite God means that, although humans are always passive in respect to God, because he is other, this passivity need not exclude activity. Indeed, the more intimate a person's relationship with God is, the more empowered they are to live out the fullness of who they have been created to be. Similarly, 'no matter how active one is as creature, one is never anything other than the recipient of God's active grace – God remains active over all'.[34]

Implications: Christocentric Trinitarian Ecclesiology

The church is initiated and upheld by God, the *main cable*, within which there is a tension between God's transcendence and his immanence. *Contra* social models of the Trinity, which either diminish God's connection with creation or undermine his freedom, the body of Christ metaphor presents the church as united to Christ as his body without amalgamating the two. Such intimacy and distinction is possible since Christ's divine transcendence enables his immanence. Through its union with Christ, the church participates in God's life in a context of overarching passivity. The church can give to God but this ability is, itself, a gift from God, enabling the church to enter into real relationship (unequal reciprocity) with him. This has the following implications for re-contextual ecclesiology.

Christocentric Trinitarianism

Paul's conception of church is not predicated on the church as an icon (or image) of the Godhead in a general sense. Rather the church is incorporated into the divine life as the body of Christ. In their pursuit of a Trinitarian ecclesiology, re-contextual thinkers should thus focus on Christ's Trinitarian role and relations. Tanner highlights Christ's role in criticism of those, such as Moltmann, who model human communities on egalitarian conceptions of the Trinity. The problem with these idealized models is that, 'unlike the peaceful and perfectly loving mutuality of the trinity, human society is full of suffering, conflict, and sin'.[35] Such models also fail to account for the otherness of God: 'How' (Tanner asks) 'is the gap between sinful, finite human beings and the trinity to be bridged so that we can see its implications for the lives we actually live?'[36] Her answer is Christ:

> Human beings are not left to their own devices in figuring out what the trinity means for human relations. Instead the trinity enters our world in Christ to show us how human relations are to be reformed in its image ... We are not called to imitate the trinity ... but brought to participate in it ... The second person of the trinity takes the humanity united to it into its own relations with Father and Spirit; and we are to enjoy those same relations through him by the power of the Spirit. In Christ we are therefore shown what the trinity looks like when it includes the human, and what humanity looks like when it is taken up within the trinity's own relationships.[37]

Christ in his human embodiedness, not speculative constructions of the Trinity, is the church's paradigm. Christ is unique in his incarnation but Paul refers to Christ's example to teach believers how to live (for example, Col. 3.12–17). Moreover, the body of Christ texts demonstrate what participation in God's life looks like (at least, should look like) in concrete historical circumstances. The contemporary church exists in a different context than the congregations to whom Paul wrote, and therefore applying these texts today is not straightforward. The discipline of biblical exegesis, however, restrains importing into God's life one's preconceived political or ecclesial agenda to then read back the same, now legitimated, conception into society or church (which Social Trinitarians are often accused of). It is therefore unnecessary (and unhelpful) to formulate a framework for church based on abstract reflections on God's essential being, particularly when such speculative explorations are allowed to trump the more clearly articulated assertions of the body of Christ texts.

Ward is an example of such abstract speculation. His proposals regarding a more relationally networked liquid mode of church are a helpful rejoinder to the over-institutionalized solid form of church that he is criticizing, and the New Testament does not promote just one structural model for church. However, exploring Paul's understanding and application of the church's nature as Christ's body would contribute stability and structure to an ecclesiology that is otherwise founded on a fluid notion of the 'in Christ' motif and the 'liquid Trinity'. As Ward himself notes, such guidance is needed to prevent a 'fluid church' becoming a 'misguided, runaway church'.[38]

Jones attempts to provide an ecclesiology for the emerging church based on Moltmann's concept of the Social Trinity. However, his criticism of Moltmann's ecclesiology as 'too idealistic' casts doubt on whether Moltmann's Social Trinitarianism really is 'an excellent basis for the twenty-first century church'.[39] For example, Jones argues that, within Moltmann's ecclesial thinking, noting God's presence in the world removes 'the sacred-secular divide evident in the ecclesiologies that demarcate the church as unique because it is indwelt by God's Spirit'.[40] In contrast, as explored below, an ecclesiology based on the body of Christ texts provides a framework for discerning God's work in the world while maintaining the church as the place God's presence dwells in a unique way.

Overall, regarding the pursuit of a Trinitarian ecclesiology, the body of Christ motif presents the church (as a unified and diverse entity) as nested in the Godhead specifically through its incorporation in Christ and the infilling of the Spirit (Col. 1.18; Rom. 12.5; 1 Cor. 12.12–13, 27; Eph. 4.3–6, 15–16; Col. 2.9–10, 19), while maintaining the Trinity's otherness and, specifically, Christ's distinct identity as separate from his body (Col. 1.18; Eph. 1.22; 5.23). Within this *Christocentric* Trinitarian ecclesiology, the church is held in the tension between God's transcendence and immanence, anchored between Christ's life, death and resurrection, on the one side, and his return, on the other.

Transcendence and Immanence Re-Examined

This examination of God's transcendence and immanence supports re-contextual thinkers' desire for rebalance where, for example, they have viewed the church as over-focused on God's transcendence at the expense of his concern for the mundane. However, this imbalance cannot be rectified by pulling harder on the 'immanent' side of the tension, as it were. Rather, the re-contextual church must refound its understanding, recognizing that God's transcendence is not opposed to, but enables his immanence. Thwaites contends that such re-conceptualizing would enable believers to see God's revelation within human relationships and wider creation alongside God's revealed word and his unique revelation in Christ. This would not diminish the authority and uniqueness of the

Incarnation and Scripture, Thwaites argues, but provides a framework within which divine revelation can be best understood and applied. Within his argumentation, Thwaites overly polarizes Greek and Hebrew mindsets. He also demonstrates a reductionist conception of the gathered church.[41] However, despite the weaknesses of certain aspects of his argument, the re-contextual conversation should heed his challenge to refound their conception of God's transcendence and immanence. In what follows, I attempt one such refounding.

Characterized by Gift-Exchange

Ecclesiology must be based upon explorations into who God is and who the church is in relation to him. At the heart of theology is 'the sense of God as the giver of all good gifts, their fount, luminous source, fecund treasury and store house'.[42] Indeed:

> The history of the world is God's working for the fuller bestowal of such gifts, each stage of this history – creation, covenant, salvation in Christ – representing a greater communication of goodness to the creature and the overcoming of any sinful opposition to these gifts' distribution.[43]

The church's participation in a Godhead characterized by gift-giving leads to the qualification of the suspension bridge metaphor with the modifier *characterized by gift-exchange*. Since the church enters into unequal reciprocity with God, wherein the church's ability to give is itself a gift from God, the church should, first and foremost, be characterized by gratitude expressed in gift-giving: to God, within the believing community, and out into the wider world. Worship is the 'normative' response to God and should be expressed through the whole of believers' lives, such that, for example, service to others is viewed as service to God. Believers' entire lives are their offering to God (Rom. 12.1). This whole-life view of worship links worship with mission; mission is part of the church's worship. Moreover, although worship is an end in itself, rather than the means to some other goal, the more intimate believers' relationship with God is, the more empowered they are to live out the fullness of who they were created to be, which includes bearing witness to Christ in mission.[44]

Up (The Suspension Cables): Spiritual and Religious – Participating in Unmediated/Mediated Gift-Exchange with God

The re-contextual movement criticizes the unhealthy dualisms and false dichotomies that they perceive exist within the inherited church. In response, re-contextual thinkers desire to root the church in a more holistic conception of human personhood and Christian praxis. Within this pursuit, however, there is an inconsistency. On the one hand, religion is conveyed negatively yet, on the other, religious practices are encouraged. I shall therefore explore the issue of holism in relation to the 'spiritual but not religious' shift within Western culture. I endeavour to see what light Pauline anthropology, as revealed within passages pertaining to the body of Christ metaphor, sheds on the re-contextual church's pursuit of holistic faith and the trend towards spirituality and away from religion.[45]

Those examining the 'spiritual but not religious' shift note the lack of clarity surrounding these terms. Principe observes that the roots of the word 'spirituality' trace back to Paul's use of spirit (*pneuma*) to depict that within a human being that is ordered, led and influenced by God's Spirit, in contrast to the flesh (*sarx*), which is all (whether thoughts, actions, will or emotions) that is opposed to God's Spirit. When 'spiritual' entered the English language in the fourteenth century, it had departed from its Pauline use and referred to the religious and devotional realm. Fuller thus maintains that, although the terms' origins are not identical, up to the twentieth century 'spiritual' and 'religious' were effectively synonyms. Principe notes that 'spiritual' then began to indicate a dualistic distinction from the corporeal and physical. Huss contends that this dualism between the spiritual and material was prominent until the start of the twentieth century, whereupon 'spirituality' entered a new juxtaposition 'with a category it was previously closely related to, namely religious'.[46]

Spirituality now, Huss asserts, refers not to the realm of religious practices, nor is it opposed to the physical (although traces of this dualism remain). Rather, spirituality refers to the subjective, experiential, individualized, self-focused conglomerate of beliefs and (predominantly) practices (such as meditation) – aimed primarily towards self-fulfilment and wellbeing – that characterize the New Age movement. Within this there is a move towards Eastern monistic views of reality. Monism depicts reality as one, denying such Western dualisms as material/spiritual, mind/body, and natural/supernatural. Monistic theories vary regarding whether this one ultimate reality is material or spiritual, although within the New Age movement the latter is more prominent. Despite this shift towards monistic conceptions of spirituality, however, as Hunt poignantly contends, '[n]onduality seems far more frequently talked than walked'.[47] Ironically, monistic views of spirituality end up dualistic since, within many New Age spiritualities, the search for the sacred has just shifted from *up* to *in*. Spirituality is not seen as encompassing the whole of life; rather, one part of a person (the part of the brain that perceives mystical experiences) is elevated as the more spiritual part. Spiritual practices are pursued to the extent that they are effective in facilitating this experience.[48]

Others see greater overlap between spiritual and religious than Huss affords. However, although it is simplistic to define these terms via the dichotomies 'individual versus institutional' or 'good versus bad', spirituality is commonly depicted as being individualized, subjective, non-institutional, non-prescribed, experiential, pick 'n' mix and privatized. Outside a church context, contemporary spirituality is exemplified by Sheilaism. Fittingly coined by an individual called Sheila, Sheilaism refers to a self-selected conglomerate of spiritual practices and beliefs. Churchgoers also display such traits, with high numbers incorporating non-church spiritual practices and philosophies alongside their more orthodox beliefs and ethics.[49] Conversely, whereas religion was once a broad concept, it is now often viewed as just institutionally prescribed rules, rituals and dogma. Even among churchgoers, religion is often seen as externally imposed rules and a self-righteous façade that hinders authentic spirituality rather than enhances it.[50]

Despite the juxtaposition, both terms (spiritual and religious) refer to a *search for the sacred* – a transcendent person, principle or object.[51] Where they differ regards the means of this search. While there is some overlap, spirituality (in common parlance) emphasizes the individual, subjective, experiential, self-focused, self-selected, holistic (in relation to holistic wellbeing), and privatized aspects of this search; religion highlights the corporate, objective, dogmatic, institutional, prescribed and public features. In sum, while 'spiritual' implies *unmediated* access to the sacred (the individual can access the transcendent without the mediation of other people, institutions, or prescribed modes of faith), 'religious' denotes a *mediated* approach (institutions, leaders, prescribed rituals, ethics and so on are integral in relating to the sacred).

Regarding the suspension bridge metaphor, I present the church's relationship with God as the suspension cables. Within a suspension bridge, these cables are supported by the bridge's main cable. So too, the church's relationship with God (up) is determined by believers' conception of God and their understanding of themselves in relation to God, particularly his transcendence and immanence (down) (see Figure 3). Critics claim that the portrayal of God's transcendence and immanence within social models of the Trinity leads to dualism and, conversely, monistic panentheism. Social models of the Trinity are unwittingly dualistic since, if God is too removed from creation, non-divine intermediaries bridge the gap, such as the human spirit, and thus activities that are seen to engage the spirit are elevated. If the gap between God and creation is removed, panentheistic monism results. As noted above, monism leads to dualism since, if creation is absorbed into the divine life, consciousness of this is only possible if the divine encounter is located in a particular arena, usually a person's 'inner self' – their experience and feelings. Social Trinitarianism

Figure 3: The Suspension Cables: Spiritual and Religious

thus appears an inadequate foundation for re-contextual thinkers' pursuit of holistic faith.[52]

In contrast to Social Trinitarianism, the body of Christ metaphor provides a firm foundation for holistic conceptions of faith. The body of Christ metaphor supports neither the unhealthy individualism of some forms of spirituality nor the self-righteous façade of some modes of religion. Indeed, Paul's conception of spirituality and religion does not accord with contemporary notions.[53] However, just as Paul criticized an understanding of spirituality that he perceived as corrupt, so too contemporary understandings of spirituality and religion must be addressed.[54] Spirituality (nowadays) means an individual's personal, subjective, spontaneous and unmediated experience of God ('one'). Religion refers to the relational, objective, structured and mediated nature of believers' relation to God ('many'). Both aspects, and the interaction between them ('one and many'), are essential components of the church's relation with God (up) – the suspension cables that hold the bridge's platform in place. The individual, subjective, spontaneous and unmediated aspects of believers' relationship with God in Christ and through the Spirit (spiritual) must be held in tension with that which is communal, objective, structured and mediated (religious). Maintaining this tension between an unmediated and mediated search for the sacred, and the holistic anthropology undergirding this, is essential for reconceptualizing a healthy holism within the church's relationship with God.

Spiritual ('One')

Paul's use of the body of Christ metaphor in reference to believers' physical bodies in 1 Corinthians 6.12–20 provides a window through which to assess his anthropology. Within this passage Paul's presentation of the church as Christ's body, as indicated through his depiction of believers as members of Christ (6.15), is predicated on believers' incorporation into Christ (6.17). Anthropology lies at the heart of ecclesiology.

'In all things I am without restraint', but not all things are profitable. 'In all things I am without restraint', but I myself will not be restrained by anything. 'Food is for the stomach and the stomach is for food, and God will do away with both', but the body is meant for the Lord, not sexual immorality, and the Lord for the body. For God raised the Lord and will also raise us through his power. Don't you know that your bodies are members of Christ? Therefore shall I take the members of Christ and make them members of a prostitute? Never! Don't you know that when you join to a prostitute you are one body with her? For it says, 'the two will become one flesh', and those who are joined to the Lord are one Spirit with him. Flee from sexual immorality. 'All sins that people do are outside the body'[55] but in committing sexual immorality, one sins against their own body. Don't you know that your body is a temple of the Holy Spirit, who is in you and whom you receive from God, and it is not your own? You have been bought at a price therefore glorify God with your body. (1 Cor. 6.12–20)

Fee notes that 1 Corinthians 6.12–20 should quash the resilient dualism between body and soul/spirit that has underscored much Western Christian thought. Given that the soul has been deemed the locus of encounter with the transcendent in both ancient and modern thought, albeit in different ways, this passage perhaps seems an odd choice of dialogue partner when seeking to affirm that the church's relationship with God (up) is unmediated, individualized and subjective. However the unmediated relationship with God promoted through this passage is not dualistic; Paul does not present human beings as having a human spirit that somehow transcends their physicality enabling direct (spiritual) union with the divine – indeed he rails against such a view. Rather than the disembodied spiritual union a dualistic anthropology might convey, Paul affirms an individual unmediated connection to God in Christ and through the Spirit that is thoroughly enfleshed.[56]

An unmediated *and* embodied construal of believers' relationship with God accords with the Pauline conception of God's transcendence and immanence that I outlined above – God's otherness from creation enables his pervasive and permeating intimacy with created beings. God's otherness from creation is not through virtue of him being *spirit* in contrast to *material*, but *creator* in contrast to *creation* – regardless of whether this creation is the material world of human physicality, or benevolent and malevolent beings in the spiritual realm. Paul does not see a person's physicality as a barrier to unmediated relationship with God. On the contrary, believers are identified as a temple of God's Spirit precisely as embodied beings (6.19).

Within this passage Paul cites Corinthian slogans in order to rebut them. The exact form and origin of these slogans is disputed. However, there is significant agreement that Paul is countering dualistic, at least hierarchical, notions of personhood among Corinthian believers with strong assertions of human beings' embodiedness. In particular, Paul rebukes those who view themselves as having a 'spiritual' essence that is separate from and superior to the body such that what they do with their bodies (here, extramarital sex) does not impinge on their relationship with God. Paul counters that such a divide is impossible: what one does with one's body, one does with the whole of one's being. Paul's rebuttal is not just an affirmation of human beings' embodiedness, however; sexual immorality is rebuked because believers are unified with Christ – one Spirit with him (6.17). This embodied union of the believer with Christ through the Spirit is emphasized further by the temple metaphor (6.19). Thus, for Paul, spirituality relates to a person's interaction with God's Spirit. Spirituality is matured as believers walk with God's Spirit (for example, Rom. 8.4) and corrupted when people resist the Spirit and are led astray by malevolent spirits (for example, Col. 1.13; 2.16–23).[57]

Paul conceives of human personhood as embodied but not reduced to the material alone.[58] A person's relationship with Christ through God's Spirit lies at the heart of their identity and being. As a temple of God's Spirit, individual believers experience an unmediated, and therefore subjective, relationship with God in Christ and through his Spirit. In 1 Corinthians 6 Paul is not, however, promoting an individualistic pick 'n' mix spirituality. Rather, into a context that was experience- and self-orientated, Paul emphasizes later in his letter that true spirituality builds up the body (namely, others) (1 Cor. 12.12–31). In addition, in contrast to an over-elevation of autonomy and local theology, Paul re-grounds the church, as a unified body, on the foundation of apostolic tradition.[59] Moreover, whereas the temple metaphor is applied to individuals in 1 Corinthians 6.19, in Ephesians 2.21 the wider church community is in view.

Religious ('Many')

> Therefore you are no longer strangers and aliens but fellow-citizens
> with the saints, members of God's family, built upon the foundation of
> the apostles and prophets, with Christ Jesus as the foundation stone, in
> whom the whole building is joined together, growing into a holy temple
> in the Lord, in whom you also are being built into the dwelling place of
> God by the Spirit. (Eph. 2.19–22)

The context of Ephesians is not identical to 1 Corinthians, but Paul again
seeks to root the church in the apostolic witness to Christ, here to combat
the danger that believers will be tossed around by false winds of teaching
(Eph. 4.14). The temple metaphor is connected to the body of Christ image
through the language of 'growth' and 'being joined together', terms which
appear in Ephesians 2.21 and 4.15–16. Believers' membership in Christ's
community is based on the church's 'normative teaching', which rests on
the historical reality of Christ's life, death, resurrection and ascension,
and the future hope of his return; the 'ultimate foundation is Christ' and
the 'apostles and prophets lay that foundation through their proclamation
of Christ and through building people up in their knowledge of Christ and
his Word' (2.19–22).[60] The subjective experience of God that believers
have through the Spirit is built on the objective foundation of Christ's acts
in history and the apostolic testimony to these acts.

Therefore, to the extent that 'religion' highlights the public, corporate,
dogmatic, institutional and prescribed, thus mediated, components of
faith, Paul promotes mediated religiosity alongside unmediated divine
encounter. Elsewhere, however, Paul utilizes the body of Christ metaphor
to reject a mode of religiosity that is disconnected from Christ:

> Therefore don't let anyone judge you by what you eat and drink or in
> regard to festivals or New Moon celebrations or Sabbaths. For these
> things were a shadow of what was to come, the reality is Christ. Let
> no-one who delights in humility and the worship of angels disqualify
> you. They go into minute detail about what they've seen, in vain puff-
> ing up their mind and their flesh, and don't hold fast to the head, from
> whom the whole body, which is supplied and joined together by its
> joints and ligaments, grows, and its growth is from God. If you have
> died with Christ to the elements of this world, why then, as one living in
> the world, do you obey its regulations? 'Do not touch, do not taste, do
> not handle', which refer to things that perish as they are used, according
> to the commandments and teaching of human beings. These things lead
> – though they have a reputation for wisdom by self-imposed piety and
> humility and harsh treatment of the body, which have no value – to the
> gratification of the flesh. (Col. 2.16–23)[61]

In this passage Paul's derision of 'human' regulations may appear to support those, like Coates, who juxtapose religion ('form and structure, rules and ritual'), seen as bad, to 'life and liberty, people and relationships, and love and community', seen as good.[62] Certainly Paul acknowledges a form of ritual, abstinence and rule-keeping that looks good to outsiders but is ineffective, indeed counterproductive, in facilitating genuine encounter with God or right behaviour (Col. 2.23). In Colossians, however, the problem is not practices and regulations per se, but those that are syncretistic, in this instance containing both Jewish and pagan elements. Moreover, the ascetic regime that Paul criticizes is not a lifestyle but rather, as Sumney contends, is engaged in for short periods to facilitate mystical visionary experiences. Most significantly, however, those promoting the regulations and practices have lost connection with the head, Christ.[63]

Aside from this rebuke in Colossians 2.16–23, which is directed into a particular context, Paul is not averse to ethical urgings, regulations, the promotion of self-discipline, and practices to help his readers understand both what transformation by the Spirit looks like in practice and their role within this (for example, 1 Cor. 6.15; 9.24–27; Eph. 4.25; 5.18–19; 6.18). Paul is not against 'religion', in the contemporary sense of externally prescribed rules, rituals and dogma.

Spiritual and Religious ('One and Many')

It is inaccurate to pit 'Jewish monism' against 'Greek dualism' in relation to human ontology. However, Greek conceptions tend to be dichotomistic and Hebraic notions holistic. More significant than the Greek tendency to differentiate between substances (body-soul-spirit), however, is its over-focus on substance.[64] In countering the dualism within many Western readings of Paul, promoting monism risks a similar tendency. Despite Green's claim to the contrary, monism is an inappropriate term to depict human personhood since it implies that human beings are self-contained singular beings, whereas, as Green affirms, Paul's anthropology is relational.[65] *Contra* the Western tendency to reduce human ontology to substance, Paul promotes a holistic view of personhood without such reductionism. For Paul, the human person is to be understood first and foremost in terms of their relation to God. This is not an ontological aside, as if a person is a unified being outside God and then accidentally brought into relationship with him. On the contrary, the believers' connection with Christ and infilling with the Spirit is, for Paul, at the heart of their identity and essence (1 Cor. 6.19; Eph. 2.21–22). Believers are made whole only by incorporation into Christ (Eph. 2.11–16).[66] Relationship with God in Christ and through the Spirit does not empty a person of their unique selfhood but completes, perfects and fulfils this uniqueness.

As Bloom notes, 'Christ has not displaced my own personhood. I am still there; but all that I should be I have become, now that it is His life that is in me.'[67]

The duality within Paul's anthropology is thus not body versus spirit/soul; rather it lies within the eschatological tension wherein believers are already 'one new person' (Christ's body) (Eph. 2.15–16) but are yet to attain to the 'full measure of the fullness Christ' (Eph. 4.13) and so must 'grow up in all things into him who is the head, Christ' (Eph. 4.15). This eschatological tension is highlighted by the progressive nature of the verbs within the temple metaphor in Ephesians 2.21–22 – 'being joined together', 'growing', 'being built'. The location of believers in the overlap of two eras leads to an eschatological ontology wherein the believers' new identity displaces their old identity. This displacement is simultaneously both an instantaneous change wrought in Christ and a transformation that is accomplished by the Spirit over time (Eph. 2.15–16; 4.13–15).[68]

Therefore, *contra* the axiological dualism of much Western anthropological ontology, the tension between spiritual and religious – 'one and many' – must be conceptualized within the eschatological tension of believers' 'now' and 'not yet' identity as Christ's body (Eph. 2.14–16; 4.15–16) and a temple of the Holy Spirit (both as individuals and a community (1 Cor. 6.19; Eph. 2.21)). God's otherness from creation enables his immanence within creation. Human physicality is not a barrier to union with God; God's presence is known *in the body*.[69] Although finite humans can never fully grasp God, the main barriers to God are sin and the world's current eschatological state. Therefore, spiritual and religious should not be pitted against each other as if 'spiritual' referred to the unmediated union of the human and divine spirit, to which 'religion' – through its focus on bodily actions and rituals – were irrelevant, or even counterproductive. On the contrary, Paul presents believers' embodied union with God as, in one sense, unmediated. Each individual believer is 'in Christ' and a temple of the Spirit (1 Cor. 6.19), and thus the body is the location of God's unmediated engagement. However, believers' union with God is, in another sense, mediated via its foundation on the historical Christ-event and the apostolic witness to this event (Eph. 2.20). The individualized, experiential, subjective component of the Christian faith (spiritual) must be held in tension with the communal, inherited, objective aspect (religious).

Implications: Christocentric Trinitarian Holism

Within the body of Christ texts, union with God in Christ and through the Spirit is presented as both mediated and unmediated. It is mediated since Christ and the Spirit are, in different ways, the mediators between believers and the Father; the church is anchored on the historicity of the Christ-event, and apostolic witness to this event, and experiences relationship with God through the accompanying outpouring of the Spirit.[70] Therefore, to the extent that 'religious' in contemporary parlance refers to mediated aspects of humanity's relation with the divine, the church is religious. The church's union with God is also unmediated in that the mediators (Christ and the Spirit) are themselves constitutive of God's essential being. Christ is the efficacious mediator par excellence between God and humanity because in Christ the fullness of God became flesh, dwelt among human beings, died on the cross for humanity's sin, and was raised back to life (cf. Col. 1.19–22). In Christ and through his Spirit, God indwells believers (Eph. 2.21–22). Therefore, insofar as 'spiritual' refers to the unmediated components of human beings' union with God, the church is spiritual. This tension between the church's mediated and unmediated access to God, which is given to the church as a gift (Eph. 2.6–9), has the following implications for re-contextual thinking. First, it provides a firm foundation for the holistic anthropology that re-contextual thinkers rightly pursue. Second, it urges the church to seek both orthopraxy *and* orthodoxy. Third, it provides a framework in which re-contextual thinkers can re-evaluate the relationship between medium and message.

Holistic Anthropology

Re-contextual thinkers desire to reground the church on a more holistic mode of faith than has commonly been engendered within Western Christianity. *Contra* Thwaites, this is not best achieved by promoting so-called Hebrew monism over Greek dualism. Such a dichotomy is inaccurately simplistic. Moreover, neither ontological monism nor axiological dualism can support a truly holistic conception of human beings' relation to God. Axiological dualism elevates the human spirit or soul above the body such that true spirituality is disconnected from human physicality (as some Corinthian Christians believed). Monism cannot support a holistic search for the divine either since 'search' indicates that the searcher is not as connected to the divine as they desire. Within monism, one can only be connected to God in some ways but not in others by relocating union with the divine to one particular aspect of self. Within much contemporary spirituality, particularly the New Age movement, this union is relocated to the inner depths of self, such that monism is 'talked' but not 'walked'.[71]

In contrast to monism and axiological dualism, a Christocentric, relational, eschatological and embodied anthropology, nested in the divine transcendence–immanence tension, supplies a truly holistic mode of relating to God in Christ and through the Spirit. Within this Trinitarian anthropology, a search for the divine (wherein greater intimacy and maturity is sought) is maintained alongside current experience of the divine (whereby immanence is already experienced) within the eschatological framework of the 'now' and 'not yet'. The entire believer exists in the overlap of two eras. Therefore, where Paul contrasts two terms (such as 'spiritual' versus 'fleshly' and 'inner' versus 'outer') he is referring to the entire person to the extent that they live in line with God's Spirit versus the entire person insofar as they resist God's Spirit. This is not to deny the conflict individual believers experience between their old and new nature. Such conflict occurs because believers are simultaneously already 'one new person' in Christ (Eph. 2.15–16) and yet still 'growing up into Christ' (Eph. 4.12–23). This eschatological conflict involves fragmentation because old creation is characterized by alienation and new creation by reconciliation.[72]

Rooting contemporary Christian anthropology within a Christocentric Trinitarian framework maintains a God-centred view of self in a self-centred culture. Self-centred does not here mean selfish per se, but refers to the contemporary trend to root identity in interiority. While some cultures have located personal identity primarily in breadth (status, role, relation to family and wider society), the contemporary self is located mainly in depth – contemporary Westerners see themselves as 'creatures with inner depths; with partly unexplored and dark interiors'.[73] This leads to 'ontological anxiety', since the interior quest's baselessness means that it cannot fulfil the human desire for belonging and wholeness. In contrast, as Tanner contends, 'ontological anxiety is dissolved as we focus on the risen Lord, whose *parousia* (presence) is both already experienced through the indwelling Holy Spirit (as its "pledge", Eph. 1.14) and still anticipated as a consummation in which God will be "all in all"'. Therefore we must 'repudiate the sin of wanting to be ourselves, and to be perfect as ourselves, independently of God's giving to us'.[74] Paul's relational anthropology has marked implications for believers' relationships with each other alongside their relation to God. The new person created in Christ is 'fundamentally restructured away from a personhood of "self"-centredness, "closedness" and alienation, towards one of reconciliation, and a new "openness" of self-giving love to the neighbour'.[75]

Orthopraxy and Orthodoxy

Despite their desire for holism, the re-contextual church's promotion of orthopraxy above orthodoxy represents an inadvertent dualism. Proponents of this rebalance do not assert that intellectual beliefs are unimportant. Rather, they criticize the Western view that right beliefs lead to right actions, countering that actions form beliefs more than beliefs form actions.[76] A truly holistic view, however, must avoid elevating either aspect to the detriment to the other. The value of orthodoxy is evident within the body of Christ texts in that, insofar as authentic Christianity is based on the historical Christ-event, what is believed about this event, and God's nature as revealed through it, is of central importance. An anthropology is required that gives full heed to body, mind and the inseparable – but complex – unity between them.

Regarding the church community, Paul maintains the equality and inseparable unity of the various parts, while acknowledging that different parts have different roles (1 Cor. 12.12–31). The re-contextual church must pursue a similarly nuanced view of human personhood. The human mind, for example, has the unique capacity to transcend its circumstances through imagination and abstract thought. Although, *contra* Engberg-Pedersen, it is reductionistic to nominate this self-reflection as the definition of personhood, a human being can 'reflect on him- or herself from a meta-position "above" the self',[77] as is poignantly expressed by Alphonse Daudet:

> *Homo duplex, homo duplex!* ... The first time I perceived that I was two was at the death of my brother Henri, when my father cried out so dramatically, 'He is dead, he is dead!' While my first self wept, my second self thought, 'How truly given was that cry, how fine it would be in the theater.' I was then fourteen years old.[78]

This ability to reflect enables human beings to observe discrepancies between their intellectual beliefs (for example, that the environment should be treated well) and their actions (mistreating the environment despite intellectually affirming its value). Practice should thus not be prioritized above reflection or vice versa; both are required. To use an analogy from Cognitive Behavioural Therapy, it is not sufficient for arachnophobes to convince themselves rationally that spiders in the UK are not dangerous. Rather action is required, such as increasing exposure, ranging from viewing photos of spiders to holding a spider in one's hand. However, the intellectual knowledge that spiders are not dangerous (in the UK at least) is still essential. If the sufferer deems this irrelevant to their cause, they have no basis on which to pursue the exposure programme.[79]

Re-contexual thinkers must guard against elevating orthopraxy at the expense of orthodoxy. However, it is important to redress an imbalance the other way. As Smith notes, the Western church has often thought too much about thinking and not given sufficient attention to deriving a philosophy and anthropology of action. An embodied anthropology places fresh emphasis on the role of Christian disciplines and practices in Christian formation; ritual is 'the way we (learn to) believe with our bodies'.[80] However, the tension between believers' mediated and unmediated relationship with God, as outlined above, reveals the need for nuance in addressing the efficacy of spiritual disciplines and practices. On the one hand, believers' embodiedness means that there is a relationship between Christian practices and believers' formation into Christ's likeness; 'the Spirit meets us where we are … as embodied agents, inviting us into that "suite" of disciplines and practices that are conduits of transformative, empowering grace'.[81] However, on the other hand, God's freedom and believers' dependence on God means that practices and disciplines are not mechanistic (cause-and-effect). Sometimes a practice leads to a profound encounter with God but at others there is no tangible effect despite a believer's best efforts. Merleau-Ponty's analogy of sleep is illustrative in this regard; by positioning ourselves for sleep, such as by lying on a bed as opposed to standing up, it is more likely (for want of a better phrase) that sleep will fall upon us (so to speak). However, sleep is not thereby assured and may come at a less convenient time. Similarly, Christian practices enable believers to posture themselves to encounter God but do not and cannot control the Spirit.[82]

Overall, a re-emphasis on Christian practices and spiritual disciplines is a necessary rejoinder to expressions of faith that are overly cerebral. However, re-contextual proponents must recognize the formational power of practice while neither viewing practices as mechanistic nor overlooking believers' ability to encounter God in all areas of life; as Marshall notes, the New Testament concept of worship incorporates a believer's whole life.[83] Believers' orientation towards God should be one of dependence and gratitude. This is not dependence that precludes activity or gratitude as emotion only. Rather, it is gratitude that 'ministers divine beneficence to others, in correspondence to Jesus' own ministering of the Father's beneficence to humanity – healing, nourishing, attending to the needs of the world – what Jesus did in his own life, a prior ministry that empowers our own'.[84]

Medium and Message

The re-contextual desire for a more holistic mode of being and doing church is evident within Ward's call for the church to think more critically about the relationship between medium and message. Ward contends, for instance, that if the Eucharist is performed with the Prodigy's 'Firestarter' played loudly in the background and a liturgical prayer shouted over the top, the meaning of the Eucharist is affected. Smith goes further, arguing that 'the very form of worship tells the Story' – 'the medium is the message'.[85] Western Christianity, Smith argues, has falsely assumed that the content of Christianity can be distilled from its historical form and implanted into newer, more accessible modes without altering its meaning. This assumption is overly intellectualist – it reduces the gospel to a propositional message, overlooking the formative power of the medium. Forms are not neutral. Rather, a church gathering in a shopping mall, for example, unwittingly teaches those who attend that Jesus can be treated as any other consumable commodity. It is not just that both form and content matter, he concludes, but that the form/content distinction must be eschewed.[86]

Moynagh voices similar concerns when disputing the 'kernel-and-husk' approach to contextualization, wherein the cultural container of the gospel can be changed according to context but the unchanging core of the gospel remains the same. This view, he argues, assumes that the centre of the gospel is a set of unchanging propositions. Although propositions are important, he contends, the centre of the faith is a person – Jesus – not a list of facts. However, in contrast to Smith, Moynagh also rejects the idea that, instead of propositions, the gospel's centre can be maintained by an ecclesial core: a set of ecclesial practices with a culture of their own. Rather, he observes, there is no 'single, definitive "church culture"' but only 'church cultures in the plural – cultures that vary according to their contexts'.[87]

The mediated and unmediated nature of believers' relationship with God has implications for this contested relationship between medium and message. The embodied nature of human anthropology supports Ward's assertion that medium matters; form affects the message conveyed. However, the complex relationship between mind and body challenges Smith's contention that the medium *is* the message, or that a message cannot be abstracted from one form and re-communicated in another with any continuity. Rather, as Smith himself notes, the human mind is able to abstract concepts from concrete experiences – albeit these 'don't drop down from the sky; they bubble up from our embodied experience'. Thus, while the x's and o's on a coach's chalkboard do not encompass the complexity of what happens on the football field, they are not simply 'useful fiction'.[88] They portray something of the reality of the football game, even if that reality is aspiration rather than actualization. Moreover, the strategy marked out on the chalkboard can be transferred to different teams and, depending on the nature of the play, even different sports.

Similarly, although the Trinity and gospel cannot be reduced to abstract concepts and propositions, communications about God can be abstracted from one context and relocated into another with continuity in meaning – albeit translation will affect the message to a degree. Indeed, even the subjective experiences of individual believers' encounters with God share common ground such that were an individual to experience God as petulant and capricious, for example, this experience would seem out of place.[89] Therefore, in rightly noting that medium and message cannot be as neatly demarcated as overly cerebral expressions of Christianity have tended to imagine, it is not necessary to disregard the notion that the same message – specifically the message of God's actions in and through Jesus – cannot be legitimately conveyed in a variety of mediums, or that changing the medium from a more traditional mode (such as an Anglican church building) to another (a shopping mall) so radically alters the message conveyed as to render it illegitimate. In other words, although an analogy such as kernel and husk may need modifying in light of an embodied anthropology, there is no need to disregard it completely – to throw the kernel out with the husk, so to speak.

In (the Stability of the Deck): Institution and Network – Facilitating Gift-Exchange within the Christian Community

Re-contextual thinkers contend that the Western church is too hierarchical, clergy-dominated and institutionalized. In pursuing more egalitarian, every member ministry, and flexible modes of church, re-contextual thinkers draw on the egalitarian Social Trinitarianism of those such as Gunton, Volf and Moltmann. For Zizioulas, however, social models of the Trinity provide the basis of a decidedly hierarchical model. As Holmes notes, it is disconcerting that, through a seemingly minor technicality (seeing the inner-Trinitarian relationships in terms of mutuality rather than the Father's priority), such markedly different notions of church governance are derived. This suggests that preconceived ecclesial structures are read into Trinitarian relations more easily than they can be read out; Social Trinitarianism thus appears an inadequate foundation for re-contextual concerns.[90]

In contrast, the ecclesiology that I am proposing is not based on abstract speculation into the Trinity's inner life but on biblical texts addressing the concrete church (as it is in history). In this section I identify the implications of the body of Christ metaphor for the church's internal relations 'in'. Ephesians 2.14–18 and 4.11–16 are particularly pertinent in this regard. Critics of the Homogeneous Unit Principle see Ephesians 2.14–18, which outlines Christ's reconciliation of different ethnic groups, as an unassailable challenge to homogenous expressions of church.[91] Given the promotion of demographically-specific churches by some re-contextual thinkers, it is important that I address this passage. Ephesians 4.11–16 outlines distinct roles for some church members, although there is dispute regarding the nature of these roles. I shall therefore explore this passage in relation to the re-contextual church's critique of hierarchy within the church and the laity–clergy divide.

Addressing the church's internal relations raises the question, what is church? The New Testament word rendered 'church' in English translations is *ekklēsia*, which highlights the importance of gathering but, in light of its use within the LXX, primarily depicts the church as Christ's New Covenant community.[92] Ward and Moynagh observe that *ekklēsia* is used of the whole church, the local church and small groups. Ward argues that the church is located within the interlocking networks that connect believers within and between these groups. Ward and Murray Williams thus suggest abandoning the term 'parachurch' and, instead, affirming the ecclesial legitimacy of cross-congregational groups. Moynagh applies the polyvalence within the term *ekklēsia* through his temple-synagogue-tent conception of church. This, he argues, is not simply a reworking of the celebration-congregation-cell model but is more fluid, with tents coming and going and the boundaries between the three overlapping and interlocking such that, for example, members of the same tent may attend different synagogues. Moynagh and Murray Williams see connections between different church groups as essential for maintaining the church's heterogeneity while legitimizing demographic-specific expressions of church. In this, they support Ward's emphasis on a flexible, networked conception of the universal church over one that is institutionally bound.[93]

The one universal or heavenly church that is conveyed in Ephesians 2.14–18 and 4.11–16 affirms Ward's emphasis on seeing the informal networked relationships between individual believers and groups of believers as 'church' ('one'). Designating informal networked relationships 'church', however, does not mean that formal institutional structures are not required. Within the body of Christ texts, there are indications that formal and established structures are necessary (such as the fulfilling of certain roles by certain people, prearranged regular gatherings and communal practices). The church is manifest and concretized when individual Christians play a committed role within a local group of Christians and groups of Christians are supportive of each other (locally, nationally and internationally), neither of which can be sustained by informality and spontaneity alone. However, there is not one clear institutional model that can be derived from the body of Christ texts; there are various forms that an institutional model could take while still fulfilling the principles of church order and structure conveyed ('many'). The unity of the whole church is not maintained by one overarching institutional structure but through the connection of believers to Christ and the infilling of the Spirit (for example, 1 Cor. 12.12–13; Eph. 2.16–18; 4.4; 5.29–32).

The predication of believers' internal relations on the church's relationship with God in Christ and through the Spirit is analogous with the fact that, although a suspension bridge's deck appears to bear the weight of the traffic going across it, the load is borne by the main cable through the suspension cables. So too the church's participation within

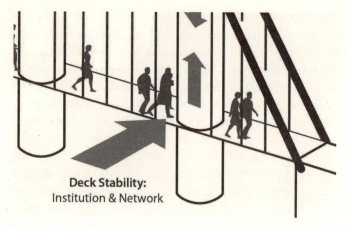

Figure 4: The Stability of the Deck: Institution and Network

the Trinity through its incorporation into Christ as Christ's body provides the foundation for the church's internal relationships. However, this does not mean that believers have no responsibility – their overarching passivity in relation to God does not exclude activity. Just as a suspension bridge's deck requires internal stability alongside the support of the cables to facilitate the flow of vehicles and goods across it, so too believers have a responsibility to form internal relationships that best facilitate gift-exchange within their community (see Figure 4).

The body of Christ metaphor legitimizes the formation and maintenance of the church's internal relationships through both informal networks and formal institutions ('one and many'). However, the contention is not that a middle path be forged between two extremes. Indeed, due to human beings' nature as embodied, the two (network and institution) cannot be neatly demarcated – where there is a network there is some level of institution and vice versa. There is no dichotomy between the divine agency that produces inside-out transformation and the habits, cultures, structures and rituals that affect outside-in change. Therefore, just as spiritual and religious must be held in dialectical tension, so too must network and institution (or informality and formality). The maintenance of this tension is essential for the facilitation of gift-exchange both within individual congregations and across distinct church groups. Moreover, this conception of church as simultaneously network and institution incorporates believers' everyday life and work without diminishing the centrality of Christian assemblies.

In what follows, I explore the notion of the church as a network as implied by the heavenly conception of church in Ephesians 2.14–18. In particular, with the polyvalence of the term *ekklēsia* in mind, the universal purview of Ephesians 2.14–18 raises the question of whether every individual congregation should be as mixed as possible or whether the reconciliation described in these verses could be fulfilled through unity between demographically-specific groups. Second, I explore the institutional features evidenced within the body of Christ texts, with particular attention to Ephesians 4.11–16. Third, I draw on Bayes' reflections on conversionism and McFadyen's treatment of institutionalism to explore the dialectical tension between informality and formality, network and institution within the church.

Network ('One')

Deinstitutionalization is a marked feature of contemporary culture. The decline in denominational churches is mirrored by a decrease in membership in non-Christian institutions. Instead of formal institutions, Castells contends, contemporary Western culture is increasingly restructuring around networks. A network is a 'netlike or complex system or collection of interrelated things'. Network-based social structures are dynamic and open to change. Re-contextual thinkers urge the church to respond to this sociological shift but base their contentions on theological justifications, not just sociological research. Ward contends that the body of Christ metaphor can help believers imagine church outside the 'institutional box' if the order is reversed from 'the church (the institution) is the body of Christ' to 'the body of Christ (the people) is the church'. The church is constituted by the networked relationships through which believers interact with each other and the wider world. Therefore these networks should be prioritized above weekly congregational gatherings.[94]

Ward's primary foundation for promoting a networked rather than institutional mode of church is the 'in Christ' motif. This motif, he argues, grants flexibility for new ways of being church beyond institutional bounds, supporting the notion that believers are 'in Christ' both when they worship and celebrate together *and* when what they do and say in the wider world is directed by God's Spirit and in accord with his character and life. As I outline below, the one heavenly or universal church conveyed in Ephesians and Colossians supports Ward's contention that the informal, networked relationships that believers form with each other and the wider world are vital expressions of the *one* body of Christ. However, as I address later on, authentic relationships cannot be sustained through informality alone.[95]

In Romans and 1 Corinthians, the body of Christ metaphor could refer to an individual local congregation or the church in a geographical region. Witherington asserts the latter, contending that in 1 Corinthians Paul refers to the Corinthian house churches as collectively Christ's body. He argues that one particular house church may not have all the gifts needed to serve as Christ's body in the city so the groups need each other. Reference to the gathering of 'the whole church' in 1 Corinthians 14.23, which met in Gaius' house (Rom. 16.23), supports Witherington's contention. However, even if the citywide church is in view, this group probably consisted of less than 50 people.[96]

Within Ephesians and Colossians a much wider body is in view but it is disputed whether this is a universal (all believers across the world) or heavenly (all believers, past, present and future, by virtue of their gathering in Christ in the heavenly realm) phenomenon.[97] Ephesians 2.14–18 indicates that the church, as Christ's body, is heavenly through its union with Christ who is, brings and proclaims 'peace' – although, as I will argue below, universal notions of church are not thereby excluded. The church manifests its heavenly identity on earth such that believers, through being reconciled to God, are reconciled with each other. As believers manifest this reconciliation through their informal and/or spontaneous networked relations, these relationships are 'church'.

> For he is our peace, the one who makes both one, having destroyed the dividing wall, that is the partition, of enmity in his flesh, having nullified the law, that is its commandments and ordinances, so that he might make the two into one new person in him, bringing peace, and reconcile them both to God in one body through the cross, having killed in himself the enmity. And he came to proclaim peace to you who were far off and peace to those who were near since through him you both in one Spirit have freedom to approach the father. (Eph. 2.14–18)

The church's heavenly identity is conveyed in this passage through: the notion of peace; the implicit temple theme; and resonance with Ephesians 2.6, where believers are described as 'raised up and seated together with Christ in the heavenly realms in Christ Jesus'. This heavenly identity is ultimately characterized by the church's access to the Father in Christ and by the Spirit.

In relation to peace, in light of the Old Testament concept of *shalom*, peace refers to life with God, who dwells in heaven, and the accompanying blessings and wholeness that this brings. Allusions to Old Testament passages regarding eschatological hope (especially in 2.17) (Isa. 52.7; 57.19 and, less strongly, Isa. 9.6) emphasize that this peace, which was once a future hope, has been brought into the present. Since Christ is now in heaven, the church is too by virtue of its union with him as 'one new person' 'in one body' (2.15–16).[98]

The church's heavenly identity is also indicated by the implicit temple theme – made explicit in 2.21–22. For example, although the law is probably the primary referent of the 'dividing wall' in 2.14, there are allusions to both the curtain separating off the Most Holy Place and the wall that separated the Gentile and non-Gentile areas. Within the Old Testament the temple, as (paradoxically) the omnipresent God's dwelling place, is the place where heaven and earth meet. In Ephesians this temple consists of Christians in union with Christ.[99]

In addition, Ephesians 2.18 elucidates 2.6, wherein believers' heavenly state is explicit. 'The heavenly realms' overlap with creation, as the abode of spiritual beings (for example, Eph. 3.10). However this phrase primarily signifies God's transcendent location. Thus *the church is a heavenly entity through its hitherto unprecedented access to the Father in Christ and through the Spirit.* Believers participate in this heavenly church as they undertake their daily life and work, not just when they gather as local communities.[100]

The church's heavenly existence should not be understood dualistically, as believers' disembodied spirits living in a realm distinct from their bodies. Rather, since God's transcendence enables his immanence, heaven infiltrates the church's *physical* existence in Christ and through the Spirit. The church's heavenly status (its access to God in Christ and through the Spirit) determines its earthly life: 'the body of Christ is a reality which partakes of or participates in the life of heaven, even though ... it is truly present here on earth'.[101] This has profound sociological and ethical implications; reconciliation with God and fellow believers are two sides of the same coin.[102]

In Ephesians 2.14–18 the new eschatological humanity created in Christ ('one new person') consists of two previously disparate groups (Jews and Gentiles), with ethnic Israel's priority relativized by Christ's work. The church is in continuity with God's people beforehand, but sufficiently distinct that it is a 'new creation'. As I noted in the previous section, Paul's presentation of the church as Christ's body must be understood in the context of a 'now' and 'not yet' eschatological schema. The church is Christ's body but must also grow to full stature (Eph. 4.15). Within this schema, reconciliation actualized in the microsphere (between individual believers or groups of believers) provides a concrete manifestation and anticipation of the ultimate reconciliation that God will achieve in the macrosphere when all things are reconciled under Christ (Eph. 1.3; 3.10). Peace in believers' individual and communal lives in the present anticipates and manifests the ultimate peace that is still to come.[103]

It is therefore apparent that, within Ephesians, the church is presented as a heavenly entity. Some proponents of the heavenly church perspective thus deny that a 'universal' church is in view. They contend that the only legitimate physical expression of the church is local gatherings, and refute the validity of cross-congregation institutional models and formal denominational structures. These proponents agree, however, that New

Testament local churches were linked organically and relationally and thus they conflate two separate issues: first, whether groups of Christians are inherently connected to each other; second, what form these relationships should take – formal and institutional, informal and networked, or a combination of the two. If these two issues are separated (the *connection* of all believers in Christ, on the one hand, and the *form* of these connections, on the other), there is significant accord.

For example, it is agreed that believers are connected to each other through their connection to Christ – the heavenly view includes all believers in all periods of time and so is a larger, not smaller, conception. Moreover, both universal and heavenly church proponents affirm the church's eschatological identity – the heavenly gathering is believers' goal and something that they already participate in through their communion with Christ. Both views maintain that there is more than one type of group that can be legitimately called church. Therefore, the conception of local congregations as imperfect anticipations of the heavenly community, perfected on Christ's return, surely applies to larger groups of Christians too. Believers' relationships both within and between individual church communities manifest the eschatological heavenly church. Indeed, Ward asserts that, to the extent that believers display their heavenly identity in the wider world, even the networked relationships between believers and non-believers contribute to the church's 'fuzzy edges'.[104]

Believers in groupings of different forms and sizes are therefore fully church in that they are communities of Christ's people. There is no basis for designating a local congregation 'church' but not a denomination, national, or even universal church – although, as I argue below, it is helpful to distinguish between 'a church' (countable noun), 'church' (uncountable noun), and 'the church' (definite noun). However, the language of manifestation and anticipation suggests that the extent to which various expressions of church (local, town-wide, national, international, formal and informal) are church in a proleptic sense (as a foretaste of God's future re-creation) depends not upon their structures but upon the quality of relationships formed.

To the extent that there is impurity, lust, falsehood, theft, rotten speech, bitterness, slander, malice, greed, foolishness, debauchery, division, envy, arrogance and immorality within believers' relationships then, regardless of their geographical purview (local, national or international) or the degree of formality (spontaneous, informal and networked, *or* structured, formal and institutionalized) the manifestation of the heavenly church is hindered (cf. Eph. 4.17–5.20) – except that such vices provide an opportunity for fellow believers to respond with truth and grace, which is intrinsic to the church's anticipatory nature. Equally, regardless of the geographical purview or extent of formalization, to the degree that love, unity, reconciliation, peace, righteousness, thanksgiving, grace, mutual edification, wisdom and gift-exchange characterize relationships, the new creation is anticipated and manifest more fully.

The view that believers are simultaneously both *fully* church (through their incorporation into Christ) and *imperfectly* church (they can anticipate the eschatological new creation to a greater or lesser degree) may seem contradictory. However, it accords with O'Brien's assertion that, in Ephesians, Paul urges believers to 'become what they already are'.[105]

Seeing the quality of relationships, rather than organizational structures, as determining the extent to which the church anticipates God's new creation, and thus *is church*, seems to support wholeheartedly Ward's contention that the church should focus more on the quality of relationships than a particular structure, such as the weekly congregational gathering. However, as I contend below, the embodied nature of human beings means that the quality of relationships and the nature of structures cannot be as neatly demarcated as this statement suggests; the relationship between divine agency and embodied practices, rituals, cultures and structures is complex and the two should not be dichotomized. Moreover, alongside being a heavenly entity, the church's earthly nature means that it is frail and weak. The church is, this side of Christ's return, 'both profoundly sick and yet healing and life-giving'.[106] Conceptions of church must not be overly idealistic.

Therefore, although Ward prioritizes spontaneity and informality, believers' existence as embodied and fallen means that institutional structures are essential for the promotion of relationships that will best manifest the heavenly church. How many people, for example, would spontaneously gather weekly for mutual edification, praise and thanksgiving with people they like and those they find harder to like without the external structure of a weekly congregation? It is unsurprising, therefore, that the body of Christ texts also support institutionalization.

Institution ('Many')

Despite criticizing the Western church for being over-institutionalized, re-contextual thinkers concede that institutionalization is inevitable. An institution is a social entity with a stable and regulated structure. The church has exhibited institutional structure from its conception and can only establish communities as an institution in some form or other; the question is what type of institution it will be. Within institutions, patterns of communication and modes of decision-making can be regulated and standardized to differing degrees, with varying levels of openness to change, innovation and spontaneity. Institutions need sufficient routinization to enable dependability and sufficient openness to facilitate transformation. As Ward notes, structures are necessary, but they should be flexible and constantly amended to best serve the church's context.[107]

Scholars dispute what level of institutionalization is revealed within the body of Christ texts. Routinization as marked by ritual (in the soft sense) is evident in the promotion of the Lord's Supper, which is affirmed as a Christian ritual by appeal to tradition (1 Cor. 11.23–26) and the specification that it can be defiled (1 Cor. 11.27–34).[108] Moreover, although 'baptised by one Spirit into one body' in 1 Corinthians 12.13 does not simply denote water baptism – it refers to conversion as a whole (with emphasis on the Spirit's agency within this) – it alludes to this ritual that proclaims and marks believers' turning to Christ. Meeks designates baptism and the Lord's Supper as the 'two great ritual complexes' within early Christianity but notes that it is hard to avoid reading back into New Testament texts the meaning(s) that these rituals have accrued over time.[109]

Institutionalization is also evident through the delineation of the Christian community implied by the body of Christ metaphor – believers have a connection to Christ, and thus each other, that non-believers do not share. Boundaries are essential for social groups to exist. Although the church was counterculturally inclusive in relation to social status and ethnicity, its identity as Christ's body excluded other religious affiliations (1 Cor. 10.16–21). Institutionalization is also apparent through regularity in relation to church gatherings. For example, 1 Corinthians 12.12–31 is situated in the context of Paul's exhortations regarding the Corinthian Christians' public and corporate gatherings (1 Cor. 11.1–14.40). While it is unclear how often they met, the early Christians gathered regularly, and regular meetings, in set groups and at set times and places, constitute a ritual.[110]

The degree of institutionalization depicted within the body of Christ texts is most disputed in relation to the existence, or not, of offices. *OED* defines office as a 'position or post to which certain duties are attached'.[111] Some deny the existence of offices within the body of Christ texts, and even the whole Pauline corpus. Fee, for example, denies that the apostles, prophets and teachers depicted in 1 Corinthians 12.28 are offices held by certain individuals, arguing that they are ministries expressed by a variety of people. However, although the gifts listed (Rom. 12.6–8; 1 Cor. 12.28; Eph. 4.11) refer to Spirit-given functions, dichotomizing function and office implies that these gifts are only given for short durations, which Turner argues is more similar to the Corinthian's distorted view of spirituality, wherein they overemphasized ecstatic experience, than Paul's portrayal of spiritual gifts. Moreover, the *Sitz im Leben* is one in which Paul is bringing order to pre-existing church structures, rather than establishing a blueprint of his own. To the degree that office means a function with some longevity, recognition by the wider church, authorization, and formal commissioning (and possibly remuneration), reference to apostles, prophets, and teachers within the body of Christ texts presupposes that such offices already existed.[112]

Ephesians 4.11–16 develops the notion of office further by asserting that those with the five giftings listed (apostles, prophets, evangelists, pastors, and teachers) have a distinctive role.

> And he gave some to be apostles, some to be prophets, some to be evangelists, some to be pastors and teachers to equip the saints for the work of service, for the building up of the body of Christ, until we all arrive into the unity of faith and knowledge of the Son of God, into the complete human, into the measure of the stature of the fullness of Christ, in order that we may no longer be children, tossed around and knocked to and fro by every wind of teaching, by people's trickery, by craftiness directed towards deceitful cunning but, telling the truth in love, let us grow in every way into him, who is the head, Christ, out of whom the whole body is joined together and united through every supporting ligament, as each part works to grow the body so it builds itself up in love. (Eph. 4.11–16)

It is disputed whether these five ministries are called to 'equip the saints' so that the saints (as a whole) do 'the work of service' and 'build up the body of Christ' or whether these five ministries perform all three (equipping, works of service, and building up the body). However, since those with the five gifts listed would obviously undertake works of service, viewing all three tasks as carried out by just these people would make this phrase redundant. Further, the wider context (particularly the parallel between 'build up' in 4.12 and 4.16) indicates that the whole body plays a part in its own growth. Therefore 'equipping' is unique to the five ministries mentioned, but the whole body undertakes the other two tasks.[113]

There is also discord regarding the end goal of the growth. Witherington asserts that the believers' aim, which Christian ministry is to facilitate, is to reach Christ's moral maturity. Morality is not insignificant within Christian maturity, but stating this as the primary goal underplays the rest of Ephesians, which presents the reconciliation of all things in and under Christ as the ultimate aim (Eph. 1.10; cf. 1.23; 4.10). Restored relationship is central to Paul's understanding of the final end of all things and, accordingly, lies at the heart of his conception of 'the measure of the stature of the fullness of Christ'. Morality is significant insofar as it flows from this restored relationship, which has horizontal and vertical dimensions, and contributes to this relationship's quality.[114]

The nature of the five ministries that empower the body towards this ultimate end is also debated, and some question whether they are applicable today. In particular, the ongoing role of apostles and prophets is a moot point. Lincoln, for example, refers to the foundational role of the apostles and prophets as expressed in Ephesians 2.20 and concludes that here, as there, their purview is restricted to the church's founding. Others argue that the twelve apostles of Jesus, along with Paul, carried a different level of apostolic authority than the gift referred to here. In Ephesians 4.11, they maintain, *apostolos* carries the sense of itinerant minister or church planter and this gift is still needed and practised today. Similarly, the role of prophecy has been much debated.[115]

I do not intend to evaluate, or even summarize, the vast swathes of literature that Ephesians 4.11 has generated; as Niewold notes, 'a full bibliography of relevant studies would exhaust many pages of small print'.[116] Rather, I put forward the less disputed point that, regardless of how many of these ministries are applicable today, certain people are recognized by the wider community as having particular ministries, which they presumably exercised regularly. These people have a distinctive role in equipping believers such that the whole church, through the Spirit's power, builds up Christ's body into fuller unity and maturity. As Lincoln concludes, 'if the ordered regular nature of a ministry and its recognition by a local church makes it an office, then the ministers in 4.11 ... are officers'.[117]

Some church movements base their structures on the five-fold pattern of Ephesians 4.11. However, the differences between the giftings listed in body of Christ texts and the church structures evident within the Pastorals indicate that the New Testament does not support just one institutional model. This passage does demonstrate, though, that dichotomies such as *charisma* versus institution are false. Ephesians 4.1–16 and 1 Corinthians 12.12–31 assume and endorse the presence of institutional elements while maintaining the body's dependence on the Spirit (1 Cor. 12.4, 7, 13; Eph. 4.3–4). *Many* different institutional models and forms may find legitimation within the body of Christ texts, but Paul could not conceive of a church with no structure or order.[118]

Network and Institution ('One and Many')

> Instead of reflecting on the kind of society we ought to create in order to accommodate individual or communal heterogeneity, I will explore what kind of selves we need to be in order to live in harmony with others.[119]

It is disputed whether the main thrust of Paul's body of Christ texts is to urge unity or encourage diversity. More significant, though, is not Paul's call to unity or diversity in and of themselves but their coexistence: union with Christ grants *unity in diversity*, not uniformity. Paul's promotion of unity in diversity stands apart from the use of the body metaphor within wider Graeco-Roman culture, wherein subordinate groups were warned against disturbing the status quo. In contrast, and in relation to gift-exchange, Paul argues for diversity and interdependence; those of higher status are to 'respect and value the contributions of those members who appear to be their inferiors, both in social status and spiritual potency'.[120] Gift-exchange depends not only on a willingness to give but a willingness to receive. Those of lower resources and status are empowered by being enabled to give, not just given to. How, then, is this interdependent gift-exchange best facilitated? In particular, to what extent should the church pursue fluid, spontaneous and informal relationships (network), and to what degree should it establish and maintain formal, institutional structures (institution)?

Answers to this question must consider the conundrum raised by Volf's emphasis on 'what kind of selves we need to be'; to what extent do people form structures, and to what extent do structures form them?[121] Bayes distinguishes a conversionist approach, wherein the wider world is seen as corrupted and so change is only achieved through individual transformation, from a utopian response, which seeks to establish uncorrupted social systems to transform the world. Bayes believes that Paul's discussion of ministry gifts in Ephesians 4.1–16 lies within a conversionist framework: conversion is a process that the ministry gifts are intended to facilitate.[122] Ephesians 2.14–18 indicates that believers' transformation into 'one new person' is dependent on divine agency, suggesting that Paul's emphasis is on the inside-out transformation that God brings over and above the outside-in transformation that habits and structures can afford. However, although Paul is not a utopian, the fact that he locates believers' growth within a community of interdependent gift-exchange means that concern for social systems (order and structure) is not absent.

The promotion of informal networks within the re-contextual conversation assumes that believers' internal transformation will enable them to naturally and spontaneously form relationships of mutual interdependence and gift-exchange with others. A formal institutional approach highlights the role of external structures within transformation. Analysis of relevant texts demonstrates that informal networks and institutional structures are both supported by body of Christ texts. However, the church is not to walk a middle path between two extremes. Rather, just as social structures and personal formation are intrinsically interconnected, so too a strict demarcation between network and institution cannot be made. As McFadyen notes, even within one-to-one relationships a degree of routinization develops over time. This 'does not represent inauthenticity … but a previously achieved mutuality of understanding which becomes a background norm for further interaction'.[123] Such institutionalization through routinization is essential so that each individual finds the relationship dependable, rather than open to infinite possibilities – imagine the insecurity that would ensue if it were never possible to gauge prior to meeting an individual, and despite previous meetings, whether they were going to offer money, request money, shout, talk politely, ask an invasive question, give a gift, say nothing, act violently, ad infinitum.

Institutionalization is essential for the establishment and sustainability of both depth within individual relationships and breadth across a range of relationships. Institutionalization regulates, providing meaning and value to, interpersonal social relationships so that people can interpret their own and other people's experiences and communications. However, although institutions are essential for stable reciprocity (and thus gift-exchange), they should be dialogical (open to change and transformation) not monological (oppressive and restrictive). The church is, paradoxically, a 'plannable institution which aims at offering opportunities for an unplannable event that escapes all institutionalizing: the event of the Holy Spirit who blows where he wills'.[124]

It is important, therefore, to avoid false dichotomies such as *charisma* versus institution, dynamic versus static, and spontaneity versus structure, as if the former in each pair were of the Spirit and the latter merely human constructions. *Both* a lack of order *and* fully closed structures can hinder believers' relationships with God and each other. An absence of structure is, in practice, a lack of commitment on the part of individuals to any routinized engagement with God and others. This, in one sense, enables infinite openness to any and all possibilities of relating. However, since unlimited openness stifles rather than facilitates relationships (as in my example above of the insecurity that would ensue if we could never anticipate a person's response), such apparent openness is in fact closedness. It is the refusal to subordinate any aspect of personal agenda to that of a larger group.[125]

> The network does not require commitment or accountability, and this same mentality is brought into small groups. Members weigh up their options before promising to attend the next meeting, and that promise is promptly broken if a better offer comes along. The individual reigns supreme.[126]

McFadyen calls this closedness 'overexpansion' – the 'absolutizing of an individual's space, time and value so that meaning and value are found only in relation or with reference to him or herself'.[127] Ironically,

> we lose ourselves if we try to bury our love, trust and hope and find meaning in ourselves alone – if we close ourselves off from God and others. Conversely, we acquire a sense of security when our unique

beings and identities are trusted, loved, and so sustained, from afar ... We can neither find meaning nor the right order of our being and identity on our own, but only through dialogue with God and others. For individual persons and human being as such are incomplete and insecure in themselves.[128]

Just as the absence of structure reveals the closedness of individuals to others and God, so too the absence of openness indicates the closedness of the institution to God and individuals. Moreover, without the openness to adapt, institutions bring about their own downfall; institutions survive and flourish through a willingness to change.[129]

Informal networked relationships between individual believers and groups of believers are a legitimate expression of the heavenly church. However, this does not mean that regular structured gatherings are unnecessary. Institutional elements are assumed within the body of Christ texts – rituals (the Lord's Supper and baptism), regular gatherings, and the designation of certain gifted people as having a distinctive role within the community. Human embodiedness means that the habits, routines and rituals that people adopt affect who they become; so too the structures, routines and rituals that church communities implement influence the relationships formed. This does not negate the pre-eminence of the Spirit's work. Just as spiritual practices are not efficacious in a cause-and-effect way, so too there is a complex relationship between individuals and communities wherein both form the other's identity but not absolutely.[130] It is in dialectical tension between informal, spontaneous, creative, networked relationships and formal, planned, stable, institutional structures that the church is best able to facilitate gift-exchange within its internal relationships.

Implications: Christocentric Trinitarian Structures

[T]he Church is built up by love: to the edifying of itself. This means that no increase is of use which does not correspond to the whole body. That man is mistaken who desires his own separate growth. For what would it profit a leg or an arm if it grew to an enormous size, or for the mouth to be stretched wider? It would merely be afflicted with a harmful tumour. So if we wish to be considered in Christ, let no man be anything for himself, but let us all be whatever we are for others. This is accomplished by love; and where love does not reign, there is no edification of the Church, but a mere scattering.[131]

My contention that Christian communities should seek to maintain a tension between being both a network and an institution has particular implications for the re-contextual church. First, it encourages re-contextual thinkers to focus on what kind of institution the church should be, rather than promote deinstitutionalization. Second, it legitimizes seeing believers dispersed into every walk of life as 'church' while maintaining the centrality of regular gatherings and committed communities. Third, it affirms Murray Williams' desire for churches in which every member plays their role but supports Ward's assertion that *every member ministry* applies to believers' roles outside the local congregation not just within it. Therefore believers need not play an equally demanding or responsible role within the local congregation as their primary gifts may be better utilized in, for example, their workplace.

What Kind of Institution?

As Dunn observes, one 'can scarcely avoid observing how frequently the charism/office debate has been played out by successive generations in practice (not just theory), usually without much awareness of the experience of former generations or of the lessons to be learned from that history'.[132] Re-contextual thinkers are not the first to explore the relationship between church structures and spiritual gifts. Engagement with the body of Christ texts challenges the re-contextual movement to think critically about what kind of institutions will best facilitate the church's growth, rather than utilizing the rhetoric of anti- or de-institutionalization. Within the body of Christ texts, the church's union with Christ and infilling of the Spirit, through which it encounters the Father, are not pitted against order, structure and ritual. Rather, informal, spontaneous, creative, networked relationships *and* formal, planned, stable, institutional structures need to be maintained in dialectical tension so that the church is best able to facilitate gift-exchange within its internal relationships. Re-contextual thinkers should explore what structures best facilitate believers' reciprocal openness to God and each other. In particular, churches must work hard to avoid the, all too commonplace, type of institutionalization that occurs when the most powerful members adapt social structures to consolidate their power. Such developments are not inevitable so can, and should, be challenged. Indeed, Paul's countercultural subversion of the Corinthians' self-imposed hierarchy in 1 Corinthians 12 is one such challenge.[133]

The flexibility to adapt structures to the needs and nature of any one community requires consideration of a number of factors, such as size. McLaren, for instance, argues,

> a new church of 45 people feels silly trying to put on the smooth, 'front-focused' program that would be perfectly appropriate for the church of 450 or 4,500. So the small church's internal environment calls for informality. But if the informality is winsome, soon the church

will have 85, not 45 ... then 145, then 245 ... And by that time, informality will no longer be winsome – it may be chaotic or strained or embarrassing or scary. The church will need to transition to a program that better suits its size.[134]

Gibbs and Coffey identify leadership principles that are pertinent to churches of all sizes and enable churches to adapt quickly and effectively to the changes and challenges that they face. These are: an emphasis on relationship rather than status/position; permission-giving and empowerment, whereby decisions are not pushed to the top of a hierarchical pyramid but entrusted to people at all levels of an organizational structure; a focus on equipping, with theory and practice well-integrated; decentralization; and a high level of accountability.[135]

More could be said about how churches can best maintain a healthy tension between informality and formality within their structures. Rather than cover this topic exhaustively, however, my aim is to prompt re-contextual practitioners to think deeply about what this might look like in their particular context, considering factors such as size and the power and personality dynamics within their group.

A Church, the Church, Church, the Church of, to Church

Believers' union with Christ means that they *are church* (Christ's body) as they undertake their daily life and work, not just when they gather as local communities. However, seeing believers' dispersed lives and informal networks as church does not mean that formal gatherings and committed local communities are redundant. On the contrary, institutional features, such as certain people playing established roles, regular gatherings, rituals and so on, are necessary. How, therefore, in a different context from Paul's, can the re-contextual church both affirm the centrality of local Christian communities while encouraging believers to see their informal networks and daily life and work as church? I believe that differentiating between the language of 'a church', 'the church', 'church', 'the church of', and 'to church' is helpful rhetoric in this regard.

A Church
The use of the countable noun (a church) highlights the importance of every believer being committed to a local church community. Paul's fluid use of the body metaphor to refer to local congregations and the wider universal/heavenly church does not detract from his assumption that believers were meeting together regularly in local communities and that, during these gatherings, there was praise, thanksgiving, teaching, prayer, the exercise of spiritual gifts, mutual edification, and participation in the sacraments

(for example, 1 Cor. 11.2–34; 14.1–40; Col. 3.16). These activities can, and should, occur in settings other than a local church gathering. However, without some institutional structures in place (if a church is too fluid) it will, as Moynagh warns, disperse into gas. Encouraging believers to be committed to 'a church' is vital if the re-contextual church is to best facilitate gift-exchange within the Christian community.[136]

The Church

The list of activities that I have given above (praise, teaching) does not include 'worship'. This is not because meeting together is not part of believers' worship but because, as Marshall notes, in the New Testament, 'the whole activity of Christians can be described as the service of God and they are engaged throughout their lives in worshipping him, yet this vocabulary is not applied in any specific way to Christian meetings'.[137] Meeting together is worship, but it is not the only way that believers worship (their whole lives should be worship). So too commitment to a local church is not all that is conveyed by the body of Christ motif. The universal or heavenly church is also referred to as Christ's body. Just as every aspect of believers' lives should be worship, so too the entirety of believers' lives should express their identify as Christ's body – 'you *are* Christ's body and individually parts of it' (1 Cor. 12.27). This supports Ward's emphasis on seeing the body of Christ (individual believers in their dispersed walks of life) as the church, as well as the church (the institution) as the body of Christ. The definite noun helps believers to see their everyday life and work as part of their incorporation into 'the church', without diminishing the importance of being committed participants in 'a church'.

Church

Carson asserts that one 'may rejoice in the presence of Christ when two or more Christians get together for Christian purposes, but it has little bearing on the church, or on the importance of the church as a body, as an institution'.[138] The church's existence as both an institution and a network suggests, however, that the informal gatherings of two or more Christians have a great deal of bearing on the church as Christ's body. Since every believer is part of the church, the activities that Christians engage in together also constitute church. Moreover, these informal relationships are more or less church (in the proleptic sense) to the extent that they are characterized by love, unity, reconciliation, peace, righteousness, thanksgiving, grace, mutual edification, wisdom and gift-exchange (Eph. 4.1–16).

Carson also rebuffs the notion that parachurch organizations can legitimately be seen as church, which is a view that Ward and Murray Williams promote. Carson contends that an organization such as the Evangelical

Theological Society (ETS) is, utilizing the body metaphor, simply a collection of stomachs: those who take in lots of food and then distribute it to the rest of the body. Such an organization, he observes, does not demonstrate the range of giftings that should be evident in the church as Christ's body. This is an important point but, in making it, Carson marginalizes the church's universal/heavenly purview. With the wider church in view, an organization such as ETS can be seen as providing a giant stomach (to continue Carson's analogy) for the church as a whole. An evangelistic organization could be viewed as a big foot, mobilizing the wider church in this area. A social action Christian charity is, to continue the analogy, a massive hand, and so on. Designating such parachurch organizations 'church' need not undermine the centrality of the local church ('a church'), but it affirms with Murray Williams and Ward the ecclesial legitimacy of such groups and their vital role in the church's life.[139]

Regarding the controversial Homogeneous Unit Principle, the universal/heavenly purview of the church in Ephesians and Colossians raises the question of whether each individual congregation should be as mixed as possible, or whether the reconciliation described in these verses could be fulfilled through unity between demographically-specific groups. Murray Williams and Moynagh support the notion of demographic-specific churches as they believe that they are missionally effective. However, they argue that, to pursue and represent the Christ-brought reconciliation of different social groups, local churches should be in active communication and relationship with the wider body. Moynagh labels this approach 'focused-and-connected'.[140] Therefore, a universal/heavenly perspective on the church may lend support to Moynagh's proposal. With this in mind, I return to the topic of demographically-specific expressions of church when I address the church's relationship with the wider world.

The Church of

Witherington contends that in 1 Corinthians, 'Paul is apparently referring to all the Corinthian house congregations *collectively* as the body of Christ', which 'might well suggest that one particular local house church would not have all the gifts needed in that city to serve the purposes of Christ's body' – the local groups need each other.[141] Whether or not Witherington's analysis of the Corinthian church is accurate, there is great value in the churches in a shared location, such as a city, seeing themselves collectively as the church in that locality and working together in areas such as community engagement and evangelism. The language of 'the church of ... *name of town or city*' could be helpful rhetoric for conveying this sense of gift-exchange between different church groups in one locale.[142]

To Church

Ward and Murray Williams argue that the language of 'I church, you church, we church' would help believers to conceive of church as something that they make rather than attend. The use of church as a verb is awkward rhetorically. Moreover, Paul does not use the verbal form of *ekklēsia* (*ekklēsiazō*). However, *ekklēsia* must be interpreted in light of its use in the LXX, wherefore it becomes apparent that the early Christians' use of *ekklēsia* identified them as God's New Covenant community. Although the sense of gathering is still present in the early Christians' use of the term, *ekklēsia* is not just applied to Christians when they are gathered but depicts the heavenly church as a whole (esp. Eph. 1.22). Therefore were Paul to have used *ekklēsiazō*, this verb (which means 'to hold an assembly') would not have adequately conveyed the New Covenant connotations contained within Paul's understanding of church. Rather, Paul presents the verbal aspect of the church through his use of the body of Christ metaphor, in particular his depiction of the body's *growth*, which occurs as *each part works* and *builds up* the other parts (Eph. 4.16). Therefore, although I am not an advocate of using the word 'church' as a verb – in contemporary usage, 'church' is a noun – I affirm the intent behind Ward and Murray Williams' proposal. The re-contextual church's emphasis on every member ministry, and the building up of the church through this ministry, is firmly supported in the body of Christ texts.[143]

Promoting the language of 'a church', 'the church', 'church', 'the church of', and 'to church' accords with Paul's multivalent use of the body of Christ metaphor, which is applied to local congregations and the larger heavenly/universal church. Paul's use of the body metaphor in turn resonates with the fluidity of Stoic notions of the body, wherein the human body, city-state and cosmos were all seen as interconnecting 'bodies'.[144] This nuance in language is helpful because it facilitates Ward's emphasis on seeing believers as 'church' both when they are gathered and when they are dispersed without undermining the centrality of local Christian communities. The tension between 'institution' and 'network', or formality and informality, is pertinent across all these entities; there is no reason why formal structures within a local congregation are valid but those across local congregations are not.

Every Member Ministry

Murray Williams argues from Ephesians 4.7–16 that the church only reaches maturity when every member contributes. But does this mean that every believer must play an equal role within Christian gatherings? The universal/heavenly scope of the body of Christ metaphor in Ephesians suggests that, on the contrary, it is reductionistic to see the church gathering as the only forum in which believers should exercise their giftings. Since believers are the body of Christ both when they are dispersed in their everyday lives and while gathered, believers can and should exercise their gifts in the wider world, not just in church gatherings. For example, someone with a gift of leadership (Rom. 12.8) may not play a large leadership role in their local church community but devote their time and efforts to leadership in a business or political setting.[145]

Ephesians 4.7–16 also indicates that people with certain giftings have a particular responsibility to equip the body so that the body as a whole builds itself up. This does not mean that only those with the gifts listed can contribute to Christian gatherings; in 1 Corinthians 14, Paul brings guidance but does not prevent the participation of different voices. However, given the nature of the giftings highlighted in Ephesians 4.11, and the fact that, in 1 Corinthians 14, the emphasis is on teaching, prophecy and edification, Paul probably imagined the bulk of the contribution within church gatherings coming from people with these gifts.[146]

Out (Dealing With Resonance): Countercultural and Cultural – Enabling Gift-Exchange with the Wider World

> [T]he church lives in a continuous tension between being for the world and being against the world. In this situation the church is threatened by two dangers. First, if it emphasizes too strongly withdrawal from the world … it threatens to become a purely sectarian apocalyptic movement that forfeits God's redemptive plan for the whole world in the death and resurrection of Christ. Second, if the church exclusively emphasizes participation in the world, it threatens to become another 'worldly' phenomenon, accommodating itself to whatever the world will buy and so becoming a part of the world.[147]

Ecclesiologies based on social models of the Trinity (particularly Volf's) have been criticized for overlooking the church's external relationships. This results when Social Trinitarians apply *perichoresis* horizontally such that Trinitarian relations are seen as a model for believers' communal lives, leading to a preoccupation with the church's internal life. When *perichoresis* is applied vertically, God is seen as permeating creation interdependently (*panentheism*), leading to universalism. Neither inattention to the church's missional purview nor universalistic tendencies support re-contextual thinkers' aim to urge the church to go to the 99 lost sheep rather than pamper the one who is found (to use Ward's metaphor). In contrast, the ecclesiology that I develop in this book, based on Paul's body of Christ texts, presents the church as missional in nature. As I argue below, although some see the body of Christ metaphor as relating only to the church's internal relationships, this motif informs the church's relationship with the wider world.[148]

Re-contextual thinkers find much to criticize in the church's engagement with the contemporary world. Ward and Moynagh highlight the Western church's failure to infiltrate every crevice of society with the good news of the kingdom. To combat this, they emphasize the importance of *listening to what the Spirit is doing (in the wider world) and joining him*. Murray Williams focuses on the church's calling to be a prophetic countercultural community and laments Christendom's role in diminishing the church's impetus in this area. He highlights the church's calling to be a beacon on a hill as well as scattered salt. He promotes a centre-set model of church in support of this, wherein there is no fixed boundary that stops people entering the church community, but those nearer the centre (in terms of their relationship with Jesus) model mature discipleship and encourage others to walk more closely with Jesus too. Moynagh agrees that the church should be an attractive countercultural community *and* permeate society; he promotes, with Murray Williams, a cyclical pattern of *come-and-see* and *go-and-tell*. Moynagh, however, complains that too often churches gather for worship but disperse for mission. He contends that believers should infiltrate society in groups, not just as individuals.[149]

Re-contextual thinkers maintain that the church has over-focused on church members, buildings and institutional structures at the expense of mission. They also criticize the modernist- (and Christendom-) induced one-size-fits-all mentality, arguing that this has hindered contextualization into different contexts. Current church culture privileges educated, modernist, middle-class people, leaving working-class and postmodern people unable to fit in. Moynagh insists on the validity and necessity of demographic-specific expressions of church; the church, he argues, needs to re-contextualize into every subculture. Ward and Murray Williams are more reticent about this approach; Murray Williams highlights the early church's countercultural diversity (*contra* Moynagh's assertion that early house churches were homogeneous) and urges the contemporary church to follow suit. However, Murray Williams and Ward note that those in inherited churches who criticize demographic-specific expressions are usually in homogeneous churches themselves (mainly modernist, middle-class, elderly and educated). Further, they concede the missional benefits of homogeneous expressions. Murray Williams and Moynagh propose similar solutions to this dilemma: demographic-specific groups need to be in active communication and relationship with the wider church body (focused-and-connected). Murray Williams observes that, given the scale of recent cultural changes, church expressions are needed that intentionally engage with this emerging culture. These churches will begin with the young but could pioneer ways to be multigenerational emerging-culture churches in the future.[150]

Therefore, as I examine the body of Christ texts in relation to the church's relationship with the wider world, there are several questions I wish to address. How can re-contextual churches best contextualize into different subcultures while remaining faithful to God's revelation in Scripture and in Christ? To what extent does the body of Christ metaphor support or challenge Ward and Moynagh's emphasis on listening to God's Spirit and joining him? How can the church infiltrate every crevice of society while maintaining its distinctive identity as a countercultural community? Are demographic-specific expressions of church legitimate manifestations of Christ's body?

Figure 5: Dealing with Resonance: Cultural and Countercultural

Regarding the suspension bridge metaphor, a suspension bridge's external environment creates challenges that designers must address. Suspension bridges need to be flexible to withstand external forces such as wind, the movement of traffic across them and earthquakes. Central to Akashi-Kaikyo suspension bridge's survival when it experienced a 7.2 magnitude earthquake was the fact that it extended by approximately 1 metre in length without being structurally damaged. However, this flexibility means that suspension bridges are susceptible to resonance. Resonance occurs when an external periodic force is applied at a similar frequency to the bridge's natural frequency(s) resulting in oscillations of increasing size. In 1831, for example, Broughton Bridge collapsed when a troop of 60 soldiers marched across it, even though the bridge was strong enough to bear their weight, because their marching cadence induced resonance. Similarly, resonance caused by the wind led to the collapse of the Tacoma Narrows Bridge in 1940.[151]

Bridge designers address the problem of resonance by minimizing the probability that external periodic forces will occur at the same frequency as the bridge's natural frequency. For example, because most humans walk at around two steps per second (2 Hz), to reduce the likelihood of resonance, designers ensure that the natural frequency of the bridge is not between 1.7 and 2.5 Hz. In addition, since the Broughton Bridge's collapse, soldiers break step when crossing bridges. Designers also ensure that there is some rigidity, particularly in the deck. The Tacoma Narrows Bridge collapsed partly because its deck was too narrow and flexible. Since its collapse, suspension bridge decks have been strengthened.[152]

Just as suspension bridge designers must balance flexibility and rigidity, so too, *the re-contextual church must maintain a right balance between flexibility and rigidity in relation to its external relationships* (see Figure 5). It must also ensure that its natural frequency is not so similar to that of the wider world that damaging resonance occurs (to push the metaphor). The re-contextual church must be 'cultural', inculturated into every context, and thus manifest in *many* different forms ('many'). It must also be countercultural, distinct in key regards from its wider context as it exhibits its identity as the *one* church of Christ ('one'). The challenge to maintain this tension is often conveyed through the term contextualization, which refers to the church's call to present and embody 'the supracultural message of the gospel in culturally relevant terms' ('one and many').[153]

In order to identify and explore inculturated and countercultural elements within Paul's use of the body of Christ metaphor, I will address 1 Corinthians 12.12–31[154] and Ephesians 1.22–23. In 1 Corinthians 12.12–31, Paul's use of the body metaphor shares similarities with the use of this metaphor in ancient political rhetoric. However, there are also marked differences.[155] This passage thus provides an example of contextualization; it demonstrates Paul's adoption and adaptation of language, models, themes and structures from the church's wider context to shape the church's self-identity and behaviour, prompting the question, on what basis did Paul make these modifications? In Ephesians 1.22–23, the church is presented as the body of him 'who fills everything in every way'. This, I contend below, provides a theological foundation for the re-contextual church's emphasis on *seeing what the Spirit is doing and joining him* and viewing mission as a defining aspect of the church's essential nature.

Cultural ('Many')

For just as the body is one and yet has many parts, and as all the parts of the body are many but the body is one, so it is with Christ. For by one Spirit we have all been baptised into one body – whether Jew or Greek, slave or free – we have all been saturated with one Spirit. For the body is not one part but many. If the foot said, 'Since I am not a hand, I'm not part of the body', would it, for this reason, not be part of the body? And if the ear said, 'Since I am not an eye, I'm not part of the body', would it, for this reason, not be part of the body? If the whole body were an eye, where would the sense of hearing be? If it were all hearing, where would the sense of smell be? Indeed, God has placed each of the parts in the body himself, as he has seen fit. If it were all one part, where would the body be? There are many parts, but one body. Therefore the eye cannot say to the hand, 'I have no need of you!' Nor, moreover, can the head say to the foot, 'I have no need of you!' In fact, more to the point, the parts of the body considered weak are indispensable. Those parts of the body that we consider less honourable, we clothe in greater honour and the unpresentable parts we treat with greater modesty, which our more respectable parts do not need. God has knit the body together, giving greater honour to the parts that lacked it. So there is no division in the body. Rather the parts are concerned about each other. And if one part suffers, all the parts suffer together; if one part is praised, all the parts rejoice together. Now you are Christ's body and individually parts of it. God has placed in the church first apostles, second prophets, third teachers, then acts of power, then gifts of healing, helping gifts, gifts of administration, and different kinds of tongues. Surely not all are apostles? Not all are prophets? Not all are teachers? Surely not all work acts of power? Not all have gifts of healing? Not all speak in tongues? Not all interpret? But eagerly desire the greater gifts, and I will show you a far superior way. (1 Cor. 12.12–31)

A commonwealth resembles in some measure a human body. For each of them is composite and consists of many parts; and no one of their parts either has the same function or performs the same services to others. If ... the feet should say that the whole body rests on them ... the mouth, that it speaks; the head, that it sees ... and then all these should say to the belly, 'And you ... what use are you to us? ... [Y]ou are actually a hindrance and a trouble to us and ... compel us to serve you ...' ... [And if they therefore stopped serving the stomach] ... could the body possibly exist for any considerable time, and not rather be destroyed within a few days by the worst of all deaths, starvation?[156]

The quotation above is taken from a fable about body parts revolting against the stomach, which Agrippa allegedly concocted in the fifth century BC to warn the plebeians not to revolt against the Senate. There are other references to the commonwealth as a body dating back to the fourth and fifth centuries BC. Plato argues in his *Republic* that states best flourish when the individual members see themselves as one body. When a finger is hurt, the whole body feels the pain. So too, the pleasure felt by one part is experienced by all. The body metaphor is also found in texts written closer to Paul's penning of 1 Corinthians. Around the turn of the first century Seneca presented the emperor as the soul or head and the state as his body. Dio Chrysostom contended that friends provide eyes to see and ears to hear. Plutarch maintained that those who do not live harmoniously are like feet tripping each other up or a body cutting off a limb. Epictetus contended that citizens should behave in relation to the community as a hand or foot behaves in relation to the body.[157]

Within 1 Corinthians 12.12–31 there are both points of departure from and similarities with the use of the body metaphor in ancient political rhetoric. Mitchell notes that Paul's construal of the body metaphor in 1 Corinthians 12.12–31 matches wider uses even in the details. Indeed, 1 Corinthians as a whole evidences the use of several rhetorical strategies commonly used to promote *homonoia* (harmony/unity).[158] Paul's approach to the church was inculturated; he adopts language, themes, and even structures that were prevalent in the ancient world and applies these to the church (albeit with notable modifications). Paul's use of the body metaphor thus serves as an example and legitimation of contextualization. To a predominantly Gentile audience, he depicts the church not simply through Old Testament images but via a common Graeco-Roman concept. He uses a culturally meaningful image to inform the church's self-understanding.

> He subjected all things under his feet and gave him to be head over everything for the church, which is his body, the fullness of him who fills everything in every way. (Eph. 1.22–23)

> We as God's people, have already begun to be God's endtime temple where his presence is manifested to the world, and we are to extend the boundaries of the new garden-temple until Christ returns, when, finally, they will be expanded worldwide.[159]

Contra those who think that the body of Christ image predominantly concerns the church's internal relations, Ephesians 1.22–23 has marked implications for mission, as does Ephesians as a whole. Turner contends that the church's mission in Ephesians is to live out unity as a light illuminating the world's darkness and alienation.[160] Accordingly, in this passage the church is presented as a gift, manifesting Christ's presence through his Spirit to the wider world. This is not to say that God's presence is only revealed through the church. Rather, the presence of him *who fills everything in every way* is located in a unique way in the church. This provides a theological foundation for the re-contextual church's focus on *listening to what God is doing and joining him* while ensuring that an emphasis on God's work in the world does not obscure the church's unique identity and calling. Since Christ dwells in the church through his Spirit, the church plays a distinctive role in both manifesting Christ's presence to the world and recognizing the Spirit's work in the world.

This passage must be interpreted in light of Ephesians as a whole, wherein the absolute nature of the filling referred to in 1.23b ('the fullness of him who fills everything in every way') is in tension with the incompleteness and growth conveyed through 3.19 ('in order that you may be filled with all the fullness of God'). This in turn resonates with the tension between the church's present existence as 'one new human' (2.15) and its growth 'in every way into him who is the head, Christ' (4.15). Moreover, as von Soden notes, the concepts of filling/fullness (1.23 and 3.19) and growth (4.15) are connected. The fullness of Christ is achieved when the body is fully grown. Beale sees resonance between this growth and the temple theme; 'in Christ' and 'in one new human' (2.15) are equivalent to 'in one Spirit' (2.18) and 'into a holy temple' (2.21), and all refer to presence of God in the new creation. The temple theme is also implicit in Ephesians 1.22–23 (cf. 3.19); the use of the noun *plērōma* (fullness) and the verb *plēroō* (to fill) induce thoughts of the Old Testament tabernacle and temple, which are filled (*pimplēmi* [LXX]) with God's glory.[161] Verses 1.23; 2.15; 3.19 and 4.15 thus all point to the same reality – the church's eschatological existence as the inaugurated end-time temple, which is filled with God's presence through its union with Christ and infilling of the Spirit – but emphasize to differing degrees the 'now' (1.23 and 2.15) and 'not yet' (3.19 and 4.15) components of this reality. Accordingly, *plērōma* in 1.23 and 3.19 refers to God's glory, which is best defined as his presence specifically in its visibility/tangibility.[162]

It is important to ascertain whether, in 1.23, *plērōma* (fullness) and *plēroō* (here used in participle form, 'who fills') have an active or passive sense.[163] *Plērōma* ('the *fullness* of him who fills everything in every way') carries passive connotations, the church is filled with Christ. This accords with the passive sense of *plēroō* in Ephesians 3.19, which describes believers as filled with the fullness of God. *Plēroō* ('the fullness of him *who fills* everything in every way') could also be passive (a divine passive), meaning that Christ is filled by God. However, although this reading is supported by Colossians 1.18–19, the resonance between 1.23 and 4.10 indicates that *plēroō* is better understood as a middle verb with an active sense, meaning that Christ fills everything in every way. Read alongside 1.10, where Paul describes the future restoration of the cosmos, 1.23 thus depicts Christ's pervasive presence moving all things towards this future goal.[164]

Combining these two parts of 1.23, Lincoln notes that, 'although Christ is in the process of filling the cosmos, at present, it is only the Church which can actually be called his fullness (or, we might add, his "body"). The Church appears, then, to be the focus for and medium of Christ's presence and rule in the cosmos.'[165] Christ is head over all, but only the church is referred to as his body and is, to some degree, Christ's extension on earth. Through Christ's Spirit, the church manifests Christ to the world (albeit imperfectly) and is thereby a gift to the world. This accords with Ephesians 3.10, where the church's witnessing role is explicit.[166]

However, although Christ's presence and glory pervade the church, as God's temple, in a 'strong' sense, as Tanner notes, by his Spirit, Christ is also present in the wider world in a 'weak' sense. 'Weak' should be understood relationally not spatially; God's Spirit is in the world but he is often not known or even recognized. Therefore, God's filling of creation is 'the gift of God's self in revelation, salvation, [and] self-presentation'.[167] The church plays a key role in this revelation but should also be attentive to what the Spirit is already doing in the world. Ward maintains, for example, that because of the Spirit's presence, believers should expect to see 'theological flow' in song lyrics, film plots, advertising and so on and, where possible, utilize these signs of God's presence in wider culture to point people to him, while recognizing that faith growth outside the Christian community will probably be limited. Adopting the language, themes, and even structures of wider culture, and utilizing their 'theological flow' to convey the message of Jesus (being 'cultural'), provides points of connection to those outside the Christian community, making it easier for this message to be understood and responded to.[168]

The presence of God's Spirit in the world also indicates some reciprocity between the church and the wider world; the church receives from, as well as gives to, the world. As Ward asserts, with DeMent's *Lifeline* album as an example, 'As theological representation flows and circulates through mediation [within culture] there is always the possibility that in the freedom of the Spirit it may become a place of epiphany and encounter.'[169] Indeed, the body metaphor within Graeco-Roman culture has proved a gift to the church; the powerful image of unity conveyed within it has, with Paul's adoption and adaptation, profoundly shaped the church's self-identity.

Countercultural ('One')

Paul wrote 1 Corinthians to a community experiencing *eris* (strife) (1 Cor. 1.11). The nature of the conflict is disputed. Theissen has influenced the new consensus that the Corinthian believers represented a variety of social statuses, rather than just the lower ranks. He maintains that those of higher social status were particularly influential within the Corinthian church and sees differentiation of status as a primary cause of the community's conflicts. Nash, in contrast, questions how precisely the believers' socio-economic status can be ascertained and suggests that they may have compensated for a lack of status in society by striving for prominence in the church. Attempts to squeeze the whole of 1 Corinthians under one causative umbrella risk prohibiting each section from speaking for itself, and thus Theissen overstates his case. Nevertheless, differences in socio-economic rank were likely influential. More significantly, regardless of the cause, Corinthian believers were chasing status and prominence and Paul saw this competitiveness, and the conflict it produced, as antithetical to the nature of the church as Christ's body.[170]

Into this context of competition and strife Paul introduces the 'parable' of the church as Christ's body. Parables are a form of indirect communication, which can circumambulate the barriers that recipients use to block direct communication. How better to convince an assured community that their understanding is flawed than to expose the absurdity of their attitudes and behaviour through the farce of talking body parts?[171]

Paul adopts the body metaphor to promote unity in the Corinthian church. However, he adapts the metaphor in key regards. For example, the body metaphor was usually applied to the state, which was hierarchically structured. Paul applies the metaphor to the church, suggesting that the church is in some way a substitute for the state; belonging to the church trumps any other citizenship. Therefore, through his use of the body metaphor, Paul challenges the high degree of societal integration that the Corinthian believers appear to enjoy; he calls the church to be open to people of any ethnicity or social standing, but recognize the difference between those inside and outside the community.[172]

Given the original metaphor's political undercurrents, it is ironic that Soskice sees the body of Christ motif as now too politicized to be a helpful image for the church. Soskice's complaint would be better directed at the metaphor's deadness. 'The body of Christ' has become so closely associated with a particular form of the Lord's Supper that it lacks its initial dynamism. Moreover, contemporary readers do not see society as a body as the ancients did and so the metaphor's original political overtones are often overlooked. However, in the context of the Graeco-Roman world, by applying the body metaphor to the church, Paul calls believers to be an alternative community, providing a template of what society should look like.[173]

In addition, despite its similarities to contemporaneous texts, Paul's parable develops in a surprising direction. In 12.22–24 Paul reverses the hierarchy that the Corinthian Christians have built up in their minds. The weak parts are indispensable, the less-honourable are clothed in greater honour, and the unpresentable are adorned. It is unclear whom the designations 'weak', 'less-honourable', and 'unpresentable' refer to. Witherington proposes that it is the seemingly less gifted believers. Best argues that Paul has in mind those whose roles and giftings are not as prominent, those who work behind the scenes and so go unnoticed. Given that the context suggests that the letter's first recipients had a penchant for the more showy gifts of tongues and prophecy, both suggestions are feasible. Regardless of the exact meaning of 'weaker', however, rather than using the body metaphor to keep subordinates in their place, as was commonly the case, Paul urges his readers to value those who appear inferior (either in status, gifting, or both). This is not merely a 'compensatory move on Paul's part, by means of which those of lower status are to be compensated for their low position ... Rather, his rhetoric pushes for an actual reversal ... The lower is made higher, and the higher lower.'[174]

Lee argues that 'status reversal' is misleading since Paul is not elevating those of previously low status to a position of authority above those of high status. Equally, however, Paul is not depicting an imaginary status change that merely reaffirms the existing hierarchy. Rather, Paul is describing two contrasting ways of seeing status. In the world's eyes, the less honourable are still less honorable. However, the Corinthian believers should now see status, indeed the whole of reality, according to the 'new age'. In this new age, those with low status as the world sees it 'will enjoy high status as those who participate in the eschatological reality and thus shame the wise and the strong (1.27–28)'.[175] Paul is not, however, referring to future equality to ease discontent in the present. Rather, this new way of viewing reality should determine believers' current relationships. The reality to which the believers are to aspire is constituted by their connection to Christ, as his body, and corresponding participation in God's life through the Spirit. Christ is the foundation for Paul's subversion of the Corinthians' hierarchy. As Horrell notes, Paul draws upon Christ's sacrificial self-giving to undergird a countercultural ethos in which the weak are honoured and the strong lower themselves to lift up others. Thus, *contra* the usual intent of the body metaphor, to promote unity through the reinforcement of existing hierarchies (disruption to the social hierarchy was seen as a disease), Paul emphasizes the need for diversity, interdependence, mutuality, empathy and self-giving (esp. 12.14–21).[176]

The introduction of 'first ... second ... third ... ' (12.28) could indicate that Paul challenges one hierarchy to implement another. However, the apparent contradiction is resolved in light of Paul's eschatological framework. Elsewhere Paul notes that as an apostle he 'suffers indignity through his hardships and has low status in the perception of the world (4.9–13)' *but* (or, as Gorman contends, *because*) his status is high in the body of Christ.[177] 'But' and 'because' are not contradictory here. Rather:

For Paul, the possession of a right to act in a certain way has an inherent, built-in mandate to exercise truly the status that provides the right by sometimes refraining from the exercise of that right out of love for others. This is not to *deny* one's apostolic or general Christian identity (and associated rights), or to void it ... but to *exercise* it as an act of Christlike love. For Paul, love does not seek its own interest or edification but rather that of others (1 Cor. 13.5; 1 Cor. 8.1b), which is the core meaning of conformity to Christ.[178]

The ranking probably regards both authority and responsibility within the church but, because of his eschatological viewpoint, Paul has a radically different view of authority than that within wider Corinthian society; his authority involves being a 'spectacle' (4.9), a 'fool' (4.10), 'hungry', 'thirsty', 'in rags', 'brutally treated', 'homeless' (4.11), 'scum of the earth', 'garbage of the world' (4.13), and 'a slave to everyone, to win as many as possible' (9.19).[179] Similarly, the greater gifts (apostles, prophets and teachers (12.31a)) are greater from the perspective of the believers' new eschatological existence, rather than affording status in the world's eyes; they 'are greater only because they more easily function to strengthen the body' (for example, 1 Cor. 14.3–5).[180] In contrast, the gift of tongues primarily values the individual (1 Cor. 14.2) and therefore – alongside the fact that the Corinthians put it first – is placed last.[181] Paul thus challenges the prevailing hierarchy and, even more significantly, turns the whole nature of status and authority on its head.

Therefore, although Paul's adoption of the body metaphor demonstrates inculturation (the church is 'cultural'), his adaptation of this metaphor reveals that the church is also countercultural. This raises the question: on what basis does Paul both adopt and adapt the body metaphor? What factors determine which elements of this motif he accords with and which he transforms and subverts? In other words, what is Paul's framework for contextualization? Paul is not arbitrary and haphazard, thus he must have some criteria.

As I argue below, rather than a dogmatic list, Paul's framework for adopting and adapting the body metaphor consists of the one ultimate vision of church that lies behind the New Testament's presentation of church. Central to this vision is the church's dependence on God's initiating and sustaining work in Christ and through the Spirit, which is constituted by the seven dimensions that I argue form the essence of the church (down, up, in, out, of, towards and between). Paul's framework for contextualization consists of these seven dimensions.

Countercultural and Cultural ('One and Many')

Paul's adaptation of the body metaphor accords with the four limits of contextualization that Moynagh identifies (up, in, out, of). However, a fuller picture is apparent if the three other trajectories are also considered (down, towards and between). Moreover, Paul's adoption and adaptation of the body metaphor accords with the tensions that, I argue in this book, are conveyed within the body of Christ image: God's immanence and transcendence (down); believers' relationship with God as both spiritual and religious (up); the church as an institution and a network (in); the church as cultural and countercultural (out); the church as inherited and innovative (of); and the church as located in the eschatological now/not yet tension (towards and between). In addition, within his adaptation, Paul highlights the notion of gift.

Down

Paul's primary alteration of the body metaphor, which forms the basis for his other adaptations, is his designation of the church as not just a body but Christ's body, composed by the Spirit (1 Cor. 12.13).[182] Thiselton notes that those who rightly emphasize the political background (and thus political implications) of the body metaphor must not understate the Christological significance. Paul connects Christ with the church, but does not merge the two, and he can do so because God's transcendence enables his immanence. Christ permeates the church through his Spirit without being dependent on the church, and thus having his freedom impinged, because, as the creator, he can be immanently involved in creation without compromising his divine identity. The church is thus not simply a community in which unity and good order must prevail; the church is a community whose life is determined by its incorporation into Christ as his body and corresponding participation in the life of the Trinity (Paul's is a Christocentric Trinitarian ecclesiology). Therefore, a believer's role is not determined by inherited status, status climbing, social manoeuvring, or hard work – as were the determinative factors within Corinth at large – but, 'God has placed each of the parts in the body himself, as he has seen fit' (1 Cor. 12.18).[183]

Moreover, Paul's subversion of the Corinthian hierarchy through his body of Christ motif can only be understood in reference to God's self-giving as revealed most clearly in and through Christ. There is power in weakness and high status in low status because, in Christ, God has demonstrated his glory as power-in-weakness; the weak do not become the strong, they are the strong, to the extent that God's power works through their weakness.[184] This is not to deny futurity within Paul's eschatology but to note the significance of the church's present eschatological existence. The 'goal of the Christian community is to allow the life and Spirit of this [cruciform] God, rather than the imperial spirit of domination and acquisition, to flow in and through it'.[185] The notion of gift thus lies at the heart of Paul's contextualization of the body metaphor.

Up

Paul's discussion on spiritual gifts must also be understood in light of 1 Corinthians as a whole, wherein one of Paul's primary aims is to redefine spirituality in terms of Christlikeness. In 12.21–26, the believers' skewed and overinflated view of their own 'spirituality' and giftedness lies behind their attitude 'I have no need of you' (12.21), which explains one of Paul's marked modifications of the metaphor: rather than urging those of lesser status to remember their dependence on those of higher status, Paul exhorts those of higher status to remember their dependence on those of lower status. Moreover, Paul does not utilize his body of Christ metaphor to promote unity and order as ends in themselves. Rather, into a context that was experience- and self-orientated, Paul redefines spirituality in relation to the building up the body (namely, others) (esp. 14.5, 12, 26, 40). Paul thus redresses the spiritual–religious tension, as these words are understood today, by urging those obsessed with the spontaneous and individualized aspects of their faith (spiritual) to elevate the orderly and collective aspects (religious).[186]

In

The institution-network tension is apparent within Paul's contextualization of the body metaphor in that, on the one hand, he introduces the metaphor to bring order, and thus a greater degree of institutionalization. 'First apostles...' (12.28) is significant given Thiselton's observation that, throughout 1 Corinthians, Paul seeks to realign the Corinthian believers with the apostolic gospel they had received, challenging their personal leadership preferences and socially constructed theology by reference to apostolic traditions. On the other hand, although the body politic is an implicitly institutional image, rather than using the body metaphor to reinforce a fixed hierarchy, Paul subverts the hierarchy that at least some Corinthian believers' had established in their minds. Rather than addressing those of lower status and urging them to submit to their rulers' authority, Paul addresses those of higher status, urging them to respect others. In addition, within the wider context of his instructions regarding corporate worship, though Paul desires to bring greater order, he does not seek to eradicate spontaneity and informality (1 Cor. 14.26–33).[187]

In addition, within the 'in' component, the prominence of gift-giving within Paul's contextualization is particularly apparent. Paul exhorts those of higher status, who presumably believed that they had far more to give than receive, to recognize their need for the gifting of others, particularly those they viewed as inferior. As Rowan Williams notes, this emphasis on every part being equally a gift to the others is now so familiar that it is easy to forget how radical this vision was in its original setting.[188]

Out

Paul's adoption and adaptation of a pre-existing metaphor demonstrates his willingness to engage with his external context. He demonstrates a contextual approach that is cultural. However, he is also counter-cultural. Moreover, Paul does not simply pave a middle path between two extremes but holds the *one* ultimate vision of the church – a relational reality predicated on the church's participation in God's life in Christ and through the Spirit – in dialectical tension with the fact that this reality must be manifest in *many* different contexts. He utilizes an image that is particularly pertinent to the specific context into which he is writing but aligns this image with his overarching vision for church.

Of

Arguing that the political use of body contributed to Paul's construction and application of the body of Christ image is not a denial of other influences. Through the language of *sōma Christou* there is an implicit connection between Paul's parable in 1 Corinthians 12.12–31 and the metaphor's eucharistic references (1 Cor. 10.16; 11.24). Although Paul adopts a common political metaphor, his specification that the church is *Christ's* body grounds his motif in wider church tradition. This is significant given Thiselton's contention that, within 1 Corinthians, one of Paul's aims is to root the Corinthian congregation more firmly in apostolic tradition in contrast to the believers' desire for autonomy. Paul's contextualization of the body metaphor is therefore inherited and innovative. It is inherited in that it both draws on an established metaphor for the city and combines this with a central church tradition. It is innovative in the way that it brings these two together and, in doing so, generates new meaning.[189]

Towards

The eschatological tenor of 1 Corinthians 12.12–31 is apparent through the sacramental overtones of *baptizō* (to baptize) and *potizō* (to drink) (12.13), which mark the Corinthian community as the New Covenant community. Moreover, Paul's adaptation of the body metaphor to challenge and subvert the Corinthian believers' existing hierarchies can only be understood eschatologically and in reference to Christ's self-giving. As I argue in the 'Towards' section, the church is an countercultural society that is called to manifest the future reality of God's consummated kingdom. In Paul's subversion of the Corinthian hierarchy through his body of Christ metaphor, Paul stresses that the future reality of the kingdom should be exhibited in the present as the Corinthian believers imitate Christ's self-giving by giving and receiving from each other. Paul's contextualization of the body metaphor thus exhibits an eschatological framework that looks towards a future reality by anticipating this reality in the present.[190]

Between

In Paul's subversion of the Corinthians' hierarchy through his body of Christ metaphor, he also accounts for the believers' location 'between' Jesus' first and second coming. In outlining the 'far superior way' (12.31), Paul stresses that, though love will remain, the gifts of prophecy, tongues and knowledge will cease (13.8). The understanding that will accompany seeing face-to-face in the future will so utterly usurp the believers' imperfect knowledge in the present as to render it redundant (13.12). Thus, as Thiselton contends, people 'do not simply "progress" to *perfection* or completion, as gnostics might propose; for the eschatological act of definitive divine judgment ... does away with piece-by-piece knowledge in a *cosmic act of God*'.[191] Paul's emphasis on the Corinthians' location *between* the start and consummation of the new age is particularly significant given that the Corinthian believers demonstrated either an over-realized eschatology or, as Barclay suggests, a 'non' eschatology.[192]

The way in which Paul relativizes the importance of the different roles and gifts by stressing their temporariness is unprecedented. One cannot imagine Senator Menenius (who used the body metaphor to urge the workers who had gone on strike to go back to work) relativizing his rhetoric on the importance of the belly being fed (governing classes) by arguing that the role of the governing classes would eventually cease. Paul's emphasis on the church's 'between' location in his adaptation and application of the body metaphor is striking.

Implications: Christocentric Trinitarian Contextualization

The body of Christ metaphor has implications for the re-contextual church's relationship with the wider world. First, I contend that *the church as a suspension bridge characterized by gift-exchange* provides a framework for contextualization. Second, I assert that the body of Christ metaphor supports, but modifies, the kernel-and-husk model of contextualization. Third, the body of Christ texts provide a foundation for seeing mission as part of the *esse* of the church. Fourth, these texts inform re-contextual thinkers' promotion of demographic-specific churches.

The Church as a Suspension Bridge Characterized by Gift-Exchange as a Framework for Contextualization

Paul's use of the body metaphor provides a case study of his approach to contextualization. Paul's adoption, adaptation and application of this metaphor evidences concern for the seven relational dimensions that compose the church (down, up, in, out, of, towards and between) and the tensions that are inherent within each dimension. Thus the metaphor of the church as a suspension bridge of gift-exchange provides a framework for contextualization that is Christocentric and Trinitarian. This framework does not offer easy answers to questions regarding, for example, the strengths and weaknesses of contextualizing worship music into contemporary pop culture. However, it can guide re-contextual thinkers as they think through this issue, and others like it.

For example, regarding contemporary worship music, the tension between God's transcendence and immanence (down), wherein God's transcendence enables his immanence, indicates that the problem with inculturation into pop culture is not the emphasis on God's immanence per se. Rather, problems arise if God's transcendence is thereby overlooked. Songs that focus on intimacy with God must ensure that they do not reduce God to the level of creature. If this occurs, God's immanence is not highlighted at the expense of his transcendence; rather both God's transcendence and immanence are diminished.

The spiritual–religious tension (up) supports Ward's concerns regarding the imbalance within contemporary sung worship towards experiential worship songs at the expense of those recounting the historical events of Jesus' life, death, resurrection and ascension. As Ward contends, this balance must be readdressed such that believers' subjective experience (spiritual) is predicated on the objective foundation of the historical events on which this experience is based (religious).

The institution–network tension (in) provides impetus for evaluating the degree of spontaneity and formality within church gatherings in relation to sung worship. Concerns should be raised when corporate worship within a Christian gathering so closely resembles a pop concert that the majority of believers become spectators rather than participants. While the genre of pop concert conveys a superficial level of informality, this actually demonstrates an imbalance towards institution, since only a designated few actually participate.[193]

The cultural–countercultural tension (out) legitimizes the inculturation of worship songs into many different genres, including contemporary styles. However, it also prompts re-contextual thinkers to assess the extent to which their worship songs are countercultural. Music genres that are not culturally relevant (because they are dated or reflective of the music tastes of those from different cultures) can remind the church and wider world of the church's calling to be countercultural. Similarly, the inherited–innovative tension (of) affirms the value of incorporating worship songs from different eras and nationalities. As well as highlighting the church's countercultural nature, variety in worship styles reminds believers that they are incorporated into a church body that stretches back 2,000 years and across the globe.

The now/not yet tension (towards and between) encourages re-contextual thinkers to evaluate the eschatology expressed within gathered worship. Some note that contemporary worship music has so focused on praise that there is no scope for darker emotions to be expressed corporately, such as sorrow and pain. Similarly, there can be a lack of space for more contemplative components, such as silence. The 'between' dimension encourages re-contextual thinkers to explore how those leading corporate gatherings could create space and opportunity for the church to address head on the suffering and pain that believers face while living between Christ's first and second coming. The 'towards' trajectory prompts re-contextual thinkers to assess the extent to which the theme of the kingdom, in both its presence (now) and futurity (not yet), is expressed within contemporary worship music.[194]

Popular music has proved a gift to the church, in that it has provided a medium through which contemporary songwriters can express their praise to God. However, it is not a gift that should be embraced uncritically. Rather, this genre of music, as with all aspects of the church's contextualization into its context, must be critically evaluated in light of the seven dimensions that constitute the church's essence and the tensions inherent within these trajectories.

Kernel and Husk

The re-contextual church's postmodern milieu has likely contributed to the recent rebuttal of a kernel-and-husk approach to contextualization. Postmodernity presents a challenge to philosophical realism (the belief that things exist apart from one's conception of them). The alternatives are creative antirealism (or irrealism) (things are created by language) and social–constructive antirealism (things exist beyond one's perception of them but it is impossible to know them as they are). Regarding a kernel-and-husk approach to contextualization, the question is whether cultural- and time-bound statements about God's nature and work can be transferred from one 'cultural container' to another with retention of meaning. The answer to this question need not, and should not, be all or nothing. To assert that meaning changes with form does not mean that there can be no continuity of message, or that the message conserved cannot point accurately to a reality that transcends the message itself. As Corcoran notes, it is not necessary to embrace antirealism to acknowledge that human beings are finite and constrained by their context and limitations; such a view is present within Christianity itself in its pronouncement of God as creator and human beings as mere creatures. Notably, however, as created beings, humans have the ability, granted by their creator, to discern truths about the creation that they are part of. Moreover, inherent to Christianity, is the belief that the creator has revealed himself to his creatures in actions and words. Corcoran thus promotes epistemic humility, wherein claiming knowledge of God and recognizing the limits of that knowledge go hand-in-hand.[195]

Therefore, while it is important to acknowledge the limitations of a kernel-and-husk approach (medium and message cannot be neatly demarcated), this analogy need not be abandoned. Rather, since the church, indeed creation, is founded on God's initiative, and human beings are made in his image, it follows that in creating speech God created a means by which transcendent truths about himself and creation can be conveyed (albeit not perfectly or exhaustively). As Vanhoozer notes, 'God is a speaking, revealing God, whose Spirit accompanies his Word from inspiration through inscripturation to appropriation.'[196] Corcoran thus astutely contends:

> I believe that God really is loving and compassionate and just. I am sure I cannot plumb the depths of God's love and compassion and justice with words or concepts. But I also don't think that when we get to heaven (or heaven in all its fullness gets to us) we will discover that God is so wholly other, and our language so completely impotent, that it turns out God is really self-absorbed, hateful, wicked, unjust, and apathetic.[197]

Although celebrating the Eucharist with the Prodigy's 'Firestarter' blaring in the background affects the message conveyed, this does not mean that it has no shared meaning with a Eucharist conducted in silence. The presence of a 'kernel' of meaning that is shared across different forms is implicit in Paul's view that not all expressions of the Eucharist are equally valid when examined against the Christ-event that the Lord's Supper remembers and points to (1 Cor. 11.26). Paul condemns the Corinthian Christian's celebration of the Lord's Supper for not aligning adequately with this Christ-event and its implications for the present. But this relates to problems within the community's relationships and not the format that is used (1 Cor. 11.17–34).[198]

Contextualization is thus not simply a matter of pragmatism (what engages people), or preference (what people like), or human ingenuity, although these have value. Rather, contextualization is grounded in God's movement to the world, in Christ and through the Spirit, which Scripture both points to and records. While finite human beings cannot fully grasp the profundity of God's nature and his work in creation, they can depict God and his acts with accuracy and communicate their conception of God in different forms with continuity.

Mission and the Church's Esse

Through its incorporation into the Trinity in Christ, the church plays an important role in God's mission (*missio Dei*), although its activity lies within overarching passivity. Within the body of Christ texts, the church is presented as a unique locus of Christ's glory and manifests this presence, through the Spirit, to a wider world in which Christ is present but often not recognized. The church is a gift to the wider world and its involvement in God's mission is a significant way in which the church brings God glory. The body of Christ metaphor thus provides an alternative theological basis for seeing mission as part of the church's *esse* to the usual foundation proffered: God's inner being. Proposals outlining how mission relates to God's inner life tend to be speculative and, when called into question, can hinder, rather than help, missiologists' aim to connect ecclesiology and missiology more closely.[199] The problem is how to articulate the paradox that *what God reveals in history accords with his nature* but, *although God is involved in history, he is not dependent on creation.* The immanent and economic Trinity must neither be amalgamated nor separated. God's actions in history *reveal* his eternal life but do not *define* (constitute) it. Rather than seeking to demonstrate how God is missional in his inner being, therefore, it is more cogent to assert with Holmes that, since God has created, he will act consistently towards creation. God acts missionally towards humanity and thus *God is missional* and *the church is missional* can be maintained without speculation on how this relates to God's life *in se.*[200]

Focused Church?

Moynagh and Ward both address consumerism within their discussions on contextualization, arguing that the problem with the inherited church is not that it has adapted to consumerism per se, but that it has only marketed itself to a limited demographic of people. They also note that consumerism has weaknesses that the church must not incorporate (mainly its 'me'-focused culture). However, church expressions, they argue, should not recoil from marketing themselves to specific groups; the church should be contextualized into every subculture, leading to a diversity of church expressions.[201]

Ephesians 1.23 indicates that Christ's presence and glory pervade the world in a weak sense. The Spirit's presence in the wider world supports the re-contextual church's emphasis on joining in with what God is doing in different contexts. Paul may not have seen the metaphor of society as a body as 'theological flow', for instance. Certainly he would not have used this language, but he affirms the body metaphor as an exponent of unity, readily adopting and adapting it to his own ends.[202] Given the plurality of subcultures within the UK, churches similarly need to focus on the context that they seek to contextualize into. This call for the church to infiltrate every crevice of society (to re-contextualize into every subculture) exists, however, in tension with the church's identity as an alternative community, one of the characteristics of which is its unity within diversity. How can the church bear witness to the breaking down of the barriers between different genders, nationalities and so on, if church expressions are monocultural?[203]

Contextualizing the church into every context *and* maintaining the church's calling to manifest unity-in-diversity cannot be achieved by paving a middle path between the two. Although the homogeneous–heterogeneous debate dichotomizes this issue, as if all churches were either entirely demographic-specific or fully mixed, both extremes are untenable. Churches exist across a spectrum and any solution must account for this complexity. The re-contextual church must both negotiate the missional imperative to avoid unnecessary cultural barriers *and* find ways to embody diversity. Moynagh's focused-and-connected church is a noteworthy solution but risks remaining just theory unless informality and spontaneity are held in tension with formality and structure in how this is outworked in practice. Churches need to be proactive about facilitating the building of relationships across different types of church if Moynagh's proposal is to be implemented in practice.

Of (Anchorage One): Inherited and Innovative – Receiving the Gift of the Past

To demonstrate that an ecclesiology based on the body of Christ texts adds substance and stability to the re-contextual movement, it is to address the 'of' component. By 'of', I mean the relationship between the local church and the wider universal/heavenly church *and*, since the heavenly church stretches across all time periods as well as every geographical location, the connection between the contemporary church and church tradition.[204]

Church tradition is a debated topic within the re-contextual conversation, with re-contextual thinkers affirming some aspects but criticizing others. Moynagh, Ward and Murray Williams identify aspects of inherited church tradition that are unhelpful, even unhealthy, in a postmodern context. Murray Williams believes that Christendom is the main perpetrator, while Ward focuses on the church's adaptation into modernity. They believe that the influence of Christendom and modernity has created weaknesses in the church's relationship with the Trinity, its structures, and its attitude to the wider world, including: an unhealthy separation of ecclesiology and missiology; a failure to engage with people's spiritual hunger; a bland one-size-fits-all approach to church gatherings; an over-emphasis on size; discrepancies between prescribed and actual beliefs; an emphasis on spectating rather than participation; controlling, hierarchical leadership and a lay–priestly divide.[205]

Other aspects of church tradition are viewed positively. Moynagh and Murray Williams believe that new monasticism, which draws from ancient monastic practices but reapplies them in contemporary culture, could enrich the church. Both Moynagh and Murray Williams promote the practice of catechesis (training and discipleship programmes for those new to the Christian faith), with Moynagh specifying that this should be centred on the concepts of kingdom, Christian identity and church to challenge the consumerism and self-centred individualism of contemporary culture. Moynagh is the most positive about inherited churches, arguing that inherited and new expressions of church must work alongside each other in a 'mixed economy'. Murray Williams is concerned by what he perceives as a postmodern pick 'n' mix approach to retrieving ancient wisdom and practices. He urges believers to familiarize themselves with their whole heritage as one antidote to this.[206]

In relation to church sacraments and ordination, Moynagh asserts that there are no practices, including the Eucharist, that are essential for a group to be called a church, although these practices are important. He sees the church as ultimately relational, not institutional. Ward, who also belongs to the Anglican Church, rejects an institutional view of church but maintains the Eucharist (indeed the Reformation 'marks' of Word and Sacrament) as requisite. Murray Williams does not explicitly state whether he sees the Eucharist as essential; he lists it as a common liturgical element. His free church background suggests that he does not believe that an ordained person must preside. Regarding church leadership, Murray Williams affirms the importance of leadership but presents ordination negatively as a hangover from Christendom. Moynagh refers to ordination more positively, noting that flexible options would mean that a church planter could stay in the community they are working in while pursuing ordination. However, Moynagh also maintains that not all church planters need get ordained.[207]

What can an ecclesiology based on the body of Christ metaphor contribute to this discussion? Re-contextual thinkers often base their ecclesiology on Social Trinitarianism, within which a fuller understanding of God's life *in se* is sought as the basis for understanding the church's true nature. However, those who base their conceptions of church on God's inner life often overlook the centrality of the Christ-event or, by way of equal but opposite error, present God's being as dependent on history. Volf, for example, notes that Jesus' death and resurrection lie at the centre of history but, in *After Our Likeness*, these historical roots recede into the background. In contrast Moltmann ties God's life to creation through problematic statements such as Jesus' suffering on the cross 'determines the inner life of the triune God from eternity to eternity'.[208] As I will elucidate below, an ecclesiology based on the body of Christ image affirms the church's anchorage in history, but denies that God is similarly tied. The church's foundation in the past does not mean that it cannot and should not adapt to the present. Rather, as I argue below, within the body of Christ texts the church is presented as both *inherited* and *innovative*. The church's shared inheritance results from the fact that the church across all eras and contexts is *one*. Critical engagement with church tradition and history is essential if contemporary churches are to be faithful expressions of this one church. However, the church is also innovative and thus there will be *many* different expressions of church in various times and places. Believers must examine what it means in their particular context to be fully inherited and, because of the novelty of their unique context, fully innovative.

The suspension bridge metaphor is illuminative here. Suspension bridges require massive external anchors. Just as suspension bridges need anchors to maintain stability and flexibility, so the church must be anchored in its past inheritance in order to innovate faithfully (demonstrate flexibility) in every new context (see Figure 6).

The church's nature as inherited is addressed in reference to 1 Corinthians 10.14–22, where Paul roots the church in its inherited story. Moreover, in this passage, 'the body of Christ' refers to the Lord's Supper alongside the Christian community, showing the importance of this particular church practice. The church's nature as innovative is examined in reference to Ephesians 3.1–7, since here the church's identity as a new entity founded on new revelation is emphasized. The church as both inherited and innovative is explored in relation to Romans 12.3–8, where it is apparent that Paul sees scope for disagreement as regards the

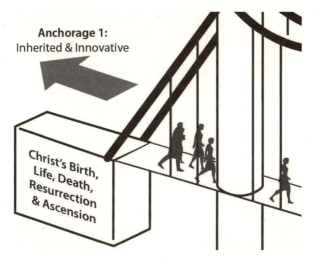

Figure 6: Anchorage One: Inherited and Innovative

practical implications of the church's inherited and innovative nature in a particular context. Paul promotes mutual respect and unity-in-diversity in contrast to uniformity.

Inherited ('One')

> Therefore, my beloved, flee from idolatry. I speak as to the wise; judge yourselves what I say. The cup of blessing that we bless, is this not fellowship in the blood of Christ? The bread that we break, is this not fellowship in the body of Christ? Because there is one bread, we who are many are one body, for we all partake of the one bread. Consider fleshly Israel; are not those who eat the sacrifice partakers of the altar? What, therefore, am I saying? That meat offered to idols is anything or that an idol is anything? No, but that those who sacrifice do so to demons and not God. I do not want you to become partakers in demons. You cannot drink the cup of the Lord and the cup of demons, nor can you partake of the table of the Lord and the table of demons. Or do we want to provoke the Lord to jealousy? Are we mightier than him? (1 Cor. 10.14–22)

Some see Paul's polemic here as contradictory to his seemingly more lenient stance on meat sacrificed to idols in 1 Corinthians 8.1–13 and 10.23–31. However, Paul addresses two distinct but related topics. Verses 8.1–13 and 10.23–33 regard meat sacrificed to idols that is eaten in the temple precinct or purchased in the market. In 10.14–22, Paul challenges participation in idolatrous cultic events. Association with a variety of cults was not considered problematic within the Graeco-Roman religious milieu. The Corinthian believers' syncretistic polytheistic background thus explains why some see no contradiction between their allegiance to Christ and engagement in other religious cults. Converted Gentiles may have imagined that all sacred rites relate to the same God. For Paul, however, Gentile syncretism and monotheistic faith are incompatible (10.21). Paul therefore underlines the centrality of covenantal loyalty and continuity, and therefore Old Testament Scripture. The church, while displaying discontinuity with what has come before, is *inherited*; 'Whatever the novelties and discontinuities brought about by the new creation in Christ, Israel and the Christian church belong to a single history of God's activity and self-disclosure.'[209]

The church's inherited nature is evident through the passage's literary context, especially 10.1–13. The depiction of Israel as 'our fathers' in 10.1 emphasizes the Corinthian church's continuity with God's actions in the past. Moreover, in his warnings from Israel's history, Paul assumes that his recipients are familiar with this history, even though they are predominantly Gentile, indicating that Israel's Scripture has become the church's Scripture and the church has become part of Israel's story (see especially 10.11). Paul applies the exodus and subsequent wilderness wanderings to the Corinthian church, bringing to mind God's gracious saving acts and Israel's unfaithful response. By re-rooting the Corinthian church in Israel's story, Paul reminds the believers that they have not been converted to just any 'god' or abstract principle, but to Israel's God, who demands full allegiance.[210]

The references to baptism into Moses (10.2) and spiritual food and drink (10.3–4) are not synonymous with Christian baptism and the Lord's Supper, but they allude to these sacraments. Baptism, in Paul's thought, signifies identification with Christ, particularly his saving death and resurrection (cf. Rom. 6.3–11). This accords with the most likely sense of baptism into Moses as identification with Moses and allegiance to his leadership. This allusion to the sacraments in 10.1–13 sets the explicit reference to the Lord's Supper in 10.14–22 in the context of Israel's unfaithfulness and subsequent judgement; just as the Israelites' covenantal membership did not make them immune from God's judgement, so the Corinthian believers' engagement in Christian rituals does not grant them the licence to participate in idol feasts. Interpreting 10.14–22 in the context of 10.1–13 thus supports Schrage's contention that at least some Corinthian believers had a magical/quasimagical view of the sacraments.[211]

Contra the Corinthian believers' emphasis on the rite of the Lord's Supper, Paul draws on the believers' inherited history to highlight that participation in 'the cup of blessing that we bless' and 'the bread that we break' involves 'fellowship in the body of Christ' (10.16). This fellowship is vertical (regarding believers' communion with Christ) and, because this union with Christ is corporate, horizontal (regarding believers' communion with each other). Believers' fellowship with Christ should result in every aspect of their lives and lifestyles being Christocentric and Christomorphic; believers are to be 'cruciform', identifying with and witnessing to 'Christ's dying for "others" and being raised by God'.[212]

Inherited rituals are important; the practice of the Lord's Supper is assumed, if not commanded. However, seeing the church as inherited does not simply mean implementing certain traditions – indeed, for Paul, covenantal disloyalty corrupts Christian rituals (10.14–22). Rather, the church's nature as inherited predominantly means being rooted in its history and shaped by what this history reveals about God and his relationship with his people. There is discontinuity between Old Testament Israel and the Corinthian church, but such is the continuity between God's previous actions and his work in Christ that, in Paul's view, Christ is both the spiritual rock that followed the Israelites through the wilderness (10.4) and the one tested (10.9). Within this, Paul is probably drawing on a Hellenistic Jewish tradition regarding the role of divine Wisdom as a protector, nourisher and guide. Regardless of exactly how these references to Christ are construed, they indicate that for Paul the pre-existent Christ was present in Israel's history. Christ was 'as much the source of the spiritual food and drink of the Israelites as he is the one present in the Lord's Supper at Corinth'.[213]

As with the Corinthian church, the contemporary church shares this inheritance as the one body of Christ that stretches back into the past, out into the present, and forwards into the future. The New Testament church's Scripture is the contemporary church's Scripture, and the New Testament is now added to this record. The *one* church of the past, present and future is anchored in God's revelation through Scripture as the Spirit breathes this Scripture into new contexts. The contemporary church has also inherited 2,000 years of heritage, which is not to ascribe the same authority to church history as the Bible, but to note that contemporary Christian identity is informed by what has come before. Examining church history involves learning from past mistakes alongside discovering lost insights. Crucially, though, this heritage should not be ignored. As Rowan Williams maintains:

> Church history, like all good history, invites us into a process of questioning and being questioned by the past; the difference is that the Christian past is unavoidably part of the Christian present in such a way that we have to be extra careful not to dismiss, caricature or give up the attempt to listen. What we are attending to is the record of encounter with God in Christ.[214]

Innovative ('Many')

> Because of this I, Paul, a prisoner of Christ (Jesus), for the benefit of you
> Gentiles, if indeed you have heard of the stewardship of God's grace
> that was given to me for you, according to the revelation made known
> to me, the mystery, as I've already written briefly about. As you read,
> you will be able to understand my insight into the mystery of Christ
> that, in other generations, was not made known to people as it has now
> been revealed to the saints through his apostles and prophets by the
> Spirit. This is that the Gentiles are co-heirs, co-members, and co-par-
> takers of the promise in Christ Jesus through the gospel, of which I have
> become a servant according to the gift of God's grace given to me by the
> working of his power. (Eph. 3.1–7)

Ephesians 3.2–13 constitutes a digression in Paul's thought from the inter-
cessory prayer that begins in 3.1 and is resumed in 3.14. The seeming
defence of Paul's apostleship offered here leads some to see this inter-
lude as evidence of pseudonymous authorship. However, the references to
Paul's incarceration (3.1) and suffering (3.13) indicate that, rather than
his apostleship, Paul is defending and explaining his current circumstance.
As Arnold asserts, Paul's imprisonment 'in no way hinders the ministry
but actually serves to magnify the triumph of God because God accomplishes his purposes in weakness'.[215] The main focus of this digression
is thus not the church but, *contra* Gombis, the church and its relationship to God's mystery are major themes. 'Mystery' appears three times
in the twelve verses (3.3, 4 and 9) and the parallels between 3.14–21 and
1.15–23, and 3.2–13 and 1.3–14, bring to mind God's plan for creation,
which was formerly a mystery but now has been made known. Therefore,
although Paul's defence of his imprisonment is the primary purpose of
the digression, expounding 'the mystery' of God's cosmic plan (1.9–10;
4.10) and the church's role within this (1.22–23; 3.6, 10; 5.32) are at the
forefront of Paul's mind. His imprisonment is addressed because it may
appear to detract from or contradict this plan.

Mystērion (mystery) was a familiar term within Judaism, referring
to something known but, because of human finitude, not fully understood, and/or something revealed by God. In the wider Graeco-Roman
world, *mystērion* referred to the mysteries or secrets that people were
told when initiated into mystery religions. The specification 'according
to the revelation made known to me' (3.3) clarifies that Paul is referring
to the Semitic sense of something revealed by God. That said, *mystērion*
perhaps appears a surprising word to use given the prevalence of mystery
language and rituals within local religions and cults. In fact, however,
this prevalence probably prompted Paul's selection of the term; in con-

trast to the carefully guarded mysteries known only to the selected few, God's mystery is proclaimed loudly and proudly such that 'the rulers and authorities in the heavenly realms' can see God's wisdom in it (3.10).[216]

'The mystery' is God's redemption plan (1.9–10; 4.8), which includes the incorporation of the Gentiles into God's covenant people (3.5–6). The extent to which this new entity (consisting of Jews and Gentiles together) is continuous or discontinuous with the covenant community before Christ is debated. Hoehner highlights the discontinuity, describing the 'one new human' (2.15), or 'one body' (2.16) that is formed as Jewish and Gentile believers become 'co-members' (3.6), as a 'race that is raceless!'[217] Hoehner's depiction requires greater nuance, however, for two reasons. First, racial differences are not obliterated in Christ, but relativized and transformed. When Ephesians was written, for example, it was possible to identify Jewish Christians, on the one hand, and Gentile Christians, on the other. Paul does not see the church as a raceless group. Rather, the two groups' distinctive identities, however much qualified, are not eradicated. Second, although the church is discontinuous with ethnic Israel, through its unprecedented access to God in Christ, the church has continuity with ethnic Israel that it does not have with the Gentile world.[218]

However, although the continuity between the former and current covenant communities must not be underplayed, neither must the discontinuity. 'The mystery' (3.3–4) of the incorporation of the Gentile believers into the covenant community is something that has *now* been revealed (3.5). The one body of which Jewish and Gentile believers are both members (3.6) has continuity with ethnic Israel but is also a new and distinct entity; it is innovative. This is not to imply that the Gentile church was simply a product of Paul's innovation, although Runesson argues that the innovative nature of Paul's engagement with his socio-cultural context is often overlooked. Rather, Paul sees this newly disclosed mystery as the result of God's initiative, not his own.[219]

The diversity of Christian communities addressed in the New Testament indicates that the church's innovative nature gave rise to different expressions. Not all of this diversity was positive; Paul rebukes the Corinthian believers for their distorted celebration of the Lord's Supper (1 Cor. 10.14–22) and the disordered nature of their gatherings (1 Cor. 14). However, Paul does not seek to abolish diversity to create uniformity (1 Cor. 12). Jewish and Gentile believers could be distinguished between; cultural differences were relativized, not eradicated, by the believers' new identity as one body in Christ (Eph. 2.15–16; 3.6).

Inherited and Innovative ('One and Many')

> For through the grace given to me, I say to all of you, do not think too highly of yourselves, beside what it is necessary to think, but think soberly, each according to the measure of faith that God has apportioned. For just as we have one body with many parts, but the parts don't all have the same function, so too we, who are many, are one body in Christ, and individually members of each other. But we have different gifts according to the grace given to us: if prophecy, according to the measure of faith; if ministry, in ministering; the teacher, in teaching; the encourager, in encouraging; the sharer in generosity; the leader in diligence; the merciful in cheerfulness. (Rom. 12.3–8)

The origin of the Roman church is uncertain, but it was likely founded by Jewish Christians in the late 30s or early 40s. It is probable that Christianity in Rome arose in the synagogue and that the church only established itself as a distinct social group when Gentiles were converted. Despite its Jewish origin, Claudius' eviction of most Jews in around AD 49 meant that for several years the Roman church predominantly consisted of Gentile believers. The absence of Jews during this time likely accelerated the Christian community's move away from Jewish cultural mores. Following Claudius' death in AD 54, the eviction edict lapsed and many Jews returned to Rome. This return probably resulted in tensions between Jewish and Gentile believers, with the latter having moved in a different direction since the Jews' eviction. Paul thus addresses his letter to a predominantly Gentile audience, challenging their indifference, even arrogance, towards the Jewish minority, while also showing the Jewish believers that they should not insist on the law.[220]

Paul probably wrote Romans from Corinth between AD 55 and 58. It is addressed to 'all those in Rome who are loved of God and chosen to be holy' (Rom. 1.7), who may have fallen into five distinct groups: the church that meets in Prisca and Aquila's 'house' (16.5); those who belong to Aristobulus (16.10); those who belong to Narcissus (16.11); Asyncritus, Phlegon, Hermes, Patrobas and Hermas, and the brothers and sisters who are with them (16.14); and Philologus, Julia, Nereus and his sister, and Olympas, and all the saints who are with them (16.15). Dunn notes that it is attractive to see these five groups listed (16.5, 10–11, 14–15) as house churches. However, Adams notes that only one is identified as a 'church at home' (16.5) and argues that here *oikos* ('house') probably refers to a workshop that doubles up as a home. The others, he asserts, may have met in homes or commercial or industrial properties.[221]

In contrast to the church in Corinth (1 Cor. 14.23), there is no indication that the Roman Christians ever met together in one location. Moreover, rather than being connected through formal institutional links, the groups were likely linked through informal personal connections, reflecting the decentralized synagogue structure from which early Christianity in Rome grew. These groups presumably acknowledged and respected wider church leadership, as this would explain the authoritative stance that Paul assumes towards a church that he did not personally establish. Individual groups may have been more Gentile or Jewish in nature, with conflict between the different church expressions. Alternatively it might be that there was conflict within the individual groups themselves. Regardless, Paul's letter indicates the existence of conflict as Paul seeks to bring reconciliation. He does so by reminding his readers that the church is in continuity with what has come before (it is inherited) and highlighting the discontinuity (the innovative changes) that has arisen with the Christ-event.[222]

The church is inherited insofar as the Roman Christians must not overlook their roots in Old Testament Judaism. The gospel Paul preaches fulfils Old Testament Scripture, particularly in relation to the law, circumcision, and Israel's role in salvation history. He even presents the unity between Jewish and Gentile believers as a fulfilment of Old Testament Scripture (15.7–13). The church is innovative, in that the incorporation of the Gentiles into the covenant community has moved the church away from certain aspects of its synagogue origins. For example, although there were probably not 'Judaizers' present when he wrote, such opponents were in the East and Paul feared that they would go to Rome (Rom. 3.8; 16.17–20). Paul seeks to ensure that the radical discontinuity accompanying the Christ-event is not undermined; 'to insist on maintaining literally all the distinctives mandated specifically for ancient Israel was to ignore the climax of salvation history, what God had accomplished in Christ'.[223]

Given the conflict between Jew and Gentile, Paul may well have introduced his body of Christ metaphor in 12.3–8 to address this area of disunity. Indeed, 12.3 alludes directly to the dispute. As Dunn notes:

> The emphatic warning against inflated thinking (v 3) recalls the similar warning against Gentile presumption in 11.7–24 (particularly 11.20), but also the similar theme of the earlier diatribes against Jewish presumption (chaps. 2–4): the 'us' over 'them' attitude which Paul saw as the heart of Jewish failure and as a potential danger for Gentile Christians must not be allowed to characterize the eschatological people of God.[224]

Moo counters that Paul's explicit concern is disunity over the matter of spiritual gifts, particularly the disunity caused by pride and comparison. However, the large amount space occupied by Paul's exhortations to Jewish and Gentile believers in the first part of the letter, and then the 'weak' and the 'strong' later on (14.1–15.13), suggests that this was a far bigger area of conflict than spiritual gifts. Therefore, even if the body of Christ metaphor is not directly directed at the disunity between Jew and Gentile, it forms a key part of Paul's overall arguments for unity. These arguments are targeted predominantly at the tension between Jewish and Gentile believers. To encourage unity, Paul grounds the Christian faith on inherited Judaism, while noting the innovative changes that have occurred as a result of the Christ-event. Within this, there is scope for disagreement regarding the practical outworkings. Paul encourages fellowship and mutual respect between the 'strong' and the 'weak'. Those who eat must not disdain those who do not eat and those who do not eat must not judge those who do eat, for God has accepted them (14.3). The diversity and unity that Paul promotes in Romans therefore includes diversity regarding the degree to which different believers' faith is more or less inherited or innovative.[225]

In the letter as a whole, Paul encourages two groups (Jewish and Gentile believers) to see themselves, in their differences, as a gift to each other – part of the same body of Christ (12.5). This is significant given Spence's view that the clash between Jewish and Gentile believers did not occur among those who had the same opinion about what church should be and how it should behave, but among those whose views differed on precisely these points. Jewish believers saw the church as a Jewish sect and desired to preserve key aspects of their Jewish identity. Gentile believers viewed the church more in terms of an Eastern cult and wished to articulate the gospel within their cultural framework. Despite these differences, Paul does not try to organize the Roman church around a particular leader, church style, or organizational structure; indeed, although spiritual gifts and 'office' must not be dichotomized, the emphasis is on spiritual gifts. Paul does not introduce a definitive list of spiritual gifts, even if he and the early church 'recognized a small number of well-defined and widely occurring gifts along with an indefinite number of other less-defined gifts'.[226] Moreover, Paul does not aim to eradicate all differences between Jewish and Gentile believers. Rather than uniformity, Paul promotes unity in diversity. He also encourages believers not to think too highly of themselves, but recognize their need for others.[227]

In conclusion, within Romans Paul seeks to establish the church on its Jewish foundation (as inherited), while preserving the discontinuity (innovative changes) brought about by the Christ-event. Within the practical outworkings of this, Paul allows scope for different believers to manifest inherited and innovative aspects to greater or lesser degrees, while urging such believers to respect, not judge, believers who see things differently. In Romans 12.3–8, Paul urges his readers towards unity in diversity, not uniformity. While the explicit tenor of the body of Christ metaphor regards spiritual gifts, the wider context indicates that differences between those who take a more or less inherited and innovative approach to their faith are also in view.

So too, in today's context, believers will manifest the church's inherited and innovative nature in different ways. What, for one, is an essential aspect of the church's inherited nature may, to another, be archaic. Sincere believers, when seeking to put into practice the church's inherited and innovative identity, may derive different conclusions as to what this looks like in practice. The *one* inherited church will express itself in *many* innovative ways and, within these various expressions, different understandings of the relationship between tradition and innovation will be evident.

Implications: Christocentric Trinitarian Innovation

What are the implications for the re-contextual movement of the church's inherited and innovative nature? Does the relationship between the early church and ethnic Israel have any application to the relationship between the contemporary and historic church? There is a radical discontinuity between ethnic Israel and the church that is not repeated between churches of different eras. The church in every era exists in the same sphere, as it were: as a body that is distinct from, and yet in continuity with, the community of God's people that preceded it. Does the relationship between distinct entities in this one sphere (different churches in different eras) bear any resemblance to the relationship between the church and ethnic Israel? An exact comparison cannot be made but some points of resonance can be identified.

First, Paul was willing to understand and communicate the changes that accompanied the Christ-event through culturally applicable concepts. For instance, Paul's adoption and adaptation of the body metaphor, a prevalent image in Graeco-Roman culture, is innovative. Runesson notes that such innovation was required for Jesus' proclamation to be exported beyond the land of Israel. Moreover, further adaptation occurred through Christianity's growth as a *voluntary association*, which, Runesson argues, was the institutional structure that the Christian *ekklēsia* (church) developed in. Such voluntary associations formed a societal sphere, distinct from the public and domestic realms, within which those of different status, ethnicity and gender (for example, slaves and slave owners) could interact in ways not possible in the other realms. The voluntary association was hospitable to the growth of the Christian church as a group open to all, not just Jews. Runesson overstates his case when he maintains that Paul's inclusive notion of 'Gentile mission' was prompted by the growth of Christianity into this institutional structure. The diaspora synagogue lacked the diversity of the early church, despite being similarly contextual-ized, and so Paul clearly had a theological impetus that diaspora Judaism lacked. However, although Runesson overemphasizes the sociological impetus for the early church's inclusive character, the contextualization of the church into a pre-existing institutional structure is noteworthy. It provides impetus for the church's continuing adaptation to its context today – continued innovation.[228]

Second, just as the early church was to see its life as rooted in God's pre-vious work and revelation, so must the church in every era. Every church in every context needs to recognize its nature as inherited. Continuity should be evident across the church in different eras, geographical loca-tions, cultural contexts, denominational distinctives, and so on. Therefore, although the relationship between *churches in different contexts* is not the same as the relationship between *the church and ethnic Israel,* just as Paul saw the early church as concurrently inherited and innovative, the same is to be true of churches in every era. Led by the Spirit, believers should explore how to live as the inherited church in their unique context, which requires innovation. As Labanow notes, engagement with the doctrine of the church is vital as churches work out what this looks like in their particular locality; 'for churches in the process of sifting and discerning their tradition in deciding what to retain, what to alter, and what to leave behind, an informed ecclesiology will prevent them from making these choices based solely on aesthetic preference or personal tastes'.[229] In addi-tion, as I explore in more detail below, in order to develop authentically *Christian* communities, churches must immerse themselves in God's story, pursue a eucharistic life, and connect to each other.

Immersion in God's Story

> Any human community that has a distinctive structure will, of course, be concerned about how to induct new members into its habits; but the Christian Church has the added concern of making sure those habits are a way of bringing believers truthfully and effectively into the pres-ence of a specific past, the incarnate reality of Jesus. What the Church conserves is seen as important because of this concept of becoming contemporary with Jesus.[230]

MacIntyre maintains that people cannot answer the question, 'What am I to do?' unless they have first answered the question, 'Of what story or stories do I find myself a part?'[231] Human beings' orientation towards the world is determined by stories. The church's nature as inherited and human beings' embodiedness should prompt re-contextual thinkers to reflect on how believers can best immerse themselves in God's story, as revealed through Scripture, particularly the Christ-event. Critical engagement and intellectual reflection is essential as believers examine how to innovate faithfully in their context. However, people's behaviour does not result from rational thinking alone (what one consciously and cognitively decides to do in any one moment). Rather, human beings navigate much of life without consciously thinking about it. The subconscious decisions that govern people's actions derive from their character, their essential desires and loves, which are in turn determined by the embodied stories that they have imbibed. These stories are reinforced through a 'pedagogy of insignificance' – 'all the mundane little micropractices that nonetheless "carry" a big Story'. The rituals and habits that people adopt are both born out of and contribute to the stories that they live by in an interconnected cycle that forms the person they become.[232]

The degree to which believers adopt Scripture's story as *their* story will affect how faithfully they conduct themselves as church, in both the subconscious and conscious decisions that they make. This involves encouraging believers to read Scripture regularly, but must extend beyond this individual practice. If the embodied nature of human personhood is to be adequately accounted for, regular habits, such as communal engagement with Scripture (teaching, preaching, discussion, etc.), individual and corporate praise and prayer, embodied rituals (such as the Eucharist), and the practical outworking of Scripture (such as caring for others), need to be incorporated. The church will be faithfully innovative and inherited to the extent that believers both live in their context and live in Scripture, as it were, allowing Scripture's revelation to shape their desires, perspective and worldview.

Immersion in God's story also requires an awareness of church history. As Chan contends, just as a person's identity is shaped by their past and their memory of this past, so too the body of Christ can only be understood in light of its shared history and its recollection of this history. While not overlooking the differences between churches of different eras, the contemporary church can learn from the past by both seeking to see God's hand at work and noting the mistakes to avoid. In addition, awareness of the broader span of church history can help prevent a postmodern pick 'n' mix approach to retrieving ancient wisdom and practices while recognizing that such traditions can be a great gift.[233] As Williams notes:

> If we begin from our axiom of common membership in the Body, there will always be gifts to be received from the past; we can expect that we shall find something that we had not grasped until a contemporary crisis had brought it into focus. Hence the extraordinary regularity with which radical renewal in the Church has come from a new appropriation of tradition of one sort or another ... [T]he movements of

greatest theological vitality are all movements of 'recovery', resource-ment, rather than simple innovation or simple repetition.[234]

Living the Eucharistic Life

Some traditions are so central to the Christian faith that to lose, neglect, or distort them is catastrophic to the integrity of faith itself. To neglect or distort the tradition of the Lord's Supper is to lose contact with the central message of the gospel that through Christ's death we have been united to each other and to God.[235]

As I argued in relation to the 'up' component (spiritual and religious), a believer's embodied nature means that there is a connection between the practices and habits that they adopt and the person that they become, but the connection is not absolute (there is not a precise cause-and-effect correlation). The transformative power of Christian practices, as they position believers for encounter with God, is received as a gift, not something that is deserved or earned. Moreover, the goal of Christian habits, practices and disciplines is deeper relationship with God. Therefore, although celebration of the Lord's Supper is an assumed aspect of the Christian community (for example, 1 Cor. 10.14–22), the sacrament is not an end in itself but points to Christ's redemptive death and the future hope of his return. The Lord's Supper also points to the solidarity that believers have with Christ, as partakers in his body, and each other, as one body together in Christ.

As re-contextual thinkers grapple with the Lord's Supper in relation to new expressions of church, these debates should go deeper than whether regular celebration of the Eucharist is an essential mark of church and, if so, how regularly it should be celebrated and who can preside (although these are, for some denominations more than others, important questions). Re-contextual thinkers should also explore what it means for the church, as Christ's body, to be a eucharistic community: a community whose life is characterized by its communion with Christ, and thus other believers, and the wider world. As Bloom maintains, a eucharistic community does not just consist of liturgical gatherings but involves being Christ's body in the world, bringing the joy, hope and love that are found in Christ to places of darkness and evil.[236]

Connected Church

Moynagh maintains that the early church consisted of demographically homogenous house churches that then met together as a whole church for town-wide gatherings. So too today, he argues, churches should be focused for mission but connected to other church groups so that homogeneity and heterogeneity are held together. Moynagh overstates the homogeneity of the early church since, although different ethnic and income groups may have lived in different areas, early churches would have contained whole households, ranging from patriarch, at one end of the social spectrum, to slave, at the other.[237] Nevertheless, Moynagh's contentions prompt the question, to what extent should (or even can) individual local congregations display the diversity of the church as a whole? Within this debate, the primary contribution Moynagh brings is to highlight that unity-in-diversity can (and indeed should) be manifest *between*, and not just *in*, local church communities. Through this diversity, local churches can be a gift to each other. Witherington argues:

> Just as gifted individuals cannot say to other Christians that they are unneeded, since no Christian has all God's gifts, so, too, this is apparently true with congregations as well. It is not accidental that different faith traditions have specialized in manifesting different gifts.[238]

Similarly, Cullmann contends that different Christian confessions have certain gifts that are a blessing to the wider body. These specific giftings should not be abandoned or overlooked in the name of homogenization but rather preserved and nurtured.[239] Therefore, while focused churches risk excluding all but an increasingly narrow segment of society, there is the equal but opposite danger that, in the name of heterogeneity, churches become one-size-fits-all, with heterogeneity within churches creating homogeneity across churches.

Towards (Anchorage Two): Now and Not Yet – Pursuing the Gift of the Future

Eschatology is a central feature of the body of Christ image. Within the body of Christ texts, God's actions in history root the church in the past, though God's being is not contingent upon history. So too, the church is anchored to a future that God determines, though God is not dependent on this future. These qualifications, regarding the anchoring of the church in the past and the future, but not God, are important since, as I have noted previously, Social Trinitarians have been criticized for presenting God as dependent on history (creation's past and future). Such a view undermines his otherness and freedom. The ecclesiology I am proposing avoids this error by emphasizing God's transcendent otherness while highlighting the church's anchorage in Christ's first and second coming.

The eschatological emphasis of the body of Christ texts, alongside the re-contextual conversation's focus on the church's eschatological nature, has prompted me to add a fifth prepositional trajectory (towards) to the four relational components (up, in, out and of) that Moynagh and others see as the essence of the church. The relationship between the church and the kingdom is central within this 'towards' trajectory. As I outline below, re-contextual thinkers raise several questions about this relationship. Their answers to these questions are best seen when set against their perception of the inherited church's views, as it is these views that they are reacting against.[240] The questions are:

To what extent is the kingdom built by God and/or human beings? To what extent is the kingdom present in the church and the world? In contrast to what Murray Williams perceives as Christendom's attempt to build the kingdom by human force, re-contextual thinkers emphasize God's role through their focus on listening to what God is doing and joining him. Ward's language of mediation, for example, refers to the Spirit-brought flow of God's kingdom within the church, from the church into the world, and within popular culture. Re-contextual thinkers emphasize that God builds his kingdom, but that this does not negate believers' responsibility. The Spirit is at work outside the church, but the church's identity as Christ's body indicates its unique connection to Jesus. As Christ's body, the church is to anticipate and manifest the future consummated kingdom (although it does so imperfectly), while being alert to Spirit-brought traces of the kingdom in the wider world.[241]

To what degree is the kingdom individualized, internalized and spiritualized, and/or externalized and materialized? Moynagh presents the kingdom as externalized by drawing on Isaiah's vision of peace, light, harmony, health, justice and abundance and exploring how this vision was manifested in Jesus' ministry. Others share his focus. Corcoran, for example, argues that '[w]herever you find people healing one another's wounds, praying and working for justice and peace, railing against injustice and oppression, wherever you discover broken lives made whole and redeemed, there you are witness to the present reality of God's kingdom'.[242] In this focus on external manifestations of the kingdom, re-contextual thinkers are combatting what they perceive as the inherited church's over-spiritualization and internalization of the kingdom.

What is the relationship between the church and the kingdom? To what extent does the kingdom inaugurated by Christ accord with, or diverge from, the theocracy in the Old Testament? Murray Williams notes that church and kingdom were unhealthily amalgamated within Christendom. Other than McKnight's contention that, when viewed eschatologically, the two concepts are the same (which I examine in more detail below), re-contextual thinkers agree that church and kingdom are overlapping, but distinct, categories. Moynagh best sums up the re-contextual church's view on this question through his language of kingdom-shaped church – in contrast to church-shaped kingdom or world-shaped kingdom. In a kingdom-shaped church perspective, the church's life and impetus is determined by its calling to be a sign and foretaste of the kingdom, but it is recognized that the Spirit brings aspects of God's kingdom outside the church too. Murray Williams complains that the amalgamation of the kingdom and the church within Christendom, and the theocratic attempts to build this kingdom, were accompanied by a bias towards Old Testament conceptions of the kingdom. He urges the church to reroot itself in the New Testament's presentation of the kingdom.[243]

Should the church's emphasis be on proclaiming or manifesting the kingdom? As I outlined in Chapter 3, some re-contextual authors are wary of the term 'evangelism', and put the emphasis on the church's call to demonstrate the good news of Christ. Other re-contextual thinkers, particularly within the Fresh Expressions subset of the discussion, highlight the centrality of proclaiming the gospel within the church's mission. Overall, though, the re-contextual church wants to pull the Western church towards a more holistic notion of mission, wherein actions and words go hand-in-hand, in contrast to what they perceive as more reductionist notions of the kingdom that focus on evangelism and conversion at the expense of a commitment to social justice and societal transformation.

To what extent is the kingdom a present and/or future reality? Re-contextual thinkers acknowledge the now/not yet of the kingdom but focus on the 'now'; they seek to see the kingdom realized in the present. This contrasts with their perception that the inherited church has over-focused on the 'not yet'. Claiming that the inherited church has over-focused on the 'not yet' might seem to contradict their complaint that the church and kingdom were equated under Christendom. Murray Williams contends that both criticisms are valid because, in Christendom, perceptions of the kingdom were either reduced to the state church or restricted to the future.[244]

The Kingdom in the Body of Christ Texts?

Basileia, 'kingdom', does not appear in any body of Christ passage. Indeed 'the kingdom' is rarely mentioned within the Pauline corpus and, in the undisputed Paulines, mainly indicates a future, not present, reality (for example, 1 Cor. 6.9; 15.24–25; Eph. 5.5), although there are some present references (1 Cor. 4.20; Rom. 14.17). This does not mean, however, that the kingdom, and its corresponding now/not yet eschatological tension, is not central to Paul's thought. Rather, as Kreitzer contends, 'while the explicit expression "kingdom of God/Christ" is not widespread within the Pauline letters, the idea is a fundamental component of Paul's eschatological perspective and underlies the whole of his teaching'.[245] For example, as I have argued elsewhere, reading 1 Corinthians 12.12–31 in light of 1 Corinthians 15.20–28 indicates that, for Paul, the church as Christ's body is an anticipation of the consummated kingdom.[246] Through its union with Christ, the church anticipates the reality that is to come when all things are under Christ's lordship. In Ephesians, this anticipatory role is also evident (Eph. 1.22–23). In Colossians, the believers' 'inheritance' (Col. 1.12) is inseparable from their transference into 'the kingdom of his beloved son' (1.13), which in turn is connected to their identity as 'Christ's body' with Christ as 'the head' (1.18).[247]

The eschatology of Ephesians and Colossians is often contrasted with the undisputed Paulines. Thompson, for example, maintains that in Ephesians and Colossians the church inhabits the kingdom but in the undisputed Paulines the kingdom is a future event. However, such variations are explained by the differing circumstances into which Paul wrote. Paul consistently presents a now/not yet eschatological tension, leading to paradoxes such as 'become what you are' and, 'thy kingdom come, for thine is the kingdom' (cf. Col. 3.1–5; Eph. 4.1–6; 1 Cor. 5.7–8). Different aspects of this tension are evident in different places depending on the context: '"what you are" may at one moment be the dominant thought, and "become!" at another moment'.[248] To demonstrate the presence of the 'now' and 'not yet' in Paul's writings, I will explore this tension, and Paul's view of the kingdom, in relation to two body of Christ passages that go against the grain of the eschatological emphasis of the letters they are located in: 1 Corinthians 11.23–26 and Ephesians 5.21–33.[249]

Regarding 1 Corinthians, Thiselton argues that the disparate issues that Paul addresses indicate both an over-realized eschatology and an overly ecstatic theology of the Spirit. Schreiner suggests that the Corinthian Christians believed that the kingdom had already been consummated. As Barclay contends, however, it may be that the Corinthian believers were simply non-eschatological – too focused on the here and now. Either way, Paul seeks to correct a lack of futurity in relation to the Corinthian church's behaviour and worldview (esp. 1 Cor. 4.8; 15.12). Despite his future emphasis, however, Paul does not deny the 'now' aspect of the now/not yet tension that lies at the heart of his eschatological understanding. Although he rectifies an either over-realized or non-eschatology in 1 Corinthians, he affirms that the Corinthian believers are already participants in 'the new covenant' (11.25).[250]

For I received from the Lord what I also handed on to you, that the Lord Jesus, on the night that he was handed over, took bread and, having given thanks, he broke it and said, 'This is my body, which is for you. Do this in remembrance of me.' And likewise, after eating, he took the cup and said, 'This is the cup, which is the new covenant in my blood. Do this as often as you drink it, in remembrance of me.' For as often as you eat this bread and drink this cup, you proclaim the Lord's death until he comes. (1 Cor. 11.23–26)

In contrast to 1 Corinthians, Ephesians demonstrates a markedly realized eschatology. Despite this realized eschatology, however, the future aspect of the now/not yet tension is also in view: 'Christ, who loved the church and made her his bride, has not yet finished freeing her from every spot and wrinkle' (5.27).[251]

… submitting to one another in reverence for Christ, wives to their own husbands as to the Lord. For the husband is head of the wife as Christ is the head of the church, who is the saviour of the body. But as the church submits to Christ, so wives to their husbands in all things. Husbands, love your wives, just as Christ loved the church and gave himself for her in order that she may be sanctified, cleansed by the washing of water in the word so that he may present to himself his glorious church, without any stain or wrinkle, for her to be holy and blameless. Likewise a man ought to love his own wife as he loves his own body. In loving his own wife he loves himself, for no-one ever hated his own flesh but nourishes and cares for it, just as Christ does for the church, since you are members of his body. For this reason a man shall leave his father and mother and be joined to his wife, and the two shall become one flesh. This is a profound mystery, now I am speaking about Christ and his church. (Eph. 5.21–32)

As I argue below, these two passages (1 Cor. 11.23–26 and Eph. 5.21–33) reveal that the kingdom is present in and through the church while also something that will come more fully in the future. The relationship between the now and not yet components of the kingdom indicates that the church, as Christ's body, is an imperfect foretaste and anticipation of the future consummated kingdom that will accompany Christ's return. Just as the church is to be anchored in the past (of), so too it must be fastened to the future: its life in the present is to be determined by its relationship to this future (towards) (see Figure 7).

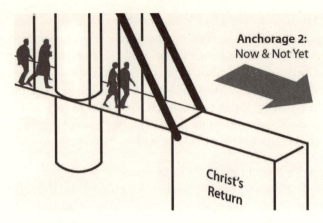

Figure 7: Anchorage Two: Now and Not Yet

Now ('Many')

Reading Paul's instructions (11.23–26) in their wider context (11.17–34) reveals that Paul is correcting a Corinthian practice that undermined the Lord's Supper and its message. Those of greater means were eating before the poorer members arrived, meaning that those from the lower classes could only eat what was left. This caused a schism between the wealthy and the poor, which ironically was a division that the Lord's Supper was meant to overcome. In bringing correction, Paul focuses his readers' attention on the centrality of the tradition established by Jesus. Within this, he highlights the historical inbreaking of the new era through Christ (11.25) and the corresponding reformulation of the believers' identity and behaviour.[252]

The kingdom is implicated by Paul's reference to 'the new covenant', with the definite article indicating that this concept is already known. The notion of the new covenant is widespread in the Old Testament, but only explicitly appears in Jeremiah 31.31–34 – the *locus classicus*. Within Jeremiah's understanding of the new covenant, to which Paul alludes, there is both continuity and discontinuity in relation to the old covenant. Kaiser argues that the points of continuity include the same God, law, divine fellowship and forgiveness – although describing the law that is written on people's hearts (Jer. 31.33) and the Mosaic Law as the 'same' requires further qualification. Aspects of discontinuity include universal peace, depth of knowledge of God, a new epoch of the Spirit, and the relocation of God's dwelling place to the new covenant community, which is the new temple (Eph. 2.19–22). These features are also aspects of the kingdom, which, alongside the new covenant, is a term used to depict the fulfilment of God's plans for creation in Christ and through the Spirit. Indeed, 'kingdom' and 'new covenant' refer to the same reality but from different angles. As regards God's reconciliation of his people to himself, and the corresponding renewal of creation that ensues, 'covenant' highlights God's relational faithfulness and 'kingdom' his sovereign rule.[253]

The new covenant, and thus the kingdom, has been inaugurated by Christ's death and therefore exists 'now', although a 'not yet' component is also evident (11.26). The believers' participation in this new covenant has marked implications for their community dynamics. In particular, although *sōma* (body) refers to Christ's physical body in 11.24, the use of *sōma* elsewhere to refer to the church (esp. 1 Cor. 12.27) brings to mind the communal implications of Christ's death. Paul plays on this double referent through his double entendre in 11.29 ('the one who eats and drinks without discerning the body (*sōma*) eats and drinks judgement on themself'). This verse is likely a call for the believers to reflect on both Christ's sacrifice and, in view of Christ's example, their relationships with one another as Christ's body. In contrast to the Corinthians' division, selfishness and indulgence, which meant that the supposedly sacred meal looked more like a pagan banquet, Paul promotes the 'radical, trans-formative, communal, noncompetitive theology of the cross and the one New Creation'.[254]

Paul's radical view of Christian relationships in light of Christ's inaugur-ated kingdom is also apparent in Ephesians 5.21–32. Household order and management was a prevalent theme in antiquity from Aristotle and Plato onwards. The proper running and ordering of the household was viewed as essential for the wellbeing and prosperity of the state. Therefore, were Paul to denounce the accepted household order, he would be con-demning what was construed as the foundation of a prosperous society, which may have induced suspicion against Christianity. New Testament teaching on household management reinforces the prevalent social order to defend Christianity against accusations that it prompted civil disorder (see Titus 2.5 and 1 Peter 3.1), but simultaneously subverts this order in key regards. In Ephesians 5.21–6.9, Paul challenges conventional social norms.[255] Paul's teaching

> presents a comprehensive vision of the *eschatological New Humanity* – the new creation *politeia* – realized under the conditions of this present fallen age. It is a manifesto for a radically new society. Because the household was a microcosm of the entire believing community, it provides a concrete model for how Paul's readers can carry out the command in Eph. 5:18–21 to be 'the household of God'.[256]

Paul's adaptation of this prevalent social framework in light of the church's eschatological existence in Christ reveals much about his view of the kingdom and its presence now. For example, although the Christchurch/husband-wife analogy is often viewed as supporting patriarchy, most striking is not Paul's reference to a husband's headship, which was a given, but Paul's radical redefinition of this headship.

The context is key in determining the meaning of 'headship' in Ephesians 5. It has been debated whether, in Koine Greek, *kephalē* ('head') means 'leader' or 'source', but neither enjoys conclusive extra-biblical support. The lack of references to *kephalē* as a metaphor prior to Paul's writings indicates that the head metaphor was a 'live' metaphor when Paul used it. It did not function, as it does today, as a dead metaphor (simply a synonym for leader). Nevertheless, justification for seeing notions of 'leader' in Paul's head metaphor is provided through the Hebrew word *rosh* ('head'), which means 'leader' in the Old Testament more often than *kephalē* does in the LXX or extra-biblical material. However, both *rosh* and *kephalē* primarily designate the literal anatomical head. Given the holistic nature of Semitic anthropology, the origin of the head-body metaphor in this literal designation invokes the notion of organic union. It is this union that I believe lies at the heart of the metaphor's intent.[257]

In particular contexts, however, notions of authority and source are evident. The context of Ephesians 1.22, which regards Christ's supremacy over the powers, demonstrates that *kephalē* connotes authority here. Notions of reconciliation with Christ, and thus union with him, are still present, however, particularly given the resonance between 1.22 and 1.10 – where God's ultimate plan is to bring together (*anakephalaioō*) everything in Christ. In Ephesians 4.15, the sense of source is invoked alongside authority and organic union: '[a]ll the life or health which is diffused through the members flows from the Head'.[258]

However, although *kephalē* likely conveys authority, as well as organic union, in Ephesians 5.21–32 too, this passage indicates four ways in which Paul's presentation of a husband's headship subverts Graeco-Roman cultural norms. First, whereas exhortations were usually only given to the subordinate members of the household, Paul focuses his instructions on the superordinate members. Second, wives' call to submit was usually matched by a charge for husbands to rule, but here husbands are instructed to love. Third, the passage is prefaced with a call for mutual submission (5.21). Fourth, Paul qualifies the head metaphor in reference to the self-giving and self-sacrificial aspect of Christ's authority and rule. This highlights the mutuality and reciprocity that Paul envisages within the husband–wife relationship wherein the *giving* involved in the wife's submission is reciprocated by the *giving* involved in the husband's self-sacrificial love.[259] As Mollenkott argues, this model of Christ's headship in relation to his radical self-giving love was offered to men and not to women because,

They [women] had no patriarchal privileges and power to surrender in the first place. Only the privileged male could 'love ... even as Christ loved the church and gave himself up for it'. Only the male could Christianize the marital structure by stepping down to equality with his wife, as Christ stepped down to equality with human beings. Only the male in patriarchal society had sufficient status to honour his wife by raising her status to the point where he loved her as much as he loved himself. This is an exceedingly exacting standard.[260]

Paul elsewhere challenges the status quo by urging those of greater responsibility, privilege and/or power to ensure the flourishing and empowerment of those who are, in any sense of the word, weaker or less advantaged (1 Cor. 8.1–13; 10.23–32; 12.21–26). Similarly, Ephesians 5.21–32 is radically countercultural; it is not mere cultural concession to the prevalent patriarchy of the day (as many commentators assume). Paul presents an idealized vision of the eschatological community, which explains his failure to mention mixed marriages (cf. 1 Cor. 7.12–16). Moreover, although marriage is the explicit target of Paul's instructions, the household is a microcosm of the believing community and therefore, what is enjoined on believing spouses has significance for every believer. This is evident from the instructions to the whole community in 5.1–21. The eschatological community is to reflect in the present the future reconciliation that is to come (Eph. 1.10; cf. 5.27). Believers, as Christ's body, anticipate this future when they demonstrate love and self-giving in their interpersonal relationship, modelling their community on Christ's love for the church.[261]

Paul's engagement with pre-existing social structures indicates that the eschatological community can demonstrate its distinctiveness in many different forms, even within structures that do not represent God's ideal. For example, Paul maintains that by submitting to their masters, those compelled to be slaves can demonstrate their allegiance to Christ and thus their membership in the alternative reality of the eschatological community. This does not mean, though, that Paul's instructions validate slavery. Rather, Paul sows seeds for the later abolition movement. So too, Paul's modification of the household code in relation to husbands and wives has similar subversive force. Therefore, in different ways and within differing social structures, the church as Christ's body, under and united with his headship, is called to live as a countercultural community, manifesting God's eschatological new creation within the wider world. In this community, love and self-giving are defining characteristics.[262]

Not Yet ('One')

1 Corinthians 11.23–26 and Ephesians 5.21–32 indicate that the kingdom is present 'now', but both passages also convey the 'not yet' of a kingdom still to come. In 1 Corinthians 11.23–26 this future purview is clearest in Paul's recitation of Jesus' words: 'for whenever you eat this bread and drink the cup you proclaim the Lord's death until he comes' (11.26), bringing to mind the consummation of the kingdom that will accompany Christ's return (15.23–24). The believers' eschatological existence is yet to reach its fulfilment.[263]

The 'not yet' of the kingdom is apparent in Ephesians 5.21–32 through the bride metaphor (5.26–27). Paul draws on Old Testament bridal imagery (esp. Ezek. 16.8–14; 36.25–27) to outline the purpose of Christ's self-giving: to cleanse his church, setting her apart for himself, 'just as a young and dazzlingly beautiful bride, in all her finery, is presented to the groom'.[264] This imagery of Christ presenting (*paristēmi*) the church as his bride (5.27) resonates with the use of *paristēmi* in Colossians 1.22 and 28, where Paul speaks of believers being 'presented' as holy, blameless and mature. Moreover, the Old Testament allusions contain new covenant connotations; in Hosea 2.14–23 (LXX), for example, the future hope of the time when God restores his people to himself includes the promise, '*On that day*, declares the Lord, you will call me "my husband"' (Hosea 2.16a [LXX]).[265]

Not everyone sees a future purview in 5.25–26, however. Best asserts that, in the context of Ephesians' realized eschatology, Paul sees the church as Christ's bride now. If Paul can see believers as seated in the heavenlies in Christ (2.6), Best argues, he can also see the church as already Christ's bride. Similarly, Lincoln maintains that the 'one flesh' marital union metaphor is applied to Christ and the church in the present, which he presumably derives from the present tenses 'this *is* a great mystery' and 'I *am talking*' (5.32). However, while noting its present scope, Lincoln highlights the paradoxical 'now' and 'not yet' purview of the bride metaphor, indeed Ephesians' eschatology. To see the church as in some sense Christ's bride now does not eliminate the possibility of a further manifestation in the future. Future fulfilment is necessary since the church is not currently without 'stain or blemish' (5.27). Moreover, the now/not yet nature of the bridal imagery accords with the assertion that Christ is head (*kephalē*) over all things (1.22) but all things are not yet gathered together (*anakephalaioō*) in him (1.10), the church is the body of Christ but is not yet 'the complete human' (4.13), and the church is 'one body' (4.4) but must grow up to attain the unity of faith (4.13).[266]

The 'not yet' component of the kingdom, as evident within 1 Corinthians 11.23–26 and Ephesians 5.21–32, highlights the point that, although there are many different ways that the church can manifest the kingdom now, there is *one* ultimate reality that creation is heading towards: the final consummation of the kingdom when the bride of Christ is without stain or blemish (5.27).

Now and Not Yet ('One and Many')

Luther contends that currently the visibility of God's kingdom is 'like beholding the sun through a cloud ... one sees the light but not the sun itself. But after the clouds have passed, both light and sun are viewed simultaneously in one and the same object.'[267] Luther sees the current manifestation of God's kingdom as primarily the proclamation of the Word and the Sacraments. This, however, is reductionistic. The church's life in its entirety, as Christ's body, is to exude this light and so provide a foretaste of the sun that will be revealed when the clouds part (to continue Luther's metaphor).[268]

This anticipatory aspect to the church's existence can be seen in 1 Corinthians 11.23–26 in that 'the fellowship gathered around the table of the Lord ... provisionally and in partial measure constitutes the pledge and first preliminary imperfect foretaste of the "Supper of the Lamb" of the final consummation to which the Lord's Supper points'.[269] Thiselton's reference to fellowship is key here since the Lord's Supper is not simply a sacred rite, although the meal itself is important, but involves 'identification with the crucified Christ who is also "here" in his raised presence'.[270] Remembrance (11.24–25) is central to this identification; it induces worship, transformation and hope by rooting believers more deeply in the narrative framework of the Christ-event in the past, the reality of Christ's risen lordship and the transformative gift of his Spirit in the present, and the hope of his return and the consummation of God's kingdom in the future.[271]

The Corinthian believers' extraction of the rite from the transformative reality of the Christ-event prompts Paul's rebuke. For Paul, it is incongruous that a believing community could celebrate the Lord's Supper in a way that so fails to identify with Christ's self-giving redemption that 'one goes hungry and another gets drunk' (11.21). Participants are called to embody the new reality that the meal points to. The referent of 'discerning the body' (1 Cor. 11.29) is *both* Christ's body *and* the church.[272] Christ and his church are so closely connected that to mistreat one is to mistreat the other (Acts 9.4). Believers' union with Christ should determine the nature of their interpersonal relationships so that the Christian community anticipates the ultimate supper that is to come: the consummation of the kingdom that will accompany Christ's return (1 Cor. 11.26; 15.24).[273]

The church's identity as an imperfect anticipation of the consummated kingdom is evident in Ephesians through the language of 'mystery' (*mystērion*) (Eph. 1.9; 3.3–4, 9; 5.32; 6.19). Throughout Ephesians *mystērion* refers to the 'once-hidden purpose of God which has now been revealed in Christ'.[274] In different places, different aspects of this purpose are highlighted. In 1.9–10 the mystery is God's plan to bring everything together in Christ (1.10), which resonates with the future consummation of the kingdom accompanying Christ's return in 1 Corinthians 15.24–28. In 3.1–10 the mystery is that the Gentiles are co-inheritors, co-members and co-sharers in the promise in Christ Jesus (3.6). Placing 1.9–10 and 3.1–10 side by side reveals that the cosmic reconciliation of all things in Christ is revealed and anticipated in the church. The horizontal component of this reconciliation is stressed in 3.6. In 5.32 the same entity is in view (the church) but the focus of the mystery is the church's union with Christ, which is so profound that it can be depicted in the language of one flesh (5.31).[275]

Within the now/not yet tension as expressed through the body of Christ image, the church as now reconciled to Christ as his body provides an imperfect foretaste of the reality that is to come when everything is brought into its rightful place in him. Therefore, the trajectory 'towards' is central to the church's essential nature. The *one* reality of the consummated kingdom is to be manifest in the *many* different situations that the church finds itself in. The church is, in every era and every context, to shine forth the light that seeps through the clouds of a futurity yet to come, when the clouds are withdrawn, and the sun itself can be seen.[276]

Implications: Christocentric Trinitarian Vision

The kingdom, although not mentioned explicitly, is a key theme within the body of Christ texts. 1 Corinthians 11.23–26 and Ephesians 5.21–32 reveal that the kingdom is imperfectly manifest in and through the church as Christ's body but there is a future consummation still to come. The church is called to orientate itself towards this future, with believers' interpersonal relationships shaped by their identity as Christ's new covenant community. This 'towards' trajectory has significant implications for the re-contextual church, which are discussed under three headings: kingdom-shaped church, church-shaped kingdom, and noting the pendulum swing.[277]

Kingdom-Shaped Church

If there is to be no poverty in the new heavens and earth, the Church should be seen as a community that cares for the poor. If there is to be no injustice, it is to be seen as a community that challenges injustice. If we will see Christ face to face, then the Church becomes the place where we learn to believe without having seen. If we will enjoy the gracious hospitality of God, the Church must be a place of welcome and hospitality.[278]

The body of Christ metaphor supports Cray's call for the church to shape its present in light of its future. Paul's ecclesiology is intertwined with his eschatology. 'Towards' is thus as vital a defining trajectory as down, up, in, out and of. Moynagh has coined the term 'kingdom-shaped church' to express this kingdom-orientation. However, as Moynagh emphasizes, the church is to be shaped by the kingdom while recognizing that the kingdom is not restricted to the church. Believers should therefore be alert to Spirit-brought splashes of the kingdom in the world.[279]

Re-contextual thinkers are right to object if and when the kingdom is overly spiritualized and internalized.[280] Re-contextual thinkers must also remember, though, that the church is an imperfect and partial foretaste of the consummated kingdom that is to come. Over-realized eschatological schemas lead to cynicism, disillusionment and burnout regardless of whether they are over-realized in terms of supernatural manifestations (people will always be healed), ethics (Christians can reach perfection this side of Christ's return), or social justice (all poverty and injustice can be eradicated before Jesus comes back). Conversely, acknowledgement of the 'not yet' aspect of the kingdom should not hinder the church from pursuing the 'now'. The church is not to seek some happy medium between enthusiastic optimism and sombre realism. Rather, empowered by the Spirit, the church should hold tightly to both ends of the tension, allowing the Christocentric Trinitarian vision of the future time when all things are unified under Christ to shape its life and purpose while persevering through the inevitable hardships, brokenness, weaknesses, imperfections and disappointments that accompany its existence prior to Christ's return.

Church-Shaped Kingdom?

Moynagh has coined the term 'church-shaped kingdom' to depict the views of those who restrict the kingdom to the church. When the church and the kingdom are too closely identified, he argues, mission is reduced to bringing people into church and thus separated from God's plan for creation; evangelism is elevated, ecological and social issues are neglected, and a sense of superiority is cultivated, rather than the recognition that believers can only serve others if they are willing to receive as well as give. Moynagh follows Hull in warning that *Mission-Shaped Church* veers towards a church-shaped kingdom view of mission since mission is primarily conceived of in relation to church planting.[281]

On this relationship between kingdom and church, McKnight provides a dissenting voice. He contends that the church and the kingdom can be equated, or are at least more closely connected than is often believed. He agrees that the inherited church over-spiritualized the kingdom by focusing on rule at the expense of people and land. The kingdom was therefore reduced to individual conversion. Cultural transformation is, McKnight maintains, only a recent strand of kingdom thinking within the inherited church. The younger generations, however, have developed this strand to such an extent that many now view the kingdom as 'good deeds done by good people (Christian or not) in the public sector for the common good' and therefore think that it 'has nothing to do with church'. In contrast, McKnight contends that the kingdom should not be reduced to social justice or personal redemption but consists of 'a people governed by a king'. Since the kingdom is a people under Christ's kingship and the church is a people under Christ's lordship, the two can be identified.[282]

McKnight maintains that people separate church and kingdom because they overlook the church's future trajectory. Instead, 'most of us think of the kingdom as a future glorious reality with only a glimmer of expression in our world while we see the church in mostly earthy and rather mundane terms – with almost no future!'[283] The kingdom is viewed in terms of the 'not yet' and contrasted with the church, which is viewed in terms of the 'now'. Instead, he argues, like must be compared with like. Once it is recognized that kingdom and church are both now/not yet eschatological entities, the differences between them dissolve; 'kingdom mission is church mission, church mission is kingdom mission, and there is no kingdom mission that is not church mission'.[284] Good deeds performed for the public good are not the kingdom, although they are valuable. Rather, the kingdom is built when Christ's kingship is proclaimed and manifest and so the people of the king, the church, grows. Kingdom work versus good deeds (which are not kingdom work) is 'the difference between our energies being focused on a local church community embodying the inaugurated kingdom and a group of local Christians going to the city council ... joining with others in some kind of good activism in order to bring about more peace and justice'.[285]

In seeking to bring church and kingdom closer together, McKnight is a vital voice. Some emerging church leaders have moved too far towards a 'world-shaped kingdom' approach, wherein the focus is so much on the kingdom's presence in the world that the church's role is almost redundant. As Moynagh counters, the church 'is to do more than embrace visible signs of the kingdom: it is to critique their absence and point to salvation in Christ'.[286] The church is called to tell the wider world about the king and, as a prophetic countercultural community, demonstrate and embody the values and distinctives of his kingdom. The church's understanding of kingdom must be rooted in the good news of Jesus' life, death, resurrection, ascension and future return. Mission is neither holistic nor redemptive if a focus on God's saving grace is lost.[287]

Therefore, although McKnight overlooks God's presence outside the church, he offers a vital corrective to any view of God's kingdom that undermines the church's unique nature and role and/or minimizes the importance of evangelism (the church verbally communicating the good news of Jesus).

Noting the Pendulum Swing

There are aspects of eschatology which have to be stated and then simply balanced by their opposites or complements. So vast are the purposes of God that the human mind can only adumbrate bits of them as thesis and antithesis, never, in this life, reaching synthesis; and consequently, it is not surprising if a single thinker is found using antithetic formulations at one and the same period of his own development.[288]

Since God's nature and purposes are beyond human comprehension, as Moule notes, sometimes they can only be expressed by juxtaposing thesis and antithesis. So too, the church is afforded both flexibility and stability when it locates itself in the midst of the tensions evident within the body of Christ texts. The presence of tensions, paradoxes, theses and antitheses, however, means that theological pendulum swings are common. When one group or individual is perceived to have held so tightly to one end of a tension that they neglect or deny the other, some other group or individual pulls harder on the overlooked end to restore equilibrium. Often, though, they pull too hard for someone else's liking and the swing persists. Admittedly, this pendulum analogy is simplistic; those criticizing a previous view often add new layers and depths to a debate. However, since they are reacting to what they perceive as misconceptions of the kingdom, re-contextual thinkers must beware lest, in seeking to correct one imbalance, they create another.

At the start of this section, I outlined some questions prompted by the re-contextual church's critique of the inherited church's conception of the kingdom. On the basis of these questions, the following points of caution are raised. Re-contextual thinkers should ensure that, in their desire to emphasize afresh God's initiative in bringing his kingdom and, therefore, the presence of the kingdom outside the church, they do not negate the unique responsibility and role of the church in God's plans. In particular the church's call to proclaim the good news of the king (evangelism) must not be overlooked. In addition, while rightly wanting to highlight external and concrete manifestations of the kingdom, re-contextual thinkers should not sideline the internal transformation and subjective experience that accompanies entry into God's kingdom. Lastly, in highlighting the kingdom's presence now, re-contextual thinkers must also emphasize the 'not yet' of the kingdom, so to avoid the perils of cynicism, disappointment, and a lack of future trajectory that accompany over-realized eschatological schemas, whatever their form. This is not to say that re-contextual thinkers have pulled too far the other way in relation to these issues, but that, when reacting against one imbalance, one must be attentive to the danger of creating another.

Between (Compression Towers): Suffering and Conflict – The Role of Suffering and Conflict in Facilitating Gift-Exchange

Re-contextual thinkers are critical of idealistic blueprint models of church and accuse the inherited church of a triumphalism that fails to account for negative experiences and emotions. Within their ecclesiology, these thinkers often draw on Social Trinitarianism even though its critics deem social models of the Trinity to be overly idealistic. Pickard, for example, asserts that modelling the church's communal relationships on the relations within the Trinity fails to account for the inevitability of conflict within human communities. Such idealism suggests that Social Trinitarianism is an inadequate foundation for re-contextual concerns. In contrast, as I elucidate below, a Christocentric Trinitarian ecclesiology based on the body of Christ image is rooted in the 'between' of the church's now/not yet eschatological existence. This 'between' dimension is highlighted through the inevitability of suffering and conflict within the church community as depicted within body of Christ texts. This suffering and conflict is particularly apparent within Colossians 1.24–29 and 3.12–17, which are the passages that I focus on in this section.[289]

Within a suspension bridge, the cables, which are under tension, transfer their forces to the towers, which are compressed. This compression is as important as the tension. The metaphor of the church as a suspension bridge cannot be pushed on every detail; I am not claiming below that suffering and conflict (analogously depicted as the compression towers (see Figure 8) are created by virtue of believers' relationship with God (analogously depicted as the suspension cables). Rather, *all* the tensions contribute to this compression because they are all located within the now/not yet eschatological framework that I outlined in the section above ('towards'). The church exists in the overlap of two eras, between Christ's life, death, resurrection and ascension, on the one end, and his return, on the other.[290]

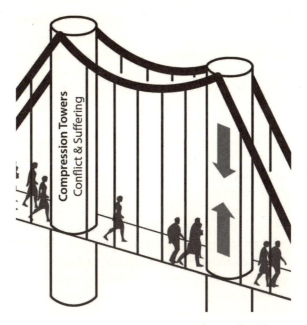

Figure 8: Compression Towers: Conflict and Suffering

Suffering (Tower One)

> Now I rejoice in my sufferings for you and I fill up in my flesh what
> is lacking in Christ's affliction for the sake of his body, which is the
> church, of which I have become a servant according to God's steward-
> ship that was given to me for you to make God's word fully known,
> the mystery, which was hidden from the ages and from the generations,
> but now has been revealed to his saints, to whom God willed to make
> known the riches of this glorious mystery among the Gentiles, which is
> Christ in you, the hope of glory. Him we proclaim, warning all people
> and teaching all people in all wisdom, in order that we might present all
> people perfect in Christ. For this I toil, striving according to his energy
> that is powerfully at work in me. (Col. 1.24–29)

This passage resonates with Jewish apocalyptic thought, wherein it was
believed that the final events of history would be triggered by the suffering of God's people. The church, however, lives between Christ's first
and second coming; it is not awaiting the Messiah's first arrival. Paul has
modified Jewish apocalypticism accordingly and thus, as Best contends,
sees Christ's suffering as 'birth-pangs' or 'woes'. Paul believes that he has
a unique role in completing these woes, which explains his belief that 'I
fill up in my flesh what is lacking in Christ's afflictions' (1.24). In this,

Paul is not implying that Christ's redemptive affliction is lacking – such thinking would contradict his assertion that Christ's death enables complete forgiveness (Col. 1.12–14, 19–22; 2.13–14) and *thlipsis* (affliction) is nowhere used of Christ's vicarious suffering. Rather, from Paul's perspective, there must be a certain number of Gentiles added before Christ returns (Rom. 11.25) and so a certain amount of suffering. This is not some arbitrary quota of affliction that must be fulfilled; rather suffering comes as a result of Paul's witness.[291]

Paul presents himself as a unique sufferer; his suffering is integral to his apostleship, particularly his proclamation of the gospel in both word and action (1.25). His relationship with the church is not reciprocal in this regard; Paul suffers for the churches that he ministers to but they do not suffer for him. Paul's uniqueness, however, does not mean that his readers are exempt from suffering. Paul locates his role within his overarching eschatological affliction framework, which Dunn maintains contains three key components: Christ's suffering and death as inaugurating the new age; participation in Christ's death as the means of transitioning into the new age; and a lifelong process of dying with Christ as leading to future resurrection in Christ. As members of Christ's body, all believers participate in Christ's sufferings in that, like Paul, their witness to Christ often results in opposition and rejection. Thus *pathēma* (suffering) (1.24) elsewhere refers to the afflictions that all Christians experience because of their connection to Christ (Rom. 8.18; 2 Cor. 1.5–7; Phil. 3.10).[292]

Although Paul rejoices in his suffering (1.24), he does not embrace or promote masochism. His view of suffering only coheres in light of the church's existence between two ages. Paul suffers to proclaim 'the mystery' of the gospel (1.26), which brings to mind God's cosmic plan for the reconciliation of creation, the consummation of which is still a future hope. Paul sees his suffering positively because of this hope; without such hope, suffering would be senseless. By rejoicing in his suffering, Paul witnesses to the transience of the current state and the glory of the one to come. Therefore, suffering is not an incidental side effect of Paul's ministry but serves as evidence for the legitimacy of his message (cf. 2 Cor. 11.23–33; 12.7b–12). For Paul, perseverance in suffering reveals God's power more profoundly than immediate deliverance from suffering; such endurance points to an alternative reality that is partially present now and yet still to come. Paul's rejoicing is thus not the result of his suffering per se (in and of itself) but what it achieves (the salvation of the Gentiles), represents (his solidarity with Christ), and points towards (the glorious vindication that will accompany Christ's return).[293]

In addition to suffering, another key aspect of the church's eschatological existence between the inauguration of the kingdom and its consummation is conflict.

Conflict (Tower Two)

> Put on, therefore, as God's elect, holy and loved, compassionate affec-
> tion, kindness, humility, gentleness, and patience, bearing with one
> another and, if anyone has a complaint against another, forgiving each
> other just as Christ has forgiven you, so you should do likewise. But,
> over all these things, put on love, which binds everything together
> perfectly. And let the peace of Christ rule in your hearts, into which
> you were called in one body; and be thankful. Let the word of Christ
> dwell richly among you, teaching and admonishing one another in all
> wisdom, singing psalms, hymns, and Spirit-inspired songs with grati-
> tude in your hearts to God. Indeed do everything, whether in word or
> deed, all in the name of the Lord Jesus, giving thanks to God the Father
> through him. (Col. 3.12–17)

Paul's view of Christian community is both idealistic and realistic, which
accords with the now/not yet nature of his eschatology. Paul urges believers
to live out their heavenly existence and instructs them how to deal with
inevitable grievances. Idealism is apparent in that the identity of those
addressed (elected by God, holy and loved) and the attributes they are
told to adopt (compassionate affection, kindness, humility, gentleness and
patience) provide a vision of what the new covenant community should
look like (3.12). This passage thus substantiates the call to take off the old
person and put on the new (3.9–10), which refers not just to an individual
new nature, but a corporate new humanity (3.11). The five virtues that
believers are told to put on (or 'clothe' themselves with) are the positive
counterparts to the five vices that the believers are instructed to take off
(3.8, 10 and 12); the vices bring disunity (anger, rage, wickedness, slander
and abusive speech), and the virtues foster unity. These virtues appear elsewhere in the New Testament (for example, Eph. 4.2; Gal. 5.22–23; Col.
1.11), implying that they are distinguishing marks of the new community.
Most importantly, these virtues are exemplified by Christ, indicating that
this vision for the new covenant community is based on him. The church
is 'one body' (3.15), Christ's (cf. 1.18, 24; 2.19).[294] As Bruce asserts:

> If the members are subject to Christ, the peace which he imparts must
> regulate their relations with one another. It was not to strife but to
> peace that God called them in the unity of the body of Christ ... In a
> healthy body harmony prevails among the various parts. Christians,
> having been reconciled to God, enjoying peace with him through Christ,
> should naturally live at peace with one another.[295]

Bruce contends that there is therefore 'no reason' why believers should not have peaceful relationships. However, he also notes that strife occurs when believers lose touch with Christ, who is the source of peace. Therefore there *is* a reason why believers might not be at peace with each other: the church's existence between the inauguration of the new covenant community and its perfection. This is not to assert that conflict is always indicative of imperfection; as Chapman notes, unlike the persons of the Trinity, human beings do not share one will and so, rather than necessarily being a sinful aberration or distortion, conflict is central to social functioning. It is, however, disagreements corrupted by sin that I particularly have in view here.[296]

In this regard, realism is evident through the call to bear with and forgive one another (3.13). 'Bear with' can refer just to putting up with people. 'Forgive each other' implies that both giving and receiving forgiveness will be required. Moreover, the idealistic characteristics that Paul urges the believers to adopt are those that will best help them to navigate their inevitable imperfections. *Compassionate affection* is a key attribute of God, referring to his compassionate mercy. This call to put on compassion (3.12) prefigures the call to forgive (3.13). *Kindness* is also associated with God's character; his kindness stands out sharply against the backdrop of his people's sin. This association with God's nature sets Paul's understanding of 'kindness' (*chrēstotēs*) apart from its meaning in wider Greek thought, wherein the word was often used disparagingly to depict weak compliance. As Dunn maintains, however, although all the virtues, particularly in this combination, might seem to encourage a '"milksop" weakness as in people whose calling in life is to be a doormat for others', these attitudes actually call for a rare kind of strength that is essential for a community to grow and flourish.[297]

Bruce observes that *humility* resonates with Jesus' nature as 'gentle and lowly in heart' (Matt. 11.29). When this characteristic is cultivated, it is less likely that pride and self-centredness will prevail. In conflict situations, Lindemann maintains, *gentleness* refers to the power that enables legitimate criticisms to be presented in such a way that they are received as help, not condemnation. Moreover, as Davies notes, although *patience* in Colossians 1.11 refers to the endurance or forbearance required to undergo external trials, in 3.12 it refers to believers' internal relations. The need for forbearance implies imperfection within the community, pre-empting the call to bear with others (3.13). Paul's exhortations to 'put on' these characteristics demonstrates his realistic approach to Christian community; believers should be prepared and equipped to respond well to each other's imperfections.[298]

Paul's idealism is apparent in his instructions regarding love and peace. The exhortations in 3.12–13 are summed up in the injunction to put on *love*, which is the 'supreme virtue' (cf. 1 Cor. 13) and the bond that holds the group together. Love is like an overcoat, put on '*over* all these things', that both holds the virtues together and completes them (Col. 3.14). Just as Christ is the model and motivation for believers to forgive so too, by implication, Christ's self-sacrifice is the model for love. Paul's language of *peace* invokes the wholeness and restoration of the Old Testament concept of *shalom*. This peace is to rule in believers' hearts (3.15), but it cannot be reduced to an internalized, spiritualized, or individualized reality. Rather, since peace was a central aspect of new covenant expectations, peace in community relations is evidence that the believers belong to the Messiah's people. In addition, there is both a 'now' and 'not yet' dimension to the new covenant *shalom* brought by Christ. As the Christian community demonstrates the peace of Christ in the present, it points to a time when this peace is extended to, and perfected in, the new creation; the Christian community is to actualize in the microsphere what will one day be realized in the macrosphere.[299]

For Paul, the ideal community is also characterized by gratitude (3.15–16). Indeed, thankfulness is a major theme in Colossians as a whole. In 1.12–14, for example, readers are encouraged to thank God for his deliverance from tyranny and their transference into Christ's kingdom. As I argued earlier in this book, gratitude and worship are the normative responses to God's love and grace. Moreover, as is much needed in the midst of the church's current imperfection, those most grateful for the grace that they have received are best equipped to extend that grace to others.[300]

These virtues that Paul urges the community to adopt in Colossians 3 do not, at first glance, seem connected to the false teaching warned of in Colossians 1—2. However, the exhortation, 'Let the word of Christ dwell richly among you' (3.16) is striking in this context.[301] Moo maintains:

> The message about Christ should take up permanent residence among the Colossians ... it should be constantly at the center of the community's activities and worship. 'Richly' suggests that this constant reference to the word of Christ should not be superficial or passing but that it should be a deep and penetrating contemplation that enables the message to have transforming power in the life of the community.[302]

Paul's exhortation that the believers not just teach but also admonish (*noutheteō*) each other (3.16) demonstrates his realism; *noutheteō* means 'to counsel about avoidance or cessation of an *improper* course of conduct' and so is only relevant to an imperfect entity.[303] The specification that believers are to admonish one another through psalms, hymns and spiritual songs does not exclude the possibility of other forms of admonishment any more than the connection of teaching to these formats eliminates oral instruction. Indeed, resonance with 1 Corinthians 14.26–33 suggests that preaching and prophecy are also in view. Leaders are not mentioned but, since the presence of leaders is assumed elsewhere (1 Cor. 12.28; Rom. 12.7), some form of leadership is presumably envisaged. However, the emphasis is on mutual instruction and admonition, which must be carried out with wisdom. Moreover, lest one think that Paul has *just* Christian gatherings in view, 3.17 extends the purview to the whole of life. Doing all things in Jesus' name means acting in line with Christ's nature and character; everything that believers say and do is to be directed by their identity as the new covenant community and contribute to their thanksgiving and worship.[304]

In summary, Paul's idealistic realism means that the community is to strive for unity and harmony as the new covenant community, foreshadowing the consummated kingdom still to come, while recognizing that imperfections are inevitable. Therefore, a key part of their identity as the new covenant community involves dealing with grievances in a Christ-like manner. Central to this is the ability and willingness of believers to mutually instruct and admonish each other. Conflict is thus an essential component of the Christian community. As Turner maintains, the 'quest for "unity" does not mean silence in disagreement. On the contrary, silence is a capitulation of my personhood to that of the other, and perhaps the failure lovingly to resist distortion in the other.'[305] Colossians 3.12–17 provides the necessary qualifications to this; conflict is not to be carried out rashly or haphazardly, but according to 'the word of Christ' and 'with all wisdom' (3.16). Moreover, the best context for healthy and godly conflict, as opposed to that which is destructive and self-serving, is a community characterized by compassionate affection, kindness, humility, gentleness, patience, love, peace and grace (3.12, 14–16), wherein people readily bear with and forgive each other (3.13).

Implications: Christocentric Trinitarian Hope

The gardener has a tree which is full of life, full of sap, capable of sharing and of giving life. He looks around for a shoot, a branch, a bush which is drooping, but which is still capable of being revived ... This is followed by an action which appears to be cruel and even violent ... The divine act of love which follows consists in pulling a branch from its roots, cutting it with a pruning knife, separating it from the life, transitory and ephemeral, which it none the less possessed, and suspending it in the possibility of total death ... And then the gardener turns towards the olive tree, to the tree he has chosen to give life, and once again he cuts, he cuts it open with his pruning knife, and it is in gash against gash, wound against wound, that the meeting between the life-giving olive and the dying branch takes place ... [T]he branch finds itself grafted on to a trunk which can give it life ... Now there begins a struggle ... Slowly, insistently, the sap of the vine, or of the olive, presses forward, seeking to penetrate the tiny capillaries of the graft ... Little by little it presses more firmly, more insistently, entering into the very life of each cell, displacing by its own life the wild, ephemeral life which led to death. And little by little the graft comes to live by a new life. Gradually its leaves unfold and it becomes alive in a more profound sense than before. But at the same time it becomes itself, in a more intense, more personal way than ever before. All its starved possibilities, which were unable to express themselves because they lacked life, flourish and come to perfection.[306]

In the above quotation, Bloom draws on the metaphor of grafting to explore the relationship between Christ and the church. Through this metaphor Bloom paints a powerful picture of the painful process of dying to self so that Christ might fill believers' lives more fully. Percy also utilizes the analogy of pruning, but does so to urge openness to change, which, he argues, often results from conflict or crisis. Without such pruning, the church produces vinegar, not new wine; thus pruning helps believers to be a gift to one another and the wider world. In line with Percy's contention, the ecclesiology that I am promoting in this book emphasizes the inevitability of both suffering and conflict in the church's life. In contrast to the Western tendency towards idealistic blueprint ecclesiologies, the re-contextual church must acknowledge the church's eschatological location, with both its 'now' and 'not yet' dimensions. Two areas that are particularly affected by the church's 'between' location are the recent focus on incarnational ministry and the church's call to be a counter-cultural community.[307]

Incarnational Ministry

The Word became flesh and blood, and moved into the neighborhood. (John 1.16a, *The Message*)

Langmead asserts that 'incarnational mission' has become a buzz term that sounds impressive but lacks clarity. He notes that, in relation to mission, any derivative of 'incarnation' can only be used in a metaphorical or secondary sense since *becoming enfleshed* can only be properly applied to a divine being; the church is already enfleshed. Guder suggests that Mackay was the first English-speaking theologian to pursue the concept of incarnational mission in print. Mackay describes the 'incarnational principle' as when Jesus' humanness becomes a missional paradigm and Christian witnesses thus identify themselves as closely as possible with their context. As Langmead notes, this definition accords with the more general use of 'incarnate' to mean 'take shape'.[308]

However, this *Jesus as a model* understanding of incarnational mission has been criticized for being idealistic and arrogant. Regarding idealism, Billings maintains that missionaries from one culture can never become one with those they are reaching as Jesus did. He argues:

> Particularly for those working among the poor (for whom incarnational ministry is most aggressively advocated), the attempt to become 'one' with the people is likely to leave a set of unanswered questions: How can I become one with the people when I have a different history and cultural background? How can I become one with the poor when I still have a network of family and mission that can bail me out of bad situations?[309]

One might cite the lyrics from Pulp's 1995 hit 'Common People' in support of Billings' point!

Regarding arrogance, Billings warns that incarnational missionaries can see identification with culture as an end in itself, implying that their own presence is redemptive. Fung argues that unhealthy pride is evident when believers assert that if you see them you see Jesus. Such thinking also leads to individualistic endeavours to 'make Christ incarnate' that undermine the importance of worshipping communities. In addition, those seeking to incarnate the gospel into a different culture implicitly equate their conception of the gospel with the divine Word, which they then contextualize into a different culture, rather than accepting that their understanding is already culturally conditioned. Langmead notes other concerns: the danger of perfectionism, legalism and works-righteousness; a diminishment of the centrality of Jesus' death and resurrection; and an overly human-centred approach.[310]

Despite the validity of these criticisms, incarnational ministry remains a vital metaphor for re-contextual thinkers. As I elucidate below, locating this concept in the Christocentric Trinitarian ecclesiology that I am promoting in this book and, in particular, the 'between' of the church's current eschatological locus, overcomes the potential weaknesses of an incarnational approach while maintaining its strengths.

Langmead asserts that incarnational ministry incorporates three strands: modelling Jesus' approach to mission (pattern); participation in Christ as his body, in which Christ is present and through which he is made present by his Spirit (power); and participation in God's incarnating mission, which began at creation and reaches its climax in Christ (premise). Most church traditions highlight one of these aspects and over-look the others. Re-contextual thinkers tend to focus on the first (pattern). Moynagh, for example, argues that the incarnation is a key paradigm for contextualization: just as Jesus was immersed in his Jewish culture so the church, as his body, must embed itself in its context. In contrast to other re-contextual thinkers, Moynagh specifies that Jesus' incarnation incorporates the entirety of Jesus' life, death, resurrection and ascension, not just his birth. In line with Jesus' ministry, Moynagh argues, Paul's mission was incarnational in that he was attentive to his context when building church communities – although Paul, and Jesus, also stood strongly against certain aspects of their context.[311]

Given this focus on patterning Jesus' ministry within the re-contextual conversation, Billings brings a vital rejoinder in highlighting the centrality of union with Christ in Paul's understanding of the church's mission. *Participation in Christ* highlights that Christ's relationship with his people is asymmetrical. Christ is the redeemer; his people point to this redemption. Believers are not incarnate; they are united with Christ, who is. *Participation in Christ*, Billings contends, is more concrete than vague notions of incarnating into another culture: it highlights the church's dependence on the Spirit to manifest Christ's living presence; it emphasizes gathering as well as sending; it is more realistic about the extent to which human beings can really inhabit a culture different to their own; and it recognizes the need to honour cultural differences rather than enforcing one's own cultural manifestation of faith onto others.[312]

Contra Billings, emphasizing union with Christ does not require aban-doning the language of incarnational mission. Rather, an ecclesiology based on Paul's body of Christ metaphor provides a framework for affirm-ing Christ's presence in and through the church while neither conflating the church and Christ nor denying Christ's freedom to act outside the church. Within the body of Christ texts, Paul sees Christ as an example to follow (esp. Col. 3.12–17). Billings asserts that 'incarnational' should not be used to depict this imitation since Christ's incarnation is, ironically, precisely that which believers cannot imitate. However, in this critique, Billings overlooks the distinction between Christ's unique incarnation and incarnation*al* as a missional model. More importantly, he overlooks the term's metaphorical force, wherein something is lost if this phrase is avoided. What is lost, as Metzger observes, is the sense in which the church is a real expression of the risen and incarnate Christ through his Spirit. The church is not, in and of itself, an incarnation, but the language of incarnational emphasizes that Christ really does continue his ministry in and through the church as his body. The church is called to embody Christ to the world, although it does so imperfectly. This is not to deny the church's calling to point people to Christ, nor Christ's presence through his Spirit outside the church. Rather, it is to affirm with Metzger that although 'the church does not continue the incarnation, Christ continues his incarnate existence through his body, the church'.[313]

Incarnational as a missional model must be located in the 'between' component of the church's essential identity. Conceptualizing incarnational ministry in the midst of the now/not yet tension facilitates optimistic enthusiasm regarding the extent to which Christ's presence is manifest in and through the church while minimizing any arrogant pretension or unrealistic compulsion to view this in an absolute sense, as if Christ were restricted to the church or there were not a fuller manifestation to come. Authentic incarnational ministry only occurs when believers recognize their own needs and failings alongside those of the community they seek to embed themselves in. Locating incarnational ministry within 'between' also supports Moynagh's emphasis on the suffering that can arise when believers give up their own preferences and norms in order to inculturate the gospel into a different context.[314] This suffering is not an end in itself, but is the prerequisite for new life. *Mission-Shaped Church* contends:

> If it is the nature of God's love to undertake such sacrifice, it must also be the nature of his Church. The Church is most true to itself when it gives itself up, in current cultural form, to be re-formed among those who do not know God's Son. In each new context the church must die to live.[315]

Therefore, while legitimate concerns have been raised regarding incarnational ministry as a missionary model, an ecclesiology based on Paul's body of Christ metaphor provides a framework in which the strengths of this concept are maintained and the weaknesses overcome. Re-contextual thinkers must emphasize believers' union with Christ alongside the call to imitate him and locate incarnational ministry in the 'between' component of the church's essential nature to avoid idealism or pride in relation to this model.

Conflict's Role in Creating and Correcting the Countercultural Community

> Faith ... wherever it develops into hope, causes not rest but unrest, not patience but impatience. It does not calm the unquiet heart, but is itself this unquiet heart in man. Those who hope in Christ can no longer put up with reality as it is, but begin to suffer under it, to contradict it. Peace with God means conflict with the world, for the goad of the promised future stabs inexorably into the flesh of every unfulfilled present.[316]

The church's orientation towards the future consummation of God's kingdom and its current existence between the 'now' and 'not yet' of this reality means that conflict with the world is inevitable. This conflict is important since a desire to be contextually accessible to non-believers can slide into syncretism. Moreover, in this conflict new truth about Christ and the church's identity is revealed. In order to maintain its identity as a countercultural community, the church also requires conflict within the Christian community. Believers must challenge and sharpen one another. This raises the issue of church discipline which, within the re-contextual discussion, Murray Williams addresses most fully. He maintains that a multi-voiced culture is best suited to the healthy implementation of discipline and that this should occur primarily through mutual accountability between church members. He promotes a centre-set model of church which, he argues, helps the church maintain its distinctive identity while remaining inclusive to people at different stages in their faith journey. Mutual accountability plays an important role in facilitating a Jesus-centred core. Murray Williams' focus on mutual accountability is supported by the body of Christ texts, particularly Colossians 3.12–17, which emphasizes the role that the members of the body have in exhorting and supporting one another.[317] As Murray Williams notes, believers

> are not lone pilgrims struggling with temptation, discouragement, misunderstandings and setbacks, but companions on the journey ... [W]e need each other, we are responsible for each other, we are accountable to each other, and we grow as disciples through our relationships with each other.[318]

Therefore, rather than seek to avoid conflict, the church should equip itself to handle conflict in a healthy and godly manner. For the church to be a countercultural community, conflict both within the Christian community and between the church and wider world is inevitable and, if handled well, beneficial.

Notes

1 C. Phillips and S. Priwer, *Bridges and Spans*, Abingdon; New York: Routledge, 2009, 56.

2 Molnar, *Freedom*, 197–233; Ge, 'One', 10–13.

3 Not that God is anchored to these events, but that the church is, and it must remember that this is so.

4 S. J. Grenz and R. E. Olson, *20th-Century Theology*, Downers Grove, IL: Paternoster, 1992, 11.

5 Grenz, *20th-Century*, 10, 12, 13.

6 Lincoln argues similarly that, for at least some of Ephesians' recipients, God

was so transcendent that moral claims could be ignored (A. T. Lincoln, 'A Re-Examination of "The Heavenlies" in Ephesians', *NTS* 19 [1972–3] 468–83, citing 483).

7 C. E. Arnold, *Power and Magic*, Cambridge: CUP, 1989, 19.

8 P. T. O'Brien, *The Letter to the Ephesians*, Leicester: Apollos, 1999, 55.

9 Arnold, *Power*, 14, 18–19, 20–3, 27; cf. Acts 19.11–20; cf. F. Thielman, *Ephesians*, Grand Rapids, MI: Baker Academic, 2010, 20; O'Brien, *Ephesians*, 54–5. Regarding the prevalence of magical practices and their influence on the Colossian Christians see C. Arnold, *The Colossian Syncretism*, Tübingen: Mohr Siebeck, 1995, 158–94 and D. J. Moo, *The Letters to Colossians and to Philemon*, Grand Rapids, MI/Cambridge: Eerdmans, 2008, 57–8.

10 J. D. G. Dunn, *The Epistles to the Colossians and to Philemon*, Carlisle: Eerdmans, 1996, 26; M. D. Hooker, 'Were There False Teachers in Colossae?' in B. Lindars and S. S. Smalley (eds), *Christ and Spirit in the New Testament*, Cambridge: CUP, 1973, 315–31, citing 323; Moo, *Colossians*, 47–8.

11 Arnold, *Syncretism*, esp. 10, 156, 208, 214–18, 226; Moo, *Colossians*, 48–50.

12 K. Tanner, 'Creation *Ex Nihilo* As Mixed Metaphor', *MTh* 29.2 (2013) 138–55, 143–64. O'Brien notes the tendency of some within the Colossian Christian community to view Christ as 'just another intermediary between God and man' (P. T. O'Brien, *Colossians and Philemon*, Waco, TX: Word, 1982, 132).

13 E.g. Psalms 104.24; Proverbs 3.19; 8.22–31; Wisdom 7.25–26; 9.1; Sirach 43.26; Dunn, *Colossians*, 88–9; cf. Moo, *Colossians*, 118–24.

14 Tanner, *Key*, 7.

15 Moo, *Colossians*, 111–14; Dunn, *Colossians*, 88–9; G. Macaskill, *Union with Christ in the New Testament*, Oxford: OUP, 2013, 158; cf. Tanner, *Key*, 5–7. As Ge notes, 'only in *creatio ex nihilo*, which is the backbone of classical theism, can we find the transcendent One, who is nonetheless radically immanent to the world' (Ge, 'One', 191).

16 Ge, 'One', 15; Tanner, *Key*, 12–13.

17 J. A. T. Robinson, *The Body: A Study in Pauline Theology*, London: SCM, 1953, 45–7; A. Perriman, '"His Body, Which is the Church …" Coming to Terms with Metaphor', *EQ* 62.2 (1990) 123–42, esp. 126–8; C. R. Campbell, *Paul and Union with Christ*, Grand Rapids, MI: Zondervan, 2012, 268 [italics his]).

18 H. Morris, 'The City as Foil (not Friend nor Foe): Conformity and Subversion in 1 Corinthians 12:12–31', in S. Walton et al. (eds), *The Urban World and the First Christians*, Grand Rapids, MI: Eerdmans, 2017.

19 P. Hanks (ed.), *Collins Dictionary of the English Language*, 2nd ed., London: Collins, 1987, 1,018.

20 Those who deny mysticism in Paul's thought do so only after narrowing this terminology down to its Hellenistic meaning (A. Wikenhauser, *Pauline Mysticism*, Edinburgh: Herder/Freiburg: Nelson, 1960, 101). Although the body of Christ metaphor conveys deep intimacy between the church and God, the Hellenistic notion of absorption into the divine is absent from Paul's thought (Wikenhauser, *Pauline*, 96).

21 J. W. Thompson, *The Church According to Paul*, Grand Rapids, MI: Baker Academic, 2014, 52.

22 Tanner, *Key*, 14–15.

23 Ge, 'Participation', 194.

24 As Ge notes, 'the most profound vision of the simultaneous transcendence and immanence of the One in relation to the Many is found in the Incarnation, in

which the wholly transcendent One became perfectly united with the Many' (Ge, 'Participation', 194–5).

25 F. F. Bruce, *The Epistles to the Colossians, to Philemon and to the Ephesians*, Grand Rapids, MI: Eerdmans, 1984, 61; Dunn, *Colossians*, 101; N. T. Wright, *Colossians and Philemon*, Leicester: IVP, 1986, 71–2; Tanner, 'Creation', 143–64.

26 Barth, *CD* IV/1, 186; cf. K. Tanner, *Jesus, Humanity and the Trinity*, Edinburgh: T&T Clark, 2001, 11–12.

27 Tanner, *Jesus*, 1–4.

28 Thielman, *Ephesians*, 386.

29 J. M. G. Barclay, 'Pure Grace? Paul's Distinctive Jewish Theology of Gift', *ST* 68.1 (2014) 4–20, citing 7 referring to J. Derrida, *Given Time*, trans. P. Kamuf, Chicago, IL: University of Chicago, 1992, 7–24.

30 Barclay, 'Grace', 15.

31 J. M. G. Barclay, *Paul and the Gift*, Grand Rapids, MI/Cambridge: Eerdmans, 2015, esp. 17, 59, 61–2, 185; M. Mauss, *The Gift*, trans. I. Cunnison, London: Cohen and West, 1966, 11.

32 Barclay 'Grace', 15.

33 O'Brien, *Ephesians*, 265; Macaskill, *Union*, 152, 298.

34 Tanner, *Jesus*, 4.

35 Tanner, *Key*, 228; cf. 207–46.

36 Tanner, *Key*, 229.

37 Tanner, *Key*, 234–5.

38 Ward, *Liquid*, 5, 6, 54.

39 Jones, *Flat*, 149.

40 Jones, *Flat*, 164.

41 *Contra* Murray Williams, Thwaites does not deny the validity of the gathered church (Murray, *Christendom*, 203–7). However, his depiction of the gathered church as a pillar to support 'the church as the fullness of the created order' – by which he means believers infiltrating every sphere of life and work – is right in what it affirms (the role of the gathered church to empower believers to serve Christ in every area of their lives) but overlooks the prophetic and worshipping role of a gathered community (Thwaithes, *Beyond*, 86–91, 178–83).

42 Tanner, *Jesus*, 1.

43 Tanner, *Jesus*, 2.

44 Tanner, *Jesus*, 3, 79–80; S. Chan, *Liturgical Theology*, Downers Grove, IL: IVP, 2006, 42; Moynagh, *Context*, 354–5.

45 Within this, I aim neither to promote the monistic (one substance) view of human personhood that Green, for example, argues characterizes the biblical portrayal of human ontology nor the substance dualism that those such as Moreland, Rae and Cooper see displayed through biblical texts (J. Green, *Body, Soul, and Human Life*, Grand Rapids, MI: Baker Academic, 2008; J. P. Moreland and S. B. Rae, *Body and Soul*, Downers Grove, IL: IVP, 2000; J. W. Cooper, *Body, Soul, and Life Everlasting, Biblical Anthropology and the Monism–Dualism Debate*, Grand Rapids, MI; Cambridge: Eerdmans, 1989). Rather, regardless of the exact ontological make-up of human personhood, Paul promotes, at the very least, a *functional holism* wherein 'the body-soul complex is a deeply integrated unity with a vastly complicated, intricate array of mutual functional dependence and causal connection' (Moreland, *Body*, 21). Martin argues that the modernist Cartesian dualism, wherein the soul or spirit is elevated above the body as the true locus of self and/or encounter with the transcendent, has influenced contemporary readings of Paul (D. B. Martin,

The Corinthian Body, New Haven, CT; London: Yale University, 1995, 6). This Cartesian dualism is the faulty view of human personhood that I contend against.

46 B. Huss, 'Spirituality: The Emergence of a New Cultural Category and its Challenge to the Religious and the Secular', *JCR* 29.1 (2014) 47–60, citing 47; R. C. Fuller, *Spiritual, But Not Religious*, Oxford: OUP, 2001, 5; W. Principe, 'Toward Defining Spirituality' *Studies in Religion* 12.2 (1983) 127–41.

47 H. T. Hunt, 'Gnostic Dilemmas in Western Psychologies of Spirituality', *The International Journal of Transpersonal Studies*, 22 (2003) 27–39, citing 37.

48 Hunt, 'Gnostic', 35–6; Huss, 'Spirituality', 53–8; J. Ankerberg and J. Weldon, *Encyclopedia of New Age Beliefs*, Eugene: Harvest House, 1996, x.

49 P. C. Hill et al., 'Conceptualizing Religion and Spirituality: Points of Commonality, Points of Departure', *Journal for the Theory of Social Behaviour* 30.1 (2000) 51–77; Fuller, *Spiritual*, 4–6, 9–10, 159. Fuller cites the startling statistic that in the USA '55 percent of all church members privately subscribe to some belief pertaining to the occult (e.g., astrology, reincarnation, fortune telling, or trance channeling)' (Fuller, *Spiritual*, 9). He also asserts, 'Church members are also among the millions who avidly read such spiritual bestsellers as *The Road Less Traveled*, *The Celestine Prophecy*, and the *Seven Spiritual Laws of Success* and strive to integrate concepts from these unchurched sources into their overall worldview' (Fuller, *Spiritual*, 9).

50 See in particular Jefferson Bethke's spoken word 'Why I Hate Religion, But Love Jesus', which has received over 28 million views on YouTube (J. Bethke, 'Why I Hate Religion, But Love Jesus', YouTube website (accessed 11 December 2014, www.youtube.com/watch?v=1IAhDGYlpqY); Hill, 'Conceptualizing', 56–60; Fuller, *Spiritual*, 5.

51 Hill, 'Conceptualizing', 64–6.

52 Molnar, *Freedom*, 197–233; Hunt, 'Gnostic', 36–7; Ge, 'Participation', 12.

53 As Wright notes, it is entirely anachronistic to examine Paul as if religion was something separate from the rest of life (N. T. Wright, *Paul and the Faithfulness of God*, London: SPCK, 2013, 52).

54 Thiselton, *First*, 225.

55 Identifying 'all sins that people do are outside the body' as a Corinthian slogan is a minority view. However, as Burk notes, in order to make sense of this clause if not a slogan, most commentators add 'other' to 'sins' with no legitimate exegetical reason (D. Burk, 'Discerning Corinthian Slogans through Paul's Use of the Diatribe in 1 Corinthians 6:12–20', *BBR* 18.1 [2008] 99–121).

56 Fee, *First*, 251; A. C. Thiselton, *The First Epistle to the Corinthians*, Grand Rapids, MI: Eerdmans/Carlisle: Paternoster, 2000, 458–9.

57 O'Brien, *Colossians*, xxix, 129–32, 149; Thiselton, *First*, 458–62. R. S. Nash, *1 Corinthians*, Macon: Smyth and Helwys, 2009, 165–6; Fee, *First*, 257. Martin warns against reading Cartesian dualism into the ancient world but notes that the body was depreciated among the elite within Graeco-Roman culture and 'Paul, by contrast, rejects a hierarchical notion of the body according to which relative importance is attached to the actions of the different levels of the human self, as if the body and food are lower on a hierarchical scale of meaningfulness than the human mind or will and therefore simply do not matter very much' (Martin, *Body*, 175–6).

58 Green, *Body*, 37–8.

59 H. W. House, 'Tongues and the Mystery Religions of Corinth', *BSac* 140 (1983) 134–50, 147; Thiselton, 'Significance', 320 and *First*, 225.

60 C. E. Arnold, *Ephesians*, Grand Rapids, MI: Zondervan, 2010, 171; cf. O'Brien, *Ephesians*, 216–18.

61 In this translation I have drawn from O'Brien, *Colossians*, 135–55 and J. L. Sumney, *Colossians*, Louisville, KY: Westminster John Knox, 2008, 160.

62 G. Coates, *Non-Religious Christianity*, Shippensburg, PA: Destiny Image, 1998, 1.

63 Moo, *Colossians*, 218, 230; Sumney, *Colossians*, 167.

64 F. L. Shults, *Reforming Theological Anthropology*, Grand Rapids, MI; Cambridge: Eerdmans, 2003, 11, 175. There were forms of both monism and dualism within both Judaism and Greek philosophy (D. E. Aune, 'Two Pauline Models of the Person', in D. E. Aune and J. McCarthy [eds], *The Whole and Divided Self*, New York: Crossroad, 1997, 89–114).

65 Green, *Body*, 37–8, 180; cf. R. S. Smith, 'Joel Green's Anthropological Monism', *CTJ* 7.2 [2010] 19–36.

66 Especially 2:14, 'for he is our peace', wherein peace (*eirēnē*) should be understood in-line with the OT notion of *shalom* as referring to wholeness rather than just the absence of conflict; *shalom* conveys completeness, soundness, welfare and peace (BDB, s.v. שָׁלוֹם); e.g. Isa. 66:12; Jer. 29.7, 11; 33.6; Ezek. 37.26.

67 A. Bloom, *The Living Body of Christ*, London: Darton, Longman and Todd, 2008, 19.

68 Turner notes that, in Ephesians, Paul does not expect the church to reach the full stature of Christ this side of the Parousia (Turner, 'Personhood', 229).

69 A. Destro and M. Pesce, 'Self, Identity, and Body in Paul and John', in A. I. Baumgarten et al. (eds), *Self, Soul and Body in Religious Experience*, Leiden: Brill, 1998, 184–97, citing 193.

70 Christ is the soteriological not ontological mediator; as Holmes notes, God can mediate his own presence (S. R. Holmes, *The Holy Trinity*, Milton Keynes: Paternoster, 2012, 200).

71 Hunt, 'Gnostic', 36–7; Thwaites, *Beyond*, e.g. 87.

72 Turner, 'Personhood', 224–5, 228; Shults, *Anthropology*, 178.

73 Taylor, *Self*, 111; cf. R. A. Di Vito, 'Here One Need Not Be Oneself: The Concept of "Self" in the Hebrew Scriptures', in D. E. Aune and J. McCarthy (eds), *The Whole and Divided Self*, New York: Crossroad, 1997, 49–88.

74 Tanner, *Jesus*, 77; cf. M. Pearse, 'Problem? What Problem? Personhood, Late Modern/Postmodern Rootlessness and Contemporary Identity Crises', *EQ* 77.1 (2005) 5–12.

75 Turner, 'Personhood', 228.

76 E.g. Frost, *Shaping*, 120–1.

77 T. Engberg-Pedersen, 'A Stoic Concept of the Person in Paul?' in C. K. Rothschild and T. W. Thompson (eds), *Christian Body, Christian Self*, Tübingen: Mohr Siebeck, 2011, 85–112, citing 91.

78 A. Daudet, *Notes Sur La Vie*, Paris: Fasquelle, 1899 as cited by W. James, *The Varieties of Religious Experience*, Cambridge: Harvard University Press, 1985, 140.

79 M. M. Antony and R. McCabe, *Overcoming Animal and Insect Phobias*, Oakland, CA: Raincoast, 2005, especially chapter 5 'Confronting Your Fear'; J. K. A. Smith, *Imagining the Kingdom*, Grand Rapids, MI: Baker Academic, 2013, 186.

80 Smith, *Imagining*, 5, 92.

81 Smith, *Imagining*, 153.

82 M. Merleau-Ponty, *Phenomenology of Perception*, trans. C. Smith, London: Routledge, 1962, 189–90 as referred to by Smith, *Imagining*, 64; cf. Chan, *Liturgical*, 94. There is no definitive list of 'Christian practices' that re-contextual thinkers share. Authors' conceptions of Christian practices range from 'extensions of the liturgical practices of gathered worship' (J. K. A. Smith, *Desiring the Kingdom*, Grand Rapids, MI: Baker, 2009, 212–13) to the mission-focused practices Frost promotes, such as 'collaborating with the neighborhood' and 'declaring God's shalom' (M. Frost, *Incarnate*, Downers Grove, IL: IVP, 2014, 167–8). Adams groups practices into those relating to solitude and withdrawal (the cave), those relating to hospitality (the refectory), and those relating to the public sphere (the road) (I. Adams, 'Cave, Refectory, Road: The Monastic Life Shaping Community and Mission', in G. Cray et al. [eds], *New Monasticism as Fresh Expressions of Church*, Norwich: Canterbury, 2010, 37–49).

83 I. H. Marshall, 'How Far Did the Early Christians *Worship* God?' *Chm* 99 (1985) 216–29.

84 Tanner, *Jesus*, 79.

85 Smith, *Imagining*, 168–9.

86 Smith, *Imagining*, 168–9; Ward, *Participation*, 66–80, 126–30.

87 Moynagh, *Context*, 156–61.

88 Smith, *Imagining*, 41, 119.

89 Corcoran, 'Realism', 17.

90 Holmes, 'Social', 83–4; Kilby, 'Problems', 442–3.

91 Referring to Ephesians 2.12–18, Cotterell argues that 'this doctrine of the community of the New Covenant ... makes the very concept of a deliberately constructed homogeneous worshipping congregation not merely unbiblical but actually counter-biblical' (P. Cotterell, *Mission and Meaninglessness*, London: SPCK, 1990, 149–50; cf. M. Turner, 'Mission and Meaning in Terms of "Unity" in Ephesians', in A. Billington et al. [eds], *Mission and Meaning*, Carlisle: Paternoster, 1995, 138–66, esp. 163–4).

92 P. Trebilco, 'Why Did the Early Christians Call Themselves ἡ ἐκκλησία?' *NTS* 57 (2011) 440–60.

93 Moynagh, *Context*, 67–8, 144, 363–4; Ward, *Liquid*, 3, 8, 98 and *Participation*, 103, 180; Murray, *Changing*, 75; *Post-Christendom*, 308 and *Christendom*, 142. Ward blurs the distinction between the local and universal church, which Moynagh and Murray Williams more strongly maintain. Within NT scholarship, it is disputed exactly what size so-called 'house churches' would be (E. Adams, *The Earliest Christian Meeting Places*, London; New York: Bloomsbury T&T Clark, 2013, 30).

94 OED, 'network, n. and adj.', *OED* website (www.oed.com/view/Entry/126342?rskey=iyqWHu&result=1); Castells, *Network*, 501–2; Ward, *Liquid*, 38.

95 Ward, *Liquid*, 14–16, 36–48, 98; cf. Moynagh, *Context*, 171–3; Cray, *Missional*, 8.

96 B. Witherington, *Conflict and Community in Corinth*, Grand Rapids, MI: Eerdmans, 1994, 262–3; J. D. G. Dunn, 'Reconstructions of Corinthian Christianity and the Interpretation of 1 Corinthians', in E. Adams and D. G. Horrell (eds), *Christianity at Corinth*, Louisville; London: Westminster John Knox, 2004, 295–310.

97 R. Banks, *Paul's Idea of Community*, Grand Rapids, MI: Baker Academic, 1995, 37–46; cf. P. T. O'Brien, 'The Church as a Heavenly and Eschatological Entity', in D. A. Carson (ed.), *The Church in the Bible and the World*, Exeter: Paternoster/Grand Rapids, MI: Baker, 1987, 88–119; K. Giles, *What on Earth is the*

Church?, London: SPCK, 1995, 127. Giles argues for a universal view in contrast to Banks (*Cultural*) and O'Brien ('Entity').

98 Lincoln, 'Re-Examination', 470, 478–9 and *Ephesians*, Dallas: Word, 1990, 140, 144; R. Schnackenburg, *Ephesians*, trans. H. Heron, Edinburgh: T&T Clark, 1991, 111–12; K. R. Snodgrass, *Ephesians*, Grand Rapids, MI: Zondervan, 1996, 124, 130.

99 D. Peterson, 'The New Temple: Christology and Ecclesiology in Ephesians and 1 Peter', in T. D. Desmond and S. Gathercole (eds), *Heaven on Earth*, Carlisle: Paternoster, 2004, 161–77; G. K. Beale, *The Temple and the Church's Mission*, Leicester: Apollos; Downers Grove, IL: IVP, 2004, 259–60; Thielman, *Ephesians*, 166–7.

100 F. Mussner, 'Contributions Made by Qumran to the Understanding of the Epistle to the Ephesians', in J. Murphy-O'Connor (ed.), *Paul and Qumran*, London: Geoffrey Chapman, 1968, 159–78; Lincoln, 'Re-Examination', 470–3, 479; O'Brien, 'Entity', 94.

101 O'Brien, 'Entity', 109.

102 F. F. Bruce, *The Epistle to the Ephesians*, London: Pickering & Inglis, 1961, 54; Lincoln, 'Re-Examination', 10–13; O'Brien, 'Entity', 117–18.

103 Lincoln, *Ephesians*, 143, 161; Peterson, 'Temple', 171; B. Witherington, *The Letters to Philemon, the Colossians, and the Ephesians*, Grand Rapids, MI; Cambridge: Eerdmans, 2007, 258.

104 Ward, *Liquid*, 48; Banks, *Cultural*, 37–46; O'Brien, 'Entity'; Giles, *What*, 115–18, 131–3, 146.

105 O'Brien, *Ephesians*, 265.

106 Bloom, *Body*, 61; cf. Healy, *Church*, 36–7.

107 Jones argues, 'It is highly unlikely that the emerging church movement can avoid institutionalization. The question now is how the movement will navigate the ambiguities of routinization as it ages' (Jones, *Flat*, 180); A. I. McFadyen, *The Call to Personhood*, Cambridge: CUP, 1990, 232–3; Giles, *What*, 18; Volf, *Likeness*, 234–5; Ward, *Liquid*, 41; *OED*, 'institution, n.', *OED* website (www.oed.com/view/Entry/97110?redirectedFrom=institution&).

108 Grimes notes that there are both 'hard' and 'soft' definitions of ritual. Hard definitions seek to delineate the notion of ritual such that there is a clear line between what constitutes a ritual and what does not. Soft definitions recognize the incipient nature of rituals, focusing on the process of ritualization rather than limiting rituals to pre-established rites (R. L. Grimes, *Beginnings in Ritual Studies*, 3rd ed., Waterloo: Ritual Studies International, 2013 [1995, 1983], 51–3). A soft notion of ritual is apt in relation to 1 Corinthians 11.23–26 as the Lord's Supper as practised within the early church must not be simplistically and inaccurately equated with established outworkings of the Lord's Supper today, such as Mass (which is a hard ritual). Defining what constitutes a ritual in the soft sense is not straight-forward although, as Bell notes, there is a notable consensus that a ritual is 'a type of critical juncture wherein some pair of opposing social or cultural forces comes together', such as belief and behaviour, the individual and the group, reality and imaginative ideals (C. Bell, *Ritual Theory, Ritual Practice*, Oxford: OUP, 1992, 16). Bell notes, however, that definitions that present rituals as integrating two seem-ingly distinct categories (e.g. thought and action) polarize these categories, usually elevating one above the other (e.g. thought above action). She argues that more holistic definitions are needed since categories perceived to be distinct (e.g. thought and action) are in reality already integrated (Bell, *Ritual*, 45–9). She defines *ritual-*

ization (demonstrating her preference for soft definitions) as 'a way of acting that is designed and orchestrated to distinguish and privilege what is being done in comparison to other, usually more quotidian, activities. As such, ritualization is a matter of various culturally specific strategies for setting some activities off from others, for creating and privileging a qualitative distinction between the "sacred" and the "profane," and for ascribing such distinctions to realities thought to transcend the powers of human actors' (Bell, *Ritual*, 74).

109 W. A. Meeks, *The First Urban Christians*, 2nd ed., New Haven, CT; London: Yale University, 2003 (1983), 142; Witherington, *Conflict*, 258; Thiselton, *First*, 997.

110 Meeks, *Urban*, 78–9, 84, 142–3, 159.

111 *OED*, 'office, n.', *OED* website (www.oed.com/view/Entry/130640?result =2&rskey=Pm3wRQ&).

112 Fee, *First*, 619; H. A. Lombard, 'Charisma and Church Office', *Neot* 10 (1976) 31–52; M. Turner, 'Spiritual Gifts Then and Now', *VE* 15 (1985) 7–63, citing 35.

113 W. J Larkin, *Ephesians*, Waco, TX: Baylor University, 2009, 78 (so too O'Brien, *Ephesians*, 301–3; Arnold, *Ephesians*, 262–4) *contra* Lincoln, *Ephesians*, 253; T. D. Gordon, '"Equipping" Ministry in Ephesians 4?' *JETS* 37.1 (1994) 69–78.

114 Turner, 'Mission', 152–7; Witherington, *Letters*, 292.

115 Arnold, *Ephesians*, 256–9; G. D. Fee, *God's Empowering Presence*, Peabody, MA: Hendrickson, 1994, 707; G. J. Lockwood, *1 Corinthians*, Saint Louis, MO: Concordia, 2000, 452; F. D. Farnell, 'Is the Gift of Prophecy for Today? Part 1', *BSac* 149 (1992) 277–303; J. D. Bayes, 'Five-Fold Ministry', *JPBL* 3.1 (2010) 113–22; M. Turner, *The Holy Spirit and Spiritual Gifts Then and Now*, Carlisle: Paternoster, 1996, 190–5.

116 J. W. Niewold, 'Set Theory and Leadership', *JBPL* 2.1 (2008) 44–63, citing 52.

117 Lincoln, *Ephesians*, 252.

118 M. Turner, 'Ecclesiology in the Major "Apostolic" Restorationist Churches', *VE* 19 (1989) 83–108; Healy, 'Church', 589–601; Lincoln, *Ephesians*, 229–33; Arnold, *Power*, 159.

119 M. Volf, *Exclusion and Embrace*, Nashville, TN: Abingdon, 1996, 20.

120 R. B. Hays, *First Corinthians*, Louisville, KY: John Knox, 1997, 213; cf. Fee, *First*, 601–2.

121 Volf does not deny the importance of social arrangements; he simply states his stress (Volf, *Embrace*, 20–1).

122 Bayes, 'Five-Fold', 117–18.

123 McFadyen, *Personhood*, 232.

124 G. Theissen, *Biblical Faith*, London: SCM, 1984, 149; McFadyen, *Personhood*, 232–6.

125 McFadyen, *Personhood*, 233; Lombard, 'Charisma', 32, 34, 49–50; Lincoln, *Ephesians*, 252.

126 Gibbs, *Next*, 225.

127 McFadyen, *Personhood*, 236.

128 McFadyen, *Personhood*, 236.

129 McFadyen, *Personhood*, 237–9.

130 McFadyen, *Personhood*, e.g. 224.

131 J. Calvin, *Galatians and Ephesians*, trans. W. Pringle, Grand Rapids, MI: Eerdmans; Carlisle: Paternoster, 1965, 185.

132 J. D. G. Dunn, *The Theology of Paul the Apostle*, 3rd ed., London; New York: T&T Clark, 2003, 569.

133 D. G. Horrell, *The Social Ethos of the Corinthian Correspondence*, Edinburgh: T&T Clark, 1996, 288–9.

134 B. McLaren, *Church on the Other Side*, Grand Rapids, MI: Zondervan, 2006, 48.

135 Gibbs, *Next*, 85–91.

136 Marshall, 'Worship', 220–3; Moynagh, *emergingchurch*, 151; Murray, *Changing*, 96.

137 Marshall, 'Worship', 220.

138 D. A. Carson, 'Why the Local Church Is More Important', *Them* 40.1 (2015) 1–9, citing 3.

139 Carson, 'Why', 1–9; Murray, *Post-Christendom*, 308; *Christendom*, 142; Ward, *Liquid*, 3.

140 Moynagh, *Context*, 171–9; cf. Murray, *Changing*, 75. Murray-Williams does not refer to Moynagh's work here but their proposed solutions are similar.

141 Witherington, *Conflict*, 262–3.

142 For instance in Loughborough, church leaders refer to 'the church of Loughborough' in order to convey and build unity across the local churches in that town (e.g. Open Heaven Church, 'Profiles: Ness Wilson', *Open Heaven* website [www.openheaven.org/profile/152]).

143 Ward, *Liquid*, 3; cf. Murray, *Post-Christendom*, 308 and *Christendom*, 142; Trebilco, 'Why', 445–6, 454, 460; O'Brien, 'Entity', 91–4.

144 Lee, *Stoics*, 46–9, 135–6.

145 Murray Williams, *Multi-Voiced*, 20; Ward, *Evangelical*, 15.

146 Murray Williams, *Multi-Voiced*, 3; Turner, 'Gifts', 35; cf. Lombard, 'Charisma', 41, 48.

147 J. C. Beker, *The Triumph of God*, trans. L. T. Stuckenbruck, Minneapolis, MN: Fortress, 1990, 29.

148 Volf, *Likeness*, 7; Flett, *Witness*, 207; Pickard, *Seeking*, 104–8; J. A. Fitzmyer, *First Corinthians*, New Haven, CT; London: Yale University, 2008, 266; Chester, *Mission*, 73; Ward, *Participation*, 5.

149 Moynagh, *Context*, 7, 95, 129, 135–50 and *emergingchurch*, 152; Ward, *Evangelical*, 3; *Participation*, 179, 189 and *Liquid*, 78–86; Murray, *Changing*, 75–6 and *Post-Christendom*, 119; Murray Williams, *Multi-Voiced*, 10.

150 Murray, *Post-Christendom*, 64, 68, 201, 235, 256 and *Changing*, 74–6; Ward, *Participation*, 5; *Evangelical*, 1–3, 153 and *Liquid*, 64, 90; Moynagh, *Context*, 171–80.

151 D. Langmead and C. Garnaut, *Encyclopedia of Architectural and Engineering Feats*, Santa Barbara: ABC-CLIO, 2001, 9; M. Denny, *Super Structures*, Baltimore, MD: Johns Hopkins, 2010, 178–82.

152 Y. Fujino, 'Vibration, Control and Monitoring of Long-Span Bridges', *Journal of Constructional Steel Research* 58 (2002) 71–97; Denny, *Structures*, 179–83.

153 Hesselgrave, *Contextualization*, 1. 'Embody' reflects Moynagh's persuasive view that it is not just the gospel that requires contextualization, but also the church (Moynagh, *Context*, 151–67).

154 Material found below in relation to 1 Corinthians 12 is also incorporated within Morris, 'Foil'.

155 M. Mitchell, *Paul and the Rhetoric of Reconciliation*, Tübingen: Mohr, 1991, 159; Martin, *Body*, 96.

156 Dionysius of Halicarnassus, *Roman Antiquities* 6.86.2–3.

157 Dionysius of Halicarnassus, *Roman Antiquities* 6.86.3–4; cf. Livy, *Ab Urbe Condita* 2.32.7–11; Seneca, *De Clementia* 1.4.3–5.1; Dio Chrysostom, *Discourses* 1.32, 3.104; Plato, *Republic* 5.462c–d; Plutarch, *Moralia* 478–9; cf. Thiselton, *First*, 992–3; Epictetus, *Dissertations* 2.10.4–5; cf. Thiselton, *First*, 992; Mitchell, *Reconciliation*, 158–60; Banks, *Cultural*, 66.

158 Mitchell, *Reconciliation*, 15, 159; Martin, *Body*, 38–9.

159 Beale, *Temple*, 395. Beale also writes, 'our task as the covenant community, the church[,] is to be God's temple, so filled with his glorious presence that we expand and fill the earth with that presence until God finally accomplishes the goal completely at the end of time!' (Beale, *Temple*, 402).

160 Turner, 'Mission', 157.

161 E.g. Exodus 40.34–5; 2 Chronicles 7.1; Ezekiel 43.1, 5; 44.4.

162 H. von Soden, *Die Briefe an die Kolosser, Epheser, Philemon*, HC, Freiburg Mohr, 1891, 111–2, as cited by J. Ernst, *Pleroma und Pleroma Christi: Geschichte und Deutung eines Begriffs der paulinischen Antilegomena, BU 5*, Regensburg: Friedrich Pustet, 1970, 114; Beale, *Temple*, 260; cf. 395; R. L. Foster, 'A Temple in the Lord Filled to the Fullness of God', *NovT* 49 (2007) 85–96; Snodgrass, *Ephesians*, 72. 'The conclusion that "fullness" is a synonym of glory here [1:23] is supported by the density of glory language throughout Ephesians 1 (e.g. in 6, 12, 17, 18)' (Macaskill, *Union*, 150).

163 A noun cannot properly be described as active or passive but *plērōma* can have either a passive sense, in that it is depicting something that is filled with something else, or an active meaning, in that it depicts something that fills something else (e.g. for a bucket filled with water, the fullness of the bucket carries a passive sense but the fullness of the water an active sense).

164 Lincoln, *Ephesians*, 75–7; O'Brien, *Ephesians*, 150.

165 Lincoln, *Ephesians*, 77.

166 Dawes, *Body*, 247; Witherington, *Letters*, 246.

167 M. Barth, *Ephesians 1 – 3*, Garden City, NY: Doubleday, 1974, 205.

168 Cf. Ward, *Participation*, e.g. 95, 105–8, 120, 126–30, 176–9; Tanner, *Key*, 8–11; Macaskill, *Union*, 151.

169 Ward, *Participation*, 177. Moynagh argues, 'Though the church offers the kingdom to the world, it receives gifts of the kingdom from the world. Thus mission is not one-way traffic from the church to people outside ... Mission involves giving and receiving' (Moynagh, *Context*, 104).

170 Differences in socio-economic status are a compelling explanation for the problems with the Lord's Supper. However, the existence of the different 'parties' (1 Cor 1:12) is better explained by the Corinthians' acquaintance with the sophist movement, within which '[a]ttachment to an eminent sophist could enhance one's own status' (Nash, *1 Corinthians*, 27; cf. 22); cf. C. B. Cousar, 'The Theological Task of 1 Corinthians', in D. M. Hay, *Pauline Theology*, vol. 2, Minneapolis, MN: Fortress, 1993, 90–102; G. Theissen, *The Social Setting of Pauline Christianity*, trans. J. H. Schütz, Philadelphia, PA: Fortress, 1975, 95–8, 124–32, 160.

171 K. E. Bailey, *Paul Through Mediterranean Eyes*, London: SPCK, 2011, 325. Since parables are now generally regarded as extended metaphors, rather than alle-

gories, designating the body of Christ metaphor as a parable need not be contentious (K. R. Snodgrass, *Stories with Intent*, Grand Rapids, MI; Cambridge: Eerdmans, 2008, 8, 13).

172 J. M. G. Barclay, 'Thessalonica and Corinth', *JSNT* 47 (1992) 49–74, citing 58 and 60; Mitchell, *Reconciliation*, 120; J. D. G. Dunn, '"The Body of Christ" in Paul', in M. J. Wilkins and T. Paige (eds), *Worship, Theology and Ministry in the Early Church*, Sheffield: Sheffield Academic, 1992, 146–62, citing 161; Lee, *Stoics*, 22; Martin, *Body*, 29, 92.

173 Soskice, *Metaphor*, 62–3; Dunn, 'Body', 162.

174 Martin, *Body*, 96; cf. M. T. Finney, *Honour and Conflict in the Ancient World*, London; New York: T&T Clark, 2012, 183; Thiselton, *First*, 1,008; Witherington, *Conflict*, 259; Best, *Body*, 103.

175 Lee, *Stoics*, 145–6.

176 Lee, *Stoics*, 148; Hays, *First*, 213; Martin, *Body*, 40, 92; Horrell, *Social*, 282–3.

177 M. Gorman, *Inhabiting the Cruciform God*, Grand Rapids, MI; Cambridge: Eerdmans, 2009, 23–4; cf. Lee, *Stoics*, 146.

178 Gorman, *Inhabiting*, 24 (italics his). Similarly, Horrell argues, 'Paul, while in places ideologically legitimating an ecclesiastical hierarchy, does not offer ideological support to the dominant social order. Although there are elements of his teaching which might be developed in this direction, on the whole he is notably critical of the behaviour and practices of the socially strong. He formulates the teaching about the cross in a way which completely inverts the values and positions of the dominant social order ... This ethos [of self-giving and self-lowering] is ... conveyed in Paul's own self-presentation and apostolic lifestyle' (Horrell, *Social*, 282–3).

179 The quotations here are from the New International Version (NIV, 2011).

180 Witherington, *Conflict*, 261; cf. Lee, *Stoics*, 152.

181 Chrysostom, *Homilies on the Epistles of Paul to the Corinthians* 32.2 as cited by G. Bray (ed.), *1 & 2 Corinthians*, Downers Grove, IL: IVP, 1999, 129; cf. Thiselton, *First*, 1015.

182 As Zizioulas asserts, the Spirit 'is not something that "animates" a Church which already somehow exists. The Spirit makes the Church *be*' (Zizioulas, *Being*, 132).

183 Thiselton, *First*, 996; K. Tanner, 'Creation Ex Nihilio', *MTh* 29.2 (2013) 138–55; Hays, *1 Corinthians*, 213.

184 Drawing on Gorman, *Cruciform*, esp. 34 and 39.

185 Gorman, *Cruciform*, 37.

186 House, 'Tongues', 147; cf. Hays, *1 Corinthians*, 206, 213; Thiselton, *First*, 225, 900.

187 Thiselton, 'Significance', 330; Nash, *1 Corinthians*, 362.

188 R. Williams, *Tokens of Trust*, Norwich: Canterbury, 2007, 106.

189 Thiselton, *First*, 866 and 'Significance', 330.

190 Lee, *Stoics*, 133, 146.

191 Thiselton, *First*, 1,065 (italics his).

192 A. C. Thiselton, 'Realized Eschatology at Corinth', *NTS* 24.4 (1978) 510–26, citing 523; Barclay, 'Corinth', 64.

193 T. Schlutz, 'Why They Don't Sing on Sunday Anymore', 21.05.14, *Holy Soup* website (https://holysoup.com/why-they-dont-sing-on-sunday-anymore/).

194 Murray, *Post-Christendom*, 255; Ward, *Selling*, 204.

195 Moynagh, for instance, does not mention postmodernism in his critique of

a kernel-and-husk approach. However, while he convincingly notes that propositions are not at the heart of the Christian faith, relationships are, his argument brings to mind DeYoung's contention that it is impossible to depict Jesus without using propositions. DeYoung sees postmodernism as influencing the diminished value placed on propositional language by at least some re-contextual thinkers (K. DeYoung and T. Kluck, *Why We're Not Emergent*, Chigago, IL: Moody, 2008, 138); cf. Corcoran, 'Realism', 3–22.

196 K. J. Vanhoozer, *Is There Meaning in This Text?*, Leicester: IVP, 1998, 458.

197 Corcoran, 'Realism', 17.

198 Fee, *First*, 558–67. Although not everyone agrees that the community is in view here (Thiselton, *First*, 892).

199 E. Arthur, 'Some Work to Be Done', 22.06.15 *Kouyanet* website (www.kouya.net/?p=7127). Citing a blog post serves to illustrate the way in which academic debates influence practioners. Arthur laments that, 'we have a situation, where some evangelical writers on mission are basing a theory of mission practice on a foundation which is repudiated by some rather serious theologians. As I said, we have a problem.'

200 S. R. Holmes, 'Trinitarian Missiology', *IJST* 8.1 (2006) 72–90; Molnar, *Freedom*, x.

201 Ward, *Liquid*, 58–64; Moynagh, *Changing*, 41–2 and *emergingchurch*, 133.

202 Ward, *Participation*, 176–9.

203 Turner, *Mission*, 163–4.

204 This is a broader conception of 'of' than that held by Moynagh and *MSC*. In Moynagh's work and *MSC* 'of' only refers to the relationship between a local church community and the wider universal church (Moynagh, *Context*, 107–8; Cray, *Mission*, 99).

205 Murray, *Post-Christendom*, 12, 60, 62, 64–8, 72, 83; Ward, *Liquid*, 3, 13–23, 72.

206 Moynagh, *Context*, xiii, 340–3, 431–47; Murray, *Changing*, 117–20 and *Post-Christendom*, 210.

207 Moynagh, *Context*, 109–11, 229–34; Ward, *Liquid*, 2, 47, 66–8, 90–1; Murray Williams, *Multi-Voiced*, xiii, 58, 68.

208 Volf, *Likeness*, 34; Moltmann, *Kingdom*, 161 criticized by Molnar, *Freedom*, 227–8 and Holmes, *Trinity*, 19–20.

209 Thiselton, *First*, 724; cf. 717–18, 750; W. A. Meeks, 'And Rose Up to Play', *JSNT* 16 (1982) 64–78.

210 Fee, *First*, 444; Nash, *1 Corinthians*, 284; Thiselton, *First*, 725, 733–4.

211 W. Schrage, *Der erste Brief an die Korinther*, Neukirchen-Vluyn: Neukirchener, 1991–2001, 2:385–6; cf. Thiselton, *First*, 724–6, 778; C. L. Blomberg, *1 Corinthians*, Grand Rapids, MI: Zondervan, 1994, 191–5, 243; Fee, *First*, 443; A. J. Bandstra, 'Interpretation in 1 Corinthians 10:1–11', *CTJ* 6 (1971) 1–21.

212 Thiselton, *First*, 751.

213 Bandstra, 'Interpretation', 14; cf. Witherington, *Conflict*, 218; Thiselton, *First*, 728–30. Thiselton gives Wisdom of Solomon 2.4 and Philo, *Legum Allegoriae* 2.86 as examples of the identification of the rock with wisdom. He provides Wisdom of Solomon 10.15–18 and 11.4 as further evidence of the association of wisdom with guidance and nourishment.

214 Williams, *Why*, 28.

215 Arnold, *Ephesians*, 179 drawing on Gombis, 'Digression', 316.

216 W. H. Mare, 'Paul's Mystery in Ephesians 3', *BETS* 8 (1965) 77–84; Snodgrass, *Ephesians*, 159; Arnold, *Ephesians*, 187–9; Lincoln, *Ephesians*, 175.

217 H. Hoehner, *Ephesians*, Grand Rapids, MI: Baker Academic, 2002, 379; cf. Arnold, *Ephesians*, 164.

218 Best, *Ephesians*, 269; Mare, 'Mystery', 81; W. S. Campbell, 'Unity and Diversity in the Church', *Transformation* 24.1 (2008) 15–30.

219 A. Runesson, 'Placing Paul', *Svensk Exegetisk Årsbok* 80 (2015) 43–67.

220 D. Moo, *Romans*, Grand Rapids, MI: Eerdmans, 1996, 19; T. R. Schreiner, *Romans*, Grand Rapids, MI, 1998, 10–14. The eviction of Jews from Rome is attested to by Suetonius, *De Vita Claudii* 25.4 (cf. C. G. Kruse, *Romans*, Grand Rapids, MI; Cambridge: Eerdmans, 2012, 1–2).

221 Adams, *Meeting*, 30–3; J. D. G. Dunn, *Romans 9–16*, Dallas, TX: Word, 1988, 891; Schreiner, *Romans*, 4.

222 Moo, *Romans*, 4–5; C. S. Keener, *Romans*, Eugene: Cascade, 2009, 4, 12; S. Spence, *The Parting of the Ways*, Leuven: Peeters, 2004, 322; Kruse, *Romans*, 460.

223 Keener, *Romans*, 8. See also Spence, *Parting*, 296; Schreiner, *Romans*, 21–2.

224 Dunn, *Romans 9–16*, 720.

225 Moo, *Romans*, 763; Keener, *Romans*, 4; Spence, *Parting*, 292; Schreiner, *Romans*, 20.

226 Moo, *Romans*, 764.

227 Spence, *Parting*, 296, 322; Moo, *Romans*, 762–3.

228 Runesson, 'Placing', 15–16.

229 Labanow, *Emerging*, 106.

230 Williams, *Why*, 91.

231 A. MacIntyre, *After Virtue*, 2nd ed., Notre Dame, IN: Notre Dame, 1984 (1981), 2.

232 Smith, *Imagining*, 3–5, 26, 109.

233 Williams, *Why*, 92; Murray, *Post-Christendom*, 210; Labanow, *Emerging*, 109.

234 Williams, *Why*, 97–8.

235 Nash, *1 Corinthians*, 348.

236 Bloom, *Body*, 234.

237 Moynagh, *Context*, 171, Padilla argues in contrast to Moynagh that the early local church communities were counterculturally mixed. He asserts, 'The apostles knew very well that if the acceptance of "people as they are" was to be more than lip-service acceptance it had to take place at the level of the local congregations. Accordingly, they sought to build communities in which right from the start Jews and Gentiles, slaves and free, poor and rich would worship together and learn the meaning of their unity in Christ, although they often had to deal with difficulties arising out of the differences in backgrounds or social status among the converts. That this was the case is well substantiated by a survey of the dealings of the apostles with the churches in the Gentile world, as reflected in the New Testament (C. R. Padilla, 'The Unity of the Church', *IBMR* 6.1 [1982] 23–30).

238 Witherington, *Conflict*, 262–3; Moynagh, *Context*, 67.

239 O. Cullmann, *Unity Through Diversity*, trans. by M. E. Boring, Philadelphia, PA: Fortress, 1988 (1986), 9.

240 This is not to affirm the accuracy of re-contextual thinkers' presentation of the inherited church. Rather, re-contextual conceptions are seen most sharply when pitted against the views they reject.

241 Moynagh, *Context*, 102–4; cf. Ward, *Participation*, 94–5, 108–14, 189–91.

242 Corcoran, 'Kingdom', 65; Moynagh, *Context*, 99–100.

243 Moynagh, *Context*, 99–104; Murray, *Post-Christendom*, 60–72, 83–124.

244 Corcoran, 'Kingdom', 65; Moynagh, *Context*, 99–104; Murray, *Post-Christendom*, 85.

245 L. J. Kreitzer, 'Kingdom of God/Christ' in G. Hawthorne et al. (eds), *Dictionary of Paul and His Letters*, Downers Grove, IL; Leicester: IVP, 1993, 524–6, citing 526.

246 Morris, 'Foil'.

247 G. Klein, 'The Kingdom of God', *Interpretation* 26.4 (1972) 378–418, citing 411; Thompson, *Church*, 14, 202–6.

248 C. F. D. Moule, 'The Influence of Circumstances on the Use of Eschatological Terms', in C. F. D. Moule (ed.), *Essays in New Testament Interpretation*, Cambridge: CUP, 1982, 184–99, citing 197–8.

249 Thompson, *Church*, 202–6; Arnold, *Ephesians*, 48; Hoehner, *Ephesians*, 284; J. Lowe, 'Development in St. Paul's Theology', *JTS* 42 (1941) 129–42.

250 Thiselton, 'Realized', 523; T. R. Schreiner, *Paul*, Leicester: Apollos; Downers Grove, IL: IVP, 2001, 92; Barclay, 'Corinth', 64.

251 Moule, 'Eschatological', 197; Lincoln, *Ephesians*, lxxxix–xc.

252 Nash, *1 Corinthians*, 347; B. D. Smith, 'Lord's Supper', *BBR* 20.4 (2010) 517–44; Schrage, *Erste*, 3:57.

253 W. C. Kaiser, 'The Old Promise and the New Covenant', *JETS* 15 (1972) 11–23.

254 Thiselton, *First*, 865–6; cf. Fee, *First*, 550–1, 564; Nash, *1 Corinthians*, 342, 348.

255 T. G. Gombis, 'Haustafel in Ephesians', *JETS* 48 (2005) 317–30; Arnold, *Ephesians*, 369–70; Witherington, *Letters*, 183–4; C. Keener, *Paul, Women and Wives*, Peabody, MA: Hendrickson, 1992, 145–8; 157–72; V. R. Mollenkott, 'Emancipative Elements in Ephesians 5.21–33', in A-J. Levine (ed.), *Feminist Companion to Paul*, London; New York: T&T Clark, 2003, 37–58.

256 Gombis, 'Haustafel', 322 (italics mine).

257 For arguments in favour of 'leader' see W. Grudem, 'Does κεφαλή ("Head") Mean "Source" Or "Authority Over"?', *TrinJ* 6.1 (1985) 38–59 and 'The Meaning of κεφαλή', *JETS* 44.1 (2001) 25–65; for 'source' see R. S. Cervin, 'Does *Kephalē* Mean "Source" or "Authority Over"', *TrinJ* 10 (1989) 85–112. Wolters argues that neither rendering enjoys much extra-biblical support (A. Wolters, 'Head as Metaphor in Paul', *Koers* 76.1 [2011] 137–53, citing 139). On OT anthropology see J. Wilkinson, 'The Body in the Old Testament', *EQ* 63.3 (1991), 195–210.

258 Calvin, *Ephesians*, 287. On Ephesians 1 see Arnold, *Ephesians*, 115; Snodgrass, *Ephesians*, 78.

259 Witherington, *Ephesians*, 187; Thielman, *Ephesians*, 379; Lincoln, *Ephesians*, 373; O'Brien, *Ephesians*, 409; Mollenkott, 'Emancipative', 45.

260 Mollenkott, 'Emancipative', 49. See also Turner, 'Mission', 155, where he writes that 'Paul simply expresses the conventional view that the husband is master of the household to whom the wife should be submissive (cf. 1 Pet. 3:1, 5–6). But in what follows Paul rescues the apparent subjugation of 5:22–23 from the possibility of its degeneration into an alienating domination. The Lord's own self-denying sacrificial love for the church is the pattern for the husband's "lordship", and it is that of the ardent lover which seeks only the good of the beloved (5:25–27).'

261 Gombis, 'Haustafel', 322; Arnold, *Ephesians*, 380; Turner, 'Mission', 153–4; Lincoln, *Ephesians*, 393.

262 Klein, 'Kingdom', 411; W. J. Webb, *Slaves, Women and Homosexuals*, Downers Grove, IL: IVP, 2001, 80; Mollenkott, 'Emancipative', 41.

263 Fee, *First*, 557.

264 Thielman, *Ephesians*, 386.

265 Arnold, *Ephesians*, 389.

266 Lincoln, *Ephesians*, 377, 389; Best, *Ephesians*, 545.

267 M. Luther, 'Commentary on 1 Corinthians 15', in H. C. Oswald (ed.), *Luther's Works*, Vol. 18, Saint Louis: Concordia, 1973, 57–213, citing 124.

268 Morris, 'Foil'.

269 Thiselton, *First*, 888.

270 Thiselton, *First*, 880.

271 Thiselton, *First*, 879–80 drawing on Ricoeur's notion of 'narrative identity' in P. Ricoeur, *Oneself as Another*, trans. K. Blamey, Chicago, IL: Chicago, 1992, 17.

272 E.g. Nash, *1 Corinthians*, 342; *contra* those who argue it must be either/or (e.g. Fee argues for the church and Thiselton Christ's body [Fee, *First*, 564; Thiselton, *First*, 893]).

273 Chan, *Liturgical*, 29.

274 Lincoln, *Ephesians*, 381.

275 O'Brien, *Ephesians*, 433–4; cf. Lincoln, *Ephesians*, 381; Gombis, 'Haustafel', 322; Schreiner, *Paul*, 233.

276 To adapt Luther's parlance (Luther, '1 Corinthians 15', 124; cf. Morris, 'Foil').

277 The inclusion of the 'towards' trajectory as part of the church's core identity is significant in light of Labanow's contention that the particular UK 'emerging' church that he examined lacked a clear teleology. He suggests that many other churches may also be teleologically deficient (Labanow, *Emerging*, 115).

278 Cray, 'Communities', 18.

279 Moynagh, *Context*, 101–4.

280 When, as McKnight expresses it, the kingdom is seen as simultaneously everywhere and nowhere (McKnight, *Kingdom*, 13).

281 Moynagh, *Context*, 100–1; Hull, *Response*, 36.

282 McKnight, *Kingdom*, 3–4, 9, 15, 74, 81, 91.

283 McKnight, *Kingdom*, 87.

284 McKnight, *Kingdom*, 96.

285 McKnight, *Kingdom*, 91–100.

286 Moynagh, *Context*, 102.

287 McKnight, *Kingdom*, 153.

288 Moule, 'Eschatological', 189.

289 Pickard, *Seeking*, 101–17; Tanner, *Key*, 228; M. Chapman, 'The Social Doctrine of the Trinity: Some Problems', *ATR* 83.2 (2001) 239–54, esp. 248.

290 Phillips, *Bridges*, 52.

291 Dunn, *Colossians*, 116; H. Stettler, 'An Interpretation of Colossians 1:24 in the Framework of Paul's Mission Theology', in J. Ådna and H. Kvalbein (eds), *The Mission of the Early Church to Jews and Gentiles*, Tübingen: Mohr Siebeck, 2000, 185–208; Best, *Body*, 136; O'Brien, *Colossians*, 77; R. J. Bauckham, 'Colossians 1:24 Again: The Apocalyptic Motif', *EQ* 47.3 (1975) 168–70; Schreiner, *Paul*, 486.

292 O'Brien, *Colossians*, 76.

293 Dunn, *Colossians*, 114, 121–3; Moo, *Colossians*, 34–5; O'Brien, *Colossians*, 76, 161; Schreiner, *Paul*, 87, 93, 97; Bruce, *Colossians*, 81; S. Hafemann, 'The Role

of Suffering in the Mission of Paul', in J. Ådna and H. Kvalbein (eds), *The Mission of the Early Church to Jews and Gentiles*, Tübingen: Mohr Siebeck, 2000, 165–84.

294 Dunn, *Colossians*, 227–8; J. Gnilka, *Der Kolosserbrief*, Freiburg: Herder, 1980, 194; A. Lindemann, *Der Kolosserbrief*, Zürich: Theologischer Verlag, 1983, 60; R.McL. Wilson, *Colossians and Philemon*, London; New York: T&T Clark, 2005, 256–7; Moo, *Colossians*, 270–9; Bruce, *Colossians*, 154; O'Brien, *Colossians*, 191, 198. By idealism I mean, 'aspiration after or pursuit of an ideal' (*OED*, 'idealism, n.', *OED* website [www.oed.com/view/Entry/90960?redirected From=idealism&]).

295 Bruce, *Colossians*, 157.

296 Chapman, 'Social', 248.

297 Dunn, *Colossians*, 230. See also Gnilka, *Kolosserbrief*, 194; O'Brien, *Colossians*, 198–200; Moo, *Colossians*, 278.

298 Bruce, *Colossians*, 154, 230; S. Walton, *Leadership and Lifestyle*, Cambridge: CUP, 2000, 76; J. Davies, *Ephesians, Colossians and Philemon*, 2nd ed., London: Macmillan, 1884, 259; Lindemann, *Kolosserbrief*, 60–1.

299 Dunn, *Colossians*, 232–4; Moo, *Colossians*, 274, 283.

300 Moo, *Colossians*, 285; O'Brien, *Colossians*, 206.

301 O'Brien, *Colossians*, 208; Moo, *Colossians*, 274–5.

302 Moo, *Colossians*, 286.

303 BDAG, s.v. νουθετέω (italics mine).

304 Moo, *Colossians*, 289–91; Bruce, *Colossians*, 158; Gnilka, *Kolosserbrief*, 200; Dunn, *Colossians*, 236–7.

305 Turner, 'Mission', 165.

306 Bloom, *Body*, 15–18.

307 M. Percy, 'A Theology of Change for the Church', in G. R. Evans and M. Percy (eds), *Managing the Church?*, Sheffield: Sheffield Academic, 2000, 174–88, esp. 184–6.

308 R. Langmead, *The Word Made Flesh*, Lanham: University Press of America, 2004, 1, 21–31, 124; D. L. Guder, 'Incarnation and the Church's Evangelistic Mission', *IRM* 83 (1994) 417–28; J. A. Mackay, *Ecumenics*, Englewood Cliffs, NJ: Prentice Hall, 1964, 173.

309 J. T. Billings, 'Incarnational Ministry and Christology', *Missiology* 32.2 (2004) 187–201, citing 188.

310 Langmead, *Flesh*, 3; Billings, *Union*, 132–7; R. Fung in a lecture on evangelism in 1993 as cited by Langmead, *Flesh*, 2.

311 Langmead, *Flesh*, 60–72, 292; Moynagh, *Context*, 181–93.

312 Billings, *Union*, 151–60.

313 P. L. Metzger, 'Fleshed Out', 26.08.12, *Uncommon God, Common Good* website (http://blogs.christianpost.com/uncommon-God-common-good/fleshed-out-the-false-dilemma-of-union-with-christ-versus-incarnational-ministry-11583/); cf. Billings, *Union*, 142; Langmead, *Flesh*, 234.

314 Moynagh, *Context*, 185–7.

315 Cray, *Mission*, 89.

316 J. Moltmann, *Theology of Hope*, Minneapolis, MN: Fortress, 1993, 21.

317 Murray Williams, *Multi-Voiced*, 91–6; Murray, *Christendom*, 26–31 and *Why*, 58–9. Murray Williams does not explicitly connect mutual accountability with the centre-set model but they clearly relate closely to each other.

318 Murray Williams, *Multi-Voiced*, 88.

Conclusion

The re-contextual movement has been largely led by practitioners who have innovatively and pragmatically sought to create more accessible modes of church within the contemporary world. Scholarly reflection has contributed to the conversation, providing theological justification and direction to support and guide practitioners' work. Within this reflection, attempts to formulate an underlying ecclesiology for the movement have often drawn on Social Trinitarian models, while predominantly assuming a free church conception of church. As I argue above, however, social models of the Trinity have received significant criticism, suggesting that they are an inadequate foundation for re-contextual concerns. In contrast, I contend that an ecclesiology based on Paul's body of Christ metaphor overcomes the weaknesses of Social Trinitarian models, adding substance and stability to the movement, while enabling the flexibility required for the church to contextualize into different subcultures.

Bringing the re-contextual church conversation into dialogue with Paul's body of Christ texts results in a series of tensions that the church must maintain in order to adapt faithfully to its current milieu. The stabilizing effect of these tensions, I argue, is best illustrated via the metaphor of a suspension bridge. Indeed, highlighting the five main components that a suspension bridge consists of helps to communicate and conceptualize my contentions. These five components are: a main cable that bears most of the tension that holds the bridge up; the vertical cables that attach the deck to the main cable; the deck; two anchorages at either end of the bridge that fasten it to the earth; and compression towers to counteract the tension in the rest of the structure. Regarding these components, I argue the following:

First, just as a suspension bridge is upheld by its main cable, so the church exists within the tension between God's transcendence and immanence, wherein God's transcendence enables his immanence *(down)*.

Second, as the suspension cables connect the deck to the main cable, so the church's relationship to God *(up)* is maintained within the tension created by its identity as spiritual and religious.

Third, the church's dependence on and orientation towards God determines its internal relationships. In this regard, just as the deck of a suspension bridge is itself held in tension in order to remain stable, so too the church's internal relationships *(in)* are maintained within the tension between the spontaneity and fluidity of relational networks and the ordered formality of institutional structures.

Fourth, the church's Godward focus has implications for its relationships with the wider world. A suspension bridge must connect to its wider context and be structured such that it avoids the damage caused by excessive resonance. So too the church must be both inculturated (cultural) and countercultural in order to connect with its context *(out)* while avoiding excessive resonance.

Fifth, the church is dependent not just on God's sustaining power but his acts in history. A suspension bridge is anchored on both sides. So too the church's anchoring in Christ's life, death, resurrection and ascension involves the church embracing its historical identity as inherited while innovatively responding to the Spirit's ongoing creativity and vitality in the present *(of)*.

Sixth, the church is an eschatological entity, anchored between Christ's historical acts in the past and his future return *(towards)*. The church is located within the now/not yet tension of the kingdom that was inaugurated with Christ and will be consummated upon his return.

Lastly, the tension within a suspension bridge is counterbalanced by compression towers. So too the church, as located within the now/not yet of the kingdom, experiences compression through suffering and conflict *(between)*.

I conceptualize these tensions through the ancient conundrum of the 'One', 'Many', and 'One and Many'. I utilize this notion because the philosophical challenge of the 'One and Many' exemplifies the need for dialectical tensions to be upheld; the 'One' and 'Many' collapse into each other if the 'One and Many' tension is not maintained (if 'One' is prioritized over 'Many' or vice versa). Similarly, for all the tensions that I have identified in this book, both sides of each tension must be maintained, rather than a central road forged between two extremes.

Down: God's Transcendence and Immanence

Ecclesiology must be based on examination into who God is and who the church is in relation to him. In this book, I propose a Trinitarian ecclesiology for the re-contextual church founded on the tension between God's transcendence and immanence. Within the body of Christ metaphor, God's transcendence and immanence are neither amalgamated nor separated since, from the creature's perspective, God's transcendence is known only through his immanence. God's transcendence is his essential otherness as a monotheistic unity in contrast to all that he has created ('one'). Within the body of Christ texts, God's immanence is expressed through the gift of himself, as three-persons-in-one (Father, Son and Spirit), and this gift is manifest in various forms as God interacts with a plurality of creatures ('many'). It is God's nature as the transcendent creator that enables his intimate presence with his creation (his transcendence enables his immanence). The myriad of interactions between God and his creation point to God's one essential being; what God reveals about himself is a true reflection of who he is even if finite human beings only ever grasp his nature partially and imperfectly ('one and many').

Re-contextual thinkers should root their understanding of church in the Christocentric Trinitarian ecclesiology provided by the body of Christ texts, rather than social models of the Trinity. Within a Christocentric Trinitarian ecclesiology, the church participates in the Trinity's life through its union with Christ; Christ's identity as the fullness of God made flesh (Col. 1.19–22) is the basis for believers' experience of this transcendent fullness through God's Spirit (Col. 2.9–10; Eph. 3.16–19). Christ is the model, however, as well as the means; Christ in his human embodiedness, not speculative constructions of the Trinity, is the church's paradigm. Christ is the incarnate Son and thus unique, but Paul urges his readers to follow Christ's example (Col. 3.12–17). Moreover, the body of Christ texts flesh out what participation in the Trinity's life as Christ's body means in concrete historical circumstances (those into which Paul wrote). The contemporary church's context is different from Paul's and therefore interpreting Paul's letters in today's world is not straightforward. Engaging in biblical exegesis, however, reduces the likelihood that one will read into the Trinity's life a preconceived ecclesial or political agenda to then apply the same, now legitimated, conception back into church or society (as Social Trinitarians have been criticized for).

Founding re-contextual ecclesiology on the body of Christ metaphor involves a re-evaluation of God's transcendence and immanence but not through 'pulling harder' on one end of this tension. Rather, re-contextual thinkers should pursue a conception of God as both more powerful and transcendent *and* more intimate and immanent than, they would maintain, the Western church has currently grasped. One consequence of this would be a nuancing of Moynagh's suggestion that the church becomes 'more immanent, more immersed in daily life, *without losing the transcendent*' to *by highlighting God's transcendence*.[1] The church must point people to God's otherness in such a way that his involvement in creation is emphasized. This is not to say that certain activities cannot have a particular focus; it could be beneficial to hold, one week, an alternative worship event that focuses on the intangible mystery of God's sovereignty in its paradoxical relationship to human responsibility and, the next, a practical workshop investigating how God's sovereignty over creation affects a believer's approach to financial stewardship. However, just as the practical exhortation 'Go to the ant, you lazybones' (Prov. 6.6, NRSV) exists in the same scriptural canon as awed statements such as 'his understanding is unsearchable' (Isa. 40.28, NRSV), both activities must be located in an overarching framework that recognizes that God is intimately involved in his creation *because of* (not in spite of) his otherness.

In addition, God's transcendence enables him to bring believers into a relationship of (unequal) reciprocity; their ability to give to God is itself a gift from him. As Chan contends, even worship is an act of God because, although it is the normative human response to God's self-disclosure, it is a response inspired by God's Spirit.[2] Nuance is vital when speaking of gift-exchange between the church and the Godhead. The church does not give to God in an absolute sense, as if it had something to offer that God needed but did not have. Rather, enabling the church to give to God is one of the most startling and profound aspects of God's self-giving.

Up: The Church as Spiritual and Religious

Second only to reflection on God himself is investigation into the church's Godward orientation, which is maintained within the tension created by believers' identity as both spiritual and religious. Although 'spiritual' and 'religious' used to be synonymous, they now represent different, but inseparable, aspects of believers' relationship with God. Spirituality (nowadays) means an individual's personal, subjective, spontaneous and unmediated experience of God ('one'). Religion refers to the relational, objective, structured and mediated nature of believers' relation to God ('many'). Again, the two cannot be separated ('one and many'); the individual, subjective, spontaneous and unmediated aspects of believers' relationship with God in Christ and through the Spirit (spiritual) must be held in tension with that which is communal, objective, structured and mediated (religious). Believers are called and empowered to participate in gift-exchange with God as embodied relational persons.

In contrast to social models of the Trinity, which have been criticized for leading either to dualism or panentheistic monism, the tension between God's transcendence and immanence as evidenced within the body of Christ texts enables a truly holistic anthropology. Believers are a temple of the Spirit as embodied beings (1 Cor. 6.19); their whole lives are under Christ's lordship and constitute their gift to him. Since believers encounter God bodily, what they do physically affects their relationship with him. Disciplines such as prayer, meditation on Scripture, solitude, silence and so on are not sacred in the sense that the rest of life is secular; nor are they cause-and-effect. However, these disciplines affect people's relationship with God since they help believers to position themselves to meet with him. Rather than restricting God's presence to such practices, spiritual disciplines help believers to experience God's presence in the entirety of their lives – just as a phone call with a friend facilitates a friendship that extends beyond the call.

A holistic anthropology based on God's otherness counteracts the contradiction within the re-contextual movement wherein, on the one hand, religion is conveyed negatively and yet, on the other, religious practices are encouraged. If this is a real contradiction, re-contextual thinkers should rethink their rhetoric. If it were an apparent contradiction, the problem would be more severe (if re-contextual thinkers were to promote spiritual practices in the individualistic pick 'n' mix mode of postmodern spirituality, whereby practices are removed from their wider narrative and incorporated into a framework of the practitioner's own making). An ecclesiology based on Paul's body of Christ texts refutes the notion that spiritual practices can be removed from the Christ-centred Christian story and remain Christian. This is not what re-contextual thinkers seek to do. However, the rhetoric of spiritual but not religious, if not nuanced, risks conveying and endorsing such an approach.

In: The Church as a Network and an Institution

The church's dependence on and orientation towards God determines its internal relationships. In this regard, the body of Christ texts indicate that the church's internal relationships are maintained within the tension between the spontaneity and fluidity of relational networks and the ordered formality of institutional structures. There is one universal/ heavenly church whose unity is not maintained via a single institutional structure but by believers' connection to Christ and thereby each other. Informal networked relationships are thus constitutive of the church ('one'). Alongside informal networks, however, this one church expresses itself in a variety of institutional forms ('many'). The health and growth of the church is dependent on the inseparable interaction between the two ('one and many'). Gift-exchange within the Christian community is best facilitated when informality and spontaneity interact and intersect with formality and structure, and vice versa.

Trinitarian ecclesiologies based on speculative reflections on the Trinity's inner nature are not just overly idealistic (underplaying the church's brokenness and sinfulness) but overlook the church's essential embodiedness. In contrast, within an ecclesiology based on the body of Christ metaphor, the church's union with Christ and infilling of the Spirit, through which it encounters the Father, are not pitted against order, structure and ritual. Indeed, in 1 Corinthians 12.12–31, Paul introduces the body of Christ metaphor in criticism of the over-elevation of individual autonomy and ecstatic spontaneity as expressed by the self-styled *pneumatikoi*.[3] There is a place for spontaneity and informality within the church's internal relationships, but informal, spontaneous, creative, networked relationships need to be maintained in dialectical tension with formal, planned, stable, institutional structures so that the church is best able to facilitate gift-exchange within its internal relationships. Moynagh and Murray Williams are right to warn that Christian communities that abandon all formal structures in favour of spontaneity and informality alone are liable to decease through dissipation. Conversely, communities whose structures become too rigid and unchangeable likely face death through stagnation.[4]

Out: The Church as Cultural (Inculturated) and Countercultural

The church's Godward focus has implications for its relationships with the wider world. A suspension bridge must connect to its wider context and be structured such that it avoids the damage caused by excessive resonance. Resonance occurs when the vibrational frequency provoked by external stimuli accords too closely with the natural frequency of the bridge, causing an exponential increase in the power of these vibrations and the eventual collapse of the bridge. So too the church must be both inculturated (cultural) and countercultural in order to connect with its context while avoiding excessive resonance.

'Cultural' represents the church's sameness to its context that is both inevitable (the church cannot be acultural) and desirable such that the church is accessible to those around it. This adaptation to the surrounding culture results in various expressions of church ('many'). 'Countercultural' emphasizes the church's calling to be prophetically distinct from its context, exhibiting redemption in place of fallenness ('one'). Determining what it means for the church to be cultural and countercultural is not straightforward. The complex interaction between message and medium, theology and culture, and content and form, as believers seek to communicate and live out the *one* vision of church that lies behind the body of Christ image, means that the two ends of the tension can neither be separated nor amalgamated ('one and many'). The body of Christ metaphor presents the church as both embedded in and distinct from its context. By being both accessible to and apart from its context, the church can best be a gift to, and receive gifts from, the wider world.

Paul's adoption and adaptation of the body metaphor (which was common in socio-political rhetoric) provides an example of how this tension can be maintained in practice. As I argue above, Paul's contextualization of the body motif accords with the suspension bridge framework that I am promoting in this book. This indicates that *the church as a suspension bridge of gift-exchange* provides a helpful model for contextualization, as well as for understanding the nature of church.

Social models of the Trinity often leave mission in the periphery or promote universalism. In contrast, an ecclesiology based on the body of Christ texts provides a foundation for seeing God as missional, and the church as joining his mission (*missio Dei*), without speculation into how this relates to God's inner being. God's presence is not restricted to the church, which re-contextual thinkers emphasize through their focus on seeing what God is doing and joining him. However, the body of Christ image also highlights the church's unique nature as a locus of God's presence and its corresponding calling to manifest this presence within the wider world.

Of: The Church as Inherited and Innovative

The church is dependent on God's sustaining power and his initiating and conclusive acts in history. Within the body of Christ image, the church's anchoring in Christ's life, death, resurrection and ascension involves the church embracing its historical identity as inherited, acknowledging the Spirit's work in the past, while innovatively responding to the Spirit's ongoing creativity and vitality in the present. 'Inherited' regards the continuity of the ('one') church through history. 'Innovative' expresses the variety of forms that this church takes ('many'). The two cannot be separated but must be addressed together ('one and many'). In every context the church must display continuity with what has gone before it, incorporating the gift of the past, while embracing certain aspects of discontinuity as it engages afresh with its current locale.

Within the body of Christ texts, the church is presented as concurrently fully inherited and fully innovative. For Paul, the continuity between God's actions in Christ and in ethnic Israel's history is so absolute that he sees Christ in this history (1 Cor. 10.4, 9). The discontinuity is such that the church, formed as Jewish and Gentile believers become 'co-members' (Eph. 3.6), is 'one new human' (Eph. 2.15) and 'the mystery' of the Christ-event (Eph. 3.3–4) is new revelation (Eph. 3.5). The church is simultaneously rooted in God's actions in history and a radically new entity. These two features of the church's nature must be held in tension. However, as regards the practical application of this tension, while Paul does not promote a middle ground between two extremes, he does indicate scope for disagreement. Within Romans 12.3–8, Paul promotes unity in diversity, not uniformity. The explicit import of the body of Christ metaphor in this passage regards the diversity of spiritual gifts, but the wider context indicates that the tension between Jewish and Gentile believers is also in view. Rather than resolve this tension by urging all the believers to accord to one particular church style, structure or leader, Paul encourages believers to see themselves in their differences as a gift to each other.

In applying this to the re-contextual church, an exact equation cannot be made between the early church's relationship with ethnic Israel and the contemporary church's connection to the church in previous eras. However, there are points of resonance. In order to work out its concurrently inherited and innovative nature, the church is called to immerse itself in God's story, live as a eucharistic community, and form connections across different expressions, recognizing that each expression has a unique gift to offer the wider body.

Towards: Pursuing the Gift of the Future

The body of Christ texts present the church as an eschatological entity, anchored between Christ's historical acts in the past and his future return. The church is located within the tension between the 'now' and 'not yet' of the kingdom that was inaugurated with Christ and will be consummated upon his return. 'Now' highlights that the church is called and empowered to manifest the future unity of all things under Christ in ('many') different ways. 'Not yet' emphasizes the hope of the ('one') future reality that believers look forward to. These two sides to the church's eschatological nature are distinct but cannot be separated ('one and many'). The church is best able to pursue the gift of the future when it embraces both the now and not yet aspects of its current eschatological existence.

Critics of Social Trinitarianism argue that its proponents present God as dependent on eschatology, undermining his freedom, and emphasize

God's presence in creation to the extent that the church's unique identity and role is overlooked. An ecclesiology based on the body of Christ texts acknowledges God's presence outside the church but highlights the church's unique nature and role. The church as Christ's body is an alternative community that imperfectly and incompletely anticipates the future consummation of God's kingdom in the present. The body of Christ texts reveal what this looks like in practice, particularly through the idealized vision of love, mutual submission and self-giving presented in Ephesians 5.21–33 (cf. Eph. 5.1–20; 1 Cor. 12.12–31; Eph. 4.1–16; Col. 3.12–17). However, the kingdom can no more be constrained to the church than God is. The body of Christ motif thus supports re-contextual thinkers' assertion that the church should be alert to Spirit-brought glimpses of the kingdom in the world.

Between: The Role of Suffering and Conflict

The tension within a suspension bridge is counterbalanced by compression towers. So too the church, as located within the 'now/not yet' of the kingdom, experiences compression through suffering and conflict. Within the body of Christ texts conflict and suffering are presented as essential parts of the church's existence this side of Christ's return, not as ends in them-

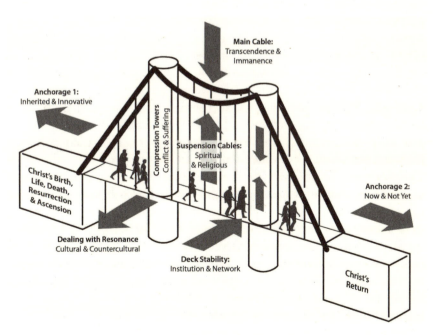

Figure 1: The Church as a Suspension Bridge Characterized by Gift-Exchange

selves but inevitable by-products of the collision between God's incoming kingdom and the fallen world it usurps. Rather than seek to avoid or deny suffering and conflict, the church must navigate both by jettisoning idealistic blueprint ecclesiologies in favour of those that intentionally address these darker aspects of the church's life and growth.

In Conclusion

What might this suspension bridge framework contribute to re-contextual expressions of church, such as those that I referred to in the introduction to this book (see Figure 1)? My hope is that the suspension bridge framework facilitates the flexibility and stability that the contemporary church needs to faithfully communicate and demonstrate the good news of Jesus in a range of different contexts. To this end, I believe that this framework provides a helpful diagnostic tool by which church expressions can evaluate their strengths and weaknesses, and identify any imbalances that may have arisen as they react to and interact with their cultural locale.

For example, re-contextual churches need to make sure that, within their efforts to highlight God's immanent concern for all aspects of work and life, the awe, majesty and mystery of God's transcendence is not overlooked. Similarly, in helpfully highlighting believers' individual and subjective experiences of God, which connects well with the contemporary church's spiritually-minded context, re-contextual expressions of church should ensure that the corporate, inherited and dogmatic components of the Christian faith are not sidelined. In rightly encouraging the growth of authentic friendships outside the weekly congregational meeting, re-contextual thinkers should not underestimate the formational power of healthy institutional structures and formal gatherings.

In creatively pursuing innovative church expressions that connect with different subcultures, re-contextual thinkers should not lose sight of the church's inherited and countercultural nature. To this end, immersion in Scripture and an informed understanding of church history are vital; a thorough knowledge of the Bible, and an awareness of the church's past, enable the church to be a faithful expression of Christ's body while adapting appropriately to its context. Genuine connections with the wider body of Christ are also essential. In addition, the re-contexual church should not lose sight of the traditions and disciplines that believers have found formative and life-giving over past centuries.

In pursuing the presence of the kingdom in the here and now, the re-contextual church should also acknowledge the church's current imperfect state by, for instance, actively preparing and equipping itself for the inevitability of suffering and conflict. And, while urging the church to manifest the kingdom in both its internal relationships and the wider world, the re-contextual church must also highlight the church's calling to proclaim afresh in every era the good news of the king.

Notes

1 Moynagh, *Context*, 86 [italics mine].

2 Chan writes, 'it is the Spirit of the Son in the assembly who rightly responds to the Father, causing us to cry out, "Abba, Father!" (Rom 8.15). In true worship there is an inherent fittingness of the response to the One who reveals himself as who he is, because it comes ultimately from the Spirit of God who indwells the body of Christ' (Chan, *Liturgical*, 47). Chan also notes that 'all true worship must begin with the truth that everything we are and have is a gift' (Chan, *Liturgical*, 53).

3 Turner, 'Gifts', esp. 27–8, 35; cf. Thiselton, 'Significance', esp. 331.

4 Murray, *Changing*, 96; Moynagh, *emergingchurch*, 151.

Bibliography

Primary Sources

Dio Chrysostom, *Discourses*, trans. J. W. Cohoon, 5 vols, LCL, Cambridge, MA: Harvard University Press, 1932–51.

Dionysius of Halicarnassus, *Roman Antiquities*, trans. E. Cary, 7 vols, LCL, Cambridge: MA: Harvard University Press, 1937–50.

Epictetus, *Dissertations*, trans. G. Long, 4 vols, ICA (http://classics.mit.edu/Epictetus/discourses.html, accessed 23 October 2015).

Holmes, M. W. (ed.), *The Greek New Testament: SBL Edition*, Bellingham: Lexham; Society of Biblical Literature, 2011–13.

John Chrysostom, *Homilies on the Epistles of Paul to the Corinthians*, CCEL (www.ccel.org/ccel/schaff/npnf112.toc.html, accessed 23 October 2015).

Livy, *History of Rome (Ab Urbe Condita Libri)*, trans. B. O. Foster et al., 14 vols, LCL, Cambridge, MA: Harvard University Press, 1919–59.

Plato, *Republic*, trans. P. Shorey, 2 vols, LCL, Cambridge, MA: Harvard University Press, 1930–35.

Plutarch, *Moralia*, trans. F. C. Babbitt et al., 16 vols, LCL, Cambridge, MA: Harvard University Press, 1927–2004.

Seneca, *Moral Essays*, trans. J. W. Basore, 3 vols, LCL, Cambridge, MA: Harvard University Press, 1928.

Secondary Sources

Adams, E. and D. G. Horrell (eds), *Christianity at Corinth: The Quest for the Pauline Church*, Louisville, KY; London: Westminster John Knox, 2004.

Adams, E., *The Earliest Christian Meeting Places: Almost Exclusively Houses?*, LNTS, London; New York: Bloomsbury; T&T Clark, 2013.

Ådna, J. and H. Kvalbein (eds), *The Mission of the Early Church to Jews and Gentiles*, WUNT 127, Tübingen: Mohr Siebeck, 2000.

Ankerberg, J. and J. Weldon, *Encyclopedia of New Age Beliefs*, Eugene, OR: Harvest House, 1996.

Arnold, C. E., *Ephesians*, ZECNT, Grand Rapids, MI: Zondervan, 2010.

Arnold, C. E., *Power and Magic: The Concept of Power in Ephesians in Light of its Historical Setting*, SNTSMS, Cambridge: CUP, 1989.

Arnold, C. E., *The Colossian Syncretism: The Interface Between Christianity and Folk Belief at Colossae*, WUNT 77, Tübingen: Mohr Siebeck, 1995.

Arthur, E., 'Some Work to Be Done', 22.06.15 *Kouyanet* website (www.kouya.net/?p=7127, accessed 6 August 2015).

Ashworth, J., Research Matters and I. Farthing, *Churchgoing in the UK: A Research Report from Tearfund on Church Attendance in the UK*, London: Tearfund, 2007.

Aune, D. E. and J. McCarthy (eds), *The Whole and Divided Self*, New York: Crossroad, 1997.

Bailey, K. E., *Paul Though Mediterranean Eyes: Cultural Studies in 1 Corinthians*, London: SPCK, 2011.

Bandstra, A. J., 'Interpretation in 1 Corinthians 10:1–11', *CTJ* 6 (1971) 1–21.

Banks, R., *Paul's Idea of Community: The Early House Churches in Their Cultural Setting*, Kindle Edition, Grand Rapids, MI: Baker Academic, 1995.

Barclay, J. M. G., 'Pure Grace? Paul's Distinctive Jewish Theology of Gift', *ST* 68.1 (2014) 4–20.

Barclay, J. M. G., *Paul and the Gift*, Grand Rapids, MI; Cambridge: Eerdmans, 2015.

Barth, M., *Ephesians 1–3*, AB. Garden City, NY: Doubleday, 1974.

Bauckham, R. J., 'Colossians 1:24 Again: The Apocalyptic Motif', *EQ* 47.3 (1975) 168–70.

Baumgarten, A. I., J. Assmann and G. G. Stroumsa (eds), *Self, Soul and Body in Religious Experience*, SHR, Leiden: Brill, 1998.

Bayes, J. D., 'Five-Fold Ministry: A Social and Cultural Texture Analysis of Ephesians 4:11–16', *JPBL* 3.1 (2010) 113–22.

Beale, G. K., *The Temple and the Church's Mission: A Biblical Theology of the Dwelling Place of God*, NSBT 17, Leicester: Apollos; Downers Grove, IL: IVP, 2004.

Beker, J. C., *The Triumph of God: The Essence of Paul's Thought*, trans. L. T. Stuckenbruck, Minneapolis, MN: Fortress, 1990.

Bell, C., *Ritual Theory, Ritual Practice*, Oxford: OUP, 1992.

Bevans, S. B., *Models of Contextual Theology*, Maryknoll, NY: Orbis, 2002 (1992).

Billings, J. T., 'Incarnational Ministry and Christology: A Reappropriation of the Way of Lowliness', *Missiology* 32.2 (2004) 187–201.

Billings, J. T., *Union with Christ: Reframing Theology and Ministry for the Church*, Grand Rapids, MI: Baker Academic, 2011.

Billington, A., T. Lane and M. Turner (eds), *Mission and Meaning: Essays Presented to Peter Cotterell*, Carlisle: Paternoster, 1995.

Blomberg, C. L., *1 Corinthians*, NIVAC, Grand Rapids, MI: Zondervan, 1994.

Bloom (of Sourozh), Metropolitan Anthony, *The Living Body of Christ*, London: Darton, Longman and Todd Ltd, 2008.

Bosch, D. J., *Transforming Mission: Paradigm Shifts in Theology of Mission*, Maryknoll, NY: Orbis, 1991.

Bray, G. (ed.), *1 & 2 Corinthians*, ACCS, Downers Grove: IVP, 1999.

Brierley, P. (ed.), *UK Christian Handbook, Religious Trends No. 2, 2000/01 Millennium Edition*, London: Christian Research, 1999.

Brierley, P. (ed.), *UK Church Statistics 2005–2015*, Tonbridge: ADBC, 2011.

Brierley, P. (ed.), *UK Church Statistics No.3 2018 Edition*, Tonbridge: ADBC, 2018.

Brierley, P., *The Tide is Running Out*, London: Christian Research, 2000.

Bruce, F. F., *The Epistle to the Ephesians: A Verse-by-Verse Exposition*, London: Pickering & Inglis, 1961.

Bruce, F. F., *The Epistles to the Colossians, to Philemon and to the Ephesians*, NICNT, Grand Rapids, MI: Eerdmans, 1984.

Burk, D., 'Discerning Corinthian Slogans through Paul's Use of the Diatribe in 1 Corinthians 6:12–20', *BBR* 18.1 (2008) 99–121.

Calvin, J., *Commentaries on the Epistles of Paul to the Galatians and Ephesians*, trans. W. Pringle, Grand Rapids, MI: Eerdmans; Carlisle: Paternoster, 1965.

Campbell, W. S., 'Unity and Diversity in the Church: Transformed Identities and the Peace of Christ in Ephesians', *Transformation* 24.1 (2008) 15–30.

Carson, D. A., 'Why the Local Church Is More Important than TGC, White Horse Inn, 9 Marks, and Maybe even ETS', *Them* 40.1 (2015) 1–9.

Carson, D. A., *Becoming Conversant with the Emerging Church: Understanding a Movement and its Implications*, Grand Rapids, MI: Zondervan, 2005.

Castells, M., *The Rise of the Network Society*, 2nd ed., Chichester: Wiley-Blackwell, 2010 (1996).

Cervin, R. S., 'Does *Kephalē* Mean "Source" or "Authority Over" in Greek Literature? A Rubuttal', *TrinJ* 10 (1989) 85–112.

Chan, S., *Liturgical Theology: The Church as Worshiping Community*, Downers Grove, IL: IVP, 2006.

Chapman, M., 'The Social Doctrine of the Trinity: Some Problems', *ATR* 83.2 (2001) 239–54.

Chester, T., *Captured by a Better Vision: Living Porn-Free*, Nottingham: IVP, 2010.

Chester, T., *Mission and the Coming of God: Eschatology, the Trinity and Mission in the Theology of Jürgen Moltmann and Contemporary Evangelicalism*, Milton Keynes: Paternoster, 2006.

Clapp, R., *A Peculiar People: The Church as Culture in a Post-Christian Society*, Downers Grove, IL: IVP, 1996.

Coates, G., *Non-Religious Christianity*, Shippensburg, PA: Destiny Image, 1998.

Cooper, J. W., *Body, Soul, and Life Everlasting: Biblical Anthropology and the Monism–Dualism Debate*, Grand Rapids, MI, Cambridge: Eerdmans, 1989.

Corcoran, K. (ed.), *Church in the Present Tense: A Candid Look at What's Emerging*, Grand Rapids, MI: Brazos, 2011.

Cotterell, P., *Mission and Meaninglessness: The Good News in a World of Suffering and Disorder*, London: SPCK, 1990.

Cray, G. (ed.), *Mission-Shaped Church: Church Planting and Fresh Expressions of Church in a Changing Culture*, London: Church House, 2004.

Cray, G., A. Kennedy and I. Mobsby (eds), *Fresh Expressions of Church and the Kingdom of God*, Norwich: Canterbury, 2012.

Cray, G., A. Kennedy and I. Mobsby (eds), *New Monasticism as Fresh Expressions of Church*, Norwich: Canterbury, 2010.

Croft, S. (ed.), *Mission-shaped Questions. Defining Issues for Today's Church*, London: Church House, 2008.

Croft, S. and I. Mobsby (eds), *Fresh Expressions in the Sacramental Tradition*, Norwich: Canterbury, 2009.

Cullmann, O., *Unity Through Diversity*, trans. M. E. Boring, Philadelphia, PA: Fortress, 1988 (1986).

Davies, J., *The Epistles of St Paul to the Ephesians, Colossians and Philemon: With Introductions and Notes, and an Essay on the Traces of Foreign Elements in the Theology of These Epistles*, 2nd edn, London: Macmillan, 1884.

Davis, S. T., D. Kendall and G. O'Collins (eds), *The Trinity: An Interdisciplinary Symposium on the Trinity*, Oxford: OUP, 1999, 123–44.

Davison, A. and A. Milbank, *For the Parish: A Critique of Fresh Expressions*, London: SCM, 2010.

Dawes, G. W., *The Body in Question: Metaphor and Meaning in the Interpretation of Ephesians 5:21–33*, BIS, Leiden: Brill, 1998.

Denny, M., *Super Structures: The Science of Bridges, Buildings, Dams, and Other Features of Engineering*, Baltimore, MD: Johns Hopkins University, 2010.

Desmond, T. D. and S. Gathercole (eds), *Heaven on Earth*, Carlisle: Paternoster, 2004.

DeYoung, K. and T. Kluck, *Why We're Not Emergent (By Two Guys Who Should Be)*, Chigago, IL: Moody, 2008.

Drane, J., *The McDonaldization of the Church*, London: Darton, Longman and Todd, 2001.

Dunn, J. D. G., *Romans 9–16*, WBC, Dallas, TX: Word, 1988.

Dunn, J. D. G., *The Epistles to the Colossians and to Philemon*, NIGTC, Carlisle: Eerdmans, 1996.

Dunn, J. D. G., *The Theology of Paul the Apostle*, 3rd ed., London/New York: T&T Clark, 2003.

Ellis R. and C. Seaton, *New Celts: Following Jesus into Millennium 3*, Eastbourne: Kingsway, 1998.

Ernst, J., *Pleroma und Pleroma Christi: Geschichte und Deutung wines Begriffs der paulinischen Antilegomena*, BU 5, Regensburg: Friedrich Putset, 1970.

Evans, G. R. and M. Percy (eds), *Managing the Church? Order and Organization in a Secular Age*, Sheffield: Sheffield Academic, 2000.

Farnell, F. D., 'Is the Gift of Prophecy for Today? Part 1 (of 4 parts): The Current Debate about New Testament Prophecy', *BSac* 149 (1992) 277–303.

Fee, G. D., *God's Empowering Presence: The Holy Spirit in the Letters of Paul*, Peabody, MA: Hendrickson, 1994.

Fee, G. D., *The First Epistle to the Corinthians*, NICNT, Grand Rapids, MI: Eerdmans, 1987.

Finney, J., *Emerging Evangelism*, London: Darton, Longman and Todd, 2004.

Finney, M. T., *Honour and Conflict in the Ancient World: 1 Corinthians in its Greco-Roman Setting*, LNTS, London; New York: T&T Clark, 2012.

Fitzmyer, J. A., *First Corinthians: A New Translation with Introduction and Commentary*, AYB 32, New Haven, CT; London: Yale University Press, 2008.

Flett, J. G., *The Witness of God: The Trinity, Missio Dei, Karl Barth, and the Nature of the Christian Community*, Grand Rapids, MI: Eerdmans, 2010.

Foord, M., 'Recent Directions in Anglican Ecclesiology', *Chm* 115.4 (2001) 316–49.

Foster, R. L., '"A Temple in the Lord Filled to the Fullness of God": Context and Intertextuality (Eph. 3:19)', *NovT* 49 (2007) 85–96.

Fox, K., *Watching the English: The Hidden Rules of English Behaviour*, rev. ed. London: Hodder & Stoughton, 2014 (2004).

Franklin, P. S., 'John Wesley in Conversation with the Emerging Church', *AsTJ* 63.1 (2008) 75–93.

Fresh Expressions, 'Stories', Fresh Expressions website (www.freshexpressions.org.uk/stories, accessed 4 May 2017).

Frost, M. and A. Hirsch, *ReJesus: A Wild Messiah for a Missional Church*, Peabody, MA: Hendrickson, 2009.

Frost, M. and A. Hirsch, *The Shaping of Things to Come: Innovation and Mission for the 21st-Century Church*, Peabody, MA: Hendrickson, 2003.

Frost, M., *Exiles: Living Missionally in a Post-Christian Culture*, Peabody, MA: Hendrickson, 2006.

Frost, M., *Incarnate: The Body of Christ in an Age of Disengagement*, Downers Grove, IL: IVP, 2014.

Fujino, Y., 'Vibration, Control and Monitoring of Long-Span Bridges – Recent Research, Developments and Practice in Japan', *Journal of Constructional Steel Research* 58 (2002) 71–97.

Fuller, R. C., *Spiritual, But Not Religious: Understanding Unchurched America*, Oxford: OUP, 2001.

Gay, D., *Remixing the Church: The Five Moves of Emerging Ecclesiology*, London: SCM, 2011.

Ge, Y., 'The Many and the One: The Metaphysics of Participation in Connection to *Creatio Ex Nihilo* in Augustine and Aquinas', PhD Thesis, Cambridge University, 2015.

Gelder, C. V. and D. J. Zscheile, *The Missional Church in Perspective: Mapping Trends and Shaping the Conversation*, Grand Rapids, MI: Baker Academic, 2011.

Gelder, C. V., 'From the Modern to the Postmodern in the West: Viewing the Twentieth Century in Perspective', *Word & World* 20.1 (2000) 32–40.

Gibbs E. and I. Coffey, *Church Next: Quantum Changes in Christian Ministry*, Leicester: IVP, 2001.

Gibbs, E. and R. K. Bolger, *Emerging Churches: Creating Community in Postmodern Cultures*, London: SPCK, 2006.

Gibbs, E., *Church Morph: How Megatrends are Reshaping Christian Communities*, Grand Rapids, MI: Baker Academic, 2009.

Giles, K., *What on Earth is the Church? A Biblical and Theological Inquiry*, London: SPCK, 1995.

Gitteos, J., B. Green and J. Heard, *Generous Ecclesiology: Church, World and the Kingdom of God*, London: SCM, 2013.

Gnilka, J., *Der Kolosserbrief*, HTKNT, Freiburg: Herder, 1980.

Gombis, T. G., 'A Radically New Humanity: The Function of the *Haustafel* in Ephesians', *JETS* 48 (2005) 317–30.

Goodhew, D. (ed.), *Church Growth in Britain: 1980 to the Present*, Farnham: Ashgate, 2012.

Gordon, T. D., '"Equipping" Ministry in Ephesians 4?' *JETS* 37.1 (1994) 69–78.

Gorman, M., *Inhabiting the Cruciform God: Kenosis, Justification and Theosis in Paul's Narrative Soteriology*, Grand Rapids, MI; Cambridge: Eerdmans, 2009.

Green, J. B., *Body, Soul and Human Life: The Nature of Humanity in the Bible*, Grand Rapids, MI: Baker Academic, 2008.

Grenz, S. J. and R. E. Olson, *20th-Century Theology: God and World in a Transitional Age*, Downers Grove, IL: Paternoster, 1992.

Grimes, R. L., *Beginnings in Ritual Studies*, 3rd ed., Waterloo, Canada: Ritual Studies International, 2013 (1995, 1983).

Grudem, W., 'Does κεφαλή ("Head") Mean "Source" or "Authority Over" in Greek Literature? A Survey of 2,336 Examples', *TrinJ* 6.1 (1985) 38–59.

Grudem, W., 'The Meaning of κεφαλή ("Head"): An Evaluation of New Evidence, Real And Alleged', *JETS* 44.1 (2001) 25–65.

Guarino, T., 'Postmodernity and Five Fundamental Theological Issues', *TS* 57 (1996) 654–89.

Guder, D. L., 'Incarnation and the Church's Evangelistic Mission', *IRM* 83 (1994) 417–28.

Gunton, C. E., *The One, the Three and the Many: God, Creation and the Culture of Modernity*, Cambridge: CUP, 1993.

Hastings, A., *A History of English Christianity 1920–2000*, London: SCM, 2001 (1986, 1987, 1991).

Hawthorne, G., R. Martin and D. Reid (eds), *Dictionary of Paul and His Letters*, Downers Grove, IL/Leicester: IVP, 1993.

Hay, D. M., *Pauline Theology*, vol. 2, Minneapolis, MN: Fortress, 1993.

Hays, R. B., *First Corinthians*, Interpretation, Louisville, KY: John Knox, 1997.

Healy, N. M., 'Christian Theology: The Church', in S. Westerholm (ed.), *The Blackwell Companion to Paul*, Chichester: Wiley-Blackwell, 2011, 589–601.

Healy, N. M., *Church, World and the Christian Life*, Cambridge: CUP, 2000.

Heelas, P. and L. Woodhead, *The Spiritual Revolution: Why Religion is Giving Way to Spirituality*, Oxford: Blackwell, 2005.

Hesselgrave D. J. and E. Rommen, *Contextualization: Meanings, Methods, and Models*, Grand Rapids, MI: Baker, 1989.

Hiebert, P. G., 'Conversion, Culture, and Cognitive Categories', *Gospel in Context* 1.4 (1978) 24–9.

Hill, P. C., K. I. Pargament, R. W. Hood, M. E. Mccullough, J. P. Swyers, D. B. Larson and B. J. Zinnbauer, 'Conceptualizing Religion and Spirituality: Points of Commonality, Points of Departure', *Journal for the Theory of Social Behaviour* 30.1 (2000) 51–77.

Hirsch, A., *The Forgotten Ways: Reactivating the Missional Church*, Grand Rapids, MI: Brazos, 2006.

Hoehner, H., *Ephesians: An Exegetical Commentary*, Grand Rapids, MI: Baker Academic, 2002.

Holmes, P. R., *Trinity in Human Community: Exploring Congregational Life in the Image of the Social Trinity*, Milton Keynes: Paternoster, 2006.

Holmes, S. R., 'Three Versus One? Some Problems of Social Trinitarianism', *JRT* 3 (2009) 77–89.

Holmes, S. R., 'Trinitarian Missiology: Towards a Theology of God as Missionary', *IJST* 8.1 (2006) 72–90.

Holmes, S. R., *The Holy Trinity: Understanding God's Life*, Milton Keynes: Paternoster, 2012.

Hooker, M. D., 'Were There False Teachers in Colossae?' in B. Lindars and S. S. Smalley (eds), *Christ and Spirit in the New Testament: Studies in Honour of Charles Francis Digby Moule*, Cambridge: CUP, 1973, 315–31.

Horrell, D. G., *The Social Ethos of the Corinthian Correspondence: Interests and Ideology from 1 Corinthians to 1 Clement*, SNTW, Edinburgh: T&T Clark, 1996.

House, H. W., 'Tongues and the Mystery Religions of Corinth', *BSac* 140 (1983) 134–50.

Hübner, H., *An Philemon, An die Kolosser, An die Epheser*, HNT 12, Tübingen: Mohr, 1997.

Hull, J. M., *Mission-Shaped Church: A Theological Response*, London: SCM, 2006.

Hunt, H. T., 'Gnostic Dilemmas in Western Psychologies of Spirituality', *The International Journal of Transpersonal Studies*, 22 (2003) 27–39.

Hunter, G. G., *Church for the Unchurched*, Nashville, TN: Abingdon, 1996.

Huss, B., 'Spirituality: The Emergence of a New Cultural Category and its Challenge to the Religious and the Secular', *JCR* 29.1 (2014) 47–60.

James, W., *The Varieties of Religious Experience*, Cambridge, MA: Harvard University Press, 1985.

Jones, A., 'March 18, 2005, EmergAnt.: 1 Emerging Vocabulary', Tall Skinny Kiwi website (http://tallskinnykiwi.typepad.com/tallskinnykiwi/2005/03/emergant_1_an_e.html, accessed 28 March 2019).

Jones, A. H., *The Church is Flat: The Relational Ecclesiology of the Emerging Church Movement*, Minneapolis, MN: JoPa, 2011.

Justin Cantuar and Sentamu Ebor, 'In Each Generation: A Programme for Reform and Renewal, GS 1976, January 2015', Church of England website (www.churchofengland.org/sites/default/files/2017-11/gs%201976%20-%20a%20note%20from%20the%20archbishops%20giving%20an%20overview%20of%20the%20task%20groups.pdf, accessed 3 January 2019).

Kahaila, 'About Us', Kahaila website (http://kahaila.com/contact-2/, accessed 8 September 2017).

Kahaila, 'Church', Kahaila website (http://kahaila.com/church, accessed 8 September 2017).

Kaiser, W. C., 'The Old Promise and the New Covenant: Jeremiah 31:31–34', *JETS* 15 (1972) 11–23.

Kandiah, K., *Paradoxology: Why Christianity Was Never Meant To Be Simple*, London: Hodder and Stoughton, 2014.

Kärkkäinen, V. M., *An Introduction to Ecclesiology: Ecumenical, Historical and Global Perspectives*, Downers Grove, IL: IVP, 2002.

Keener, C. S., *Paul, Women and Wives: Marriage and Women's Ministry in the Letters of Paul*, Peabody, MA: Hendrickson, 1992.

Keener, C. S., *Romans*, NCC, Eugene, OR: Cascade, 2009.

Kilby, K., 'Perichoresis and Projection: Problems with Social Doctrines of the Trinity', *NB* 81 (2000) 432–45.

Kimball, D., *The Emerging Church: Vintage Christianity for New Generations*, Grand Rapids, MI: Zondervan, 2003.

Klein, G., 'The Biblical Understanding of "The Kingdom of God"', *Interpretation* 26.4 (1972) 378–418.

Kruse, C. G., *Paul's Letter to the Romans*, PNTC, Grand Rapids, MI; Cambridge: Eerdmans, 2012.

Labanow, C. E., *Evangelicalism and the Emerging Church: A Congregational Study of a Vineyard Church*, Farnham: Ashgate, 2009.

Lakoff, G., *Women, Fire and Dangerous Things: What Categories Reveal about the Mind*, Chicago, IL: University of Chicago Press, 1987.

Langmead D. and C. Garnaut, *Encyclopedia of Architectural and Engineering Feats*, Santa Barbara, CA: ABC-CLIO, 2001.

Langmead, R., *The Word Made Flesh: Towards an Incarnational Missiology*, ASMDS, Lanham, MD: University Press of America, 2004.

Larkin, W. J., *Ephesians: A Handbook on the Greek Text*, BHGBT, Waco, TX: Baylor University, 2009.

Law, S., 'Anticipating Change: Missions and Paradigm Shifts in Emergence', *AsTJ* 67.1 (2012) 4–26.

Lee, M. V., *Paul, the Stoics, and the Body of Christ*, SNTSMS, Cambridge: CUP, 2006.

Lichtenstein, B. B. and D. A. Plowman, 'The Leadership of Emergence: A Complex Systems Leadership Theory of Emergence at Successive Organizational Levels', *LQ* 20 (2009) 617–30.

Lincoln, A. T., 'A Re-Examination of "The Heavenlies" in Ephesians', *NTS* 19 (1972–73) 468–83.

Lincoln, A. T., *Ephesians*, WBC, Dallas, TX: Word, 1990.

Lindemann, A., *Der Kolosserbrief*, ZBNT, Zürich: Theologischer Verlag, 1983.

Lings, G. (ed.), *Messy Church Theology: Exploring the Significance of Messy Church for the Wider Church*, Abingdon: BRF, 2013.

Littell, F. H., 'The Historical Free Church Defined', *Brethren Life and Thought* 50.3–4 (2005) 51–65 (reproduced from F. H. Littell, 'The Historical Free Church Defined', *Brethren Life and Thought*, 9.4 [1964] 78–90).

Lockwood, G. J., *1 Corinthians*, ConcC, Saint Louis, MO: Concordia, 2000.

Lohse, E. and H. Koester, *Colossians and Philemon: A Commentary on the Epistles to the Colossians and to Philemon*, Hermeneia, Philadelphia, PA: Fortress, 1971.

Lombard, H. A., 'Charisma and Church Office', *Neot* 10 (1976) 31–52.

Lowe, J., 'An Examination of Attempts to Detect Development in St. Paul's Theology', *JTS* 42 (1941) 129–42.

Macaskill, G., *Union with Christ in the New Testament*, Oxford: OUP, 2013.

MacIntyre, A., *After Virtue*, 2nd ed., Notre Dame, IN: University of Notre Dame, 1984 (1981).

Mackay, J. A., *Ecumenics: The Science of the Church Universal*, Englewood Cliffs, NJ: Prentice Hall, 1964.

Mare, W. H., 'Paul's Mystery in Ephesians 3', *BETS* 8 (1965) 77–84.

Marshall, I. H., 'How Far Did the Early Christians *Worship* God?', *Chm* 99 (1985) 216–29.

Marti, G. and G. Ganiel, *The Deconstructed Church: Understanding Emerging Christianity*, Oxford: OUP, 2014.

Martin, D. B., *The Corinthian Body*, New Haven; London: Yale University Press, 1995.

Mauss, M., *The Gift: Forms and Functions of Exchange in Archaic Societies*, trans. I. Cunnison, London: Cohen and West, 1966.

Mazarr, M. J., *Global Trends 2005: An Owner's Manual for the Next Decade*, New York: St Martin's, 1999.

McFadyen, A. I., *The Call to Personhood: A Christian Theory of the Individual in Social Relationships*, Cambridge: CUP, 1990.

McGavran, D. A., *Understanding Church Growth*, 2nd ed., Grand Rapids, MI: Eerdmans, 1980 (1970).

McKnight, S., 'Five Streams of the Emerging Church: Key Elements of the Most Controversial and Misunderstood Movement in the Church Today', *Christianity Today* website (www.christianitytoday.com/ct/2007/february/11.35.html?paging=off, accessed 17 June 2013).

McKnight, S., *Kingdom Conspiracy: Returning to the Radical Mission of the Local Church*, Grand Rapids, MI: Brazos, 2014.

McLaren, B., *Church on the Other Side: Exploring the Radical Future of the Local Congregation*, Grand Rapids, MI: Zondervan, 2006.

McLaren, B., *More Ready than you Realize: Evangelism as Dance in the Postmodern Matrix*, Grand Rapids, MI: Zondervan, 2002.

Meeks, W. A., 'And Rose Up to Play: Midrash and Paraenesis in 1 Corinthians 10:1–22', *JSNT* 16 (1982) 64–78.

Meeks, W. A., *The First Urban Christians: The Social World of the Apostle Paul*, 2nd ed., New Haven, CT/London: Yale University Press, 2003 (1983).

Metzger, P. L., 'Fleshed Out: the False Dilemma of Union with Christ versus Incarnational Ministry', 26.08.12, *Uncommon God, Common Good* website (http://blogs.christianpost.com/uncommon-God-common-good/fleshed-out-the-false-dilemma-of-union-with-christ-versus-incarnational-ministry-11583/, accessed 7 July 2015).

Michener, R. T., 'The Kingdom of God and Postmodern Ecclesiologies: A Compatibility Assessment', *ERT* 34.2 (2010) 119–30.

Miles, S., *Consumerism – As a Way of Life*, London: SAGE, 1998.

Miller, V. J., *Consuming Religion: Christian Faith and Practice in a Consumer Culture*, New York: Continuum, 2003.

Minear, P. S., *Images of the Church in the New Testament*, NTL, Louisville, KY: Westminster John Knox Press, 2004.

Mitchell, M., *Paul and the Rhetoric of Reconciliation*, HUTh, Tübingen: Mohr, 1991.

Mobsby, I., *Emerging and Fresh Expressions of Church: How Are They Authentically Church and Anglican?*, London: Moot Community, 2006.

Mobsby, I., *God Unknown: The Trinity in Contemporary Spirituality*, Norwich: Canterbury, 2012.

Mollenkott, V. R., 'Emancipative Elements in Ephesians 5.21–33: Why Feminist Scholarship Has (Often) Left Them Unmentioned and Why They Should Be Emphasized', in A-J. Levine (ed.), *Feminist Companion to Paul: The Deutero-Pauline Epistles*, London/New York: T&T Clark, 2003, 37–58.

Molnar, P. D., *Divine Freedom and the Doctrine of the Immanent Trinity: In Dialogue with Karl Barth and Contemporary Theology*, Edinburgh/New York: T&T Clark, 2002.

Moltmann, J., *God in Creation: A New Theology of Creation and the Spirit of God*, trans. M. Kohl, Minneapolis, MN: Fortress, 1993.

Moltmann, J., *The Church in the Power of the Spirit: A Contribution to Messianic Ecclesiology*, trans. M. Kohl, London: SCM, 1975.

Moltmann, J., *The Coming of God: Christian Eschatology*, trans. M. Kohl, London: SCM, 1996.

Moltmann, J., *The Trinity and the Kingdom of God*, London: SCM, 1981.

Moltmann, J., *Theology of Hope: On the Ground and the Implications of a Christian Eschatology*, Minneapolis, MN: Fortress, 1993.

Moo, D. J., *The Epistle to the Romans*, NICNT, Grand Rapids, MI: Eerdmans, 1996.

Moo, D. J., *The Letters to Colossians and to Philemon*, PNTC, Grand Rapids, MI; Cambridge: Eerdmans, 2008.

Moreland, J. P. and S. B. Rae, *Body and Soul: Human Nature and the Crisis in Ethics*, Downers Grove, IL: IVP, 2000.

Morris, H., 'Emerging Father, Traditional Son? Luke 15:11–32, the Older Son and the pre-Emerging Church', MA Thesis, London School of Theology, 2010.

Morris, H., 'The City as Foil (not Friend nor Foe): Conformity and Subversion in 1 Corinthians 12:12–31', in S. Walton, D. W. J. Gill and P. Trebilco (eds), *The Urban World and the First Christians*, Grand Rapids, MI: Eerdmans, 2017.

Moule, C. F. D. (ed.), *Essays in New Testament Interpretation*, Cambridge: CUP, 1982.

Moynagh, M., *Being Church, Doing Life: Creating Gospel Communities Where Life Happens*, Oxford: Lion Hudson, 2014.

Moynagh, M., *Changing World, Changing Church*, London/Grand Rapids, MI: Monarch, 2001.

Moynagh, M., *Church for Every Context: An Introduction to Theology and Practice*, London: SCM, 2012.

Moynagh, M., *Church in Life: Innovation, Mission and Ecclesiology*, London: SCM, 2017.

Moynagh, M., *emergingchurch.intro*, Oxford; Grand Rapids, MI: Monarch, 2004.

Murphy-O'Connor, J. (ed.), *Paul and Qumran: Studies in New Testament Exegesis*, London: Geoffrey Chapman, 1968.

Murray Williams, S. and S., *Multi-Voiced Church*, Milton Keynes: Paternoster, 2012.

Murray, S., *Changing Mission: Learning from the Newer Churches*, London: Churches Together in Britain and Ireland, 2006.

Murray, S., *Church After Christendom*, Milton Keynes: Paternoster, 2004.

Murray, S., *Church Planting: Laying Foundations*, Carlisle: Paternoster, 1998.

Murray, S., *Post-Christendom: Church and Mission in a Strange New World*, Carlisle; Waynesboro, VA: Paternoster, 2004.

Nash, R. S., *1 Corinthians*, SHBC, Macon, GA: Smyth and Helwys, 2009.

Newbigin, L., *The Gospel in a Pluralist Society*, London: SPCK, 1986.

Niewold, J. W., 'Set Theory and Leadership: Reflections on Missional Communities in the Light of Ephesians 4:11–12', *JBPL* 2.1 (2008) 44–63.

O'Brien, P. T., 'The Church as a Heavenly and Eschatological Entity', in D. A. Carson (ed.), *The Church in the Bible and the World*, Exeter: Paternoster/Grand Rapids, MI: Baker, 1987, 88–119.

O'Brien, P. T., *Colossians and Philemon*, WBC, Waco, TX: Word, 1982.

O'Brien, P. T., *The Letter to the Ephesians*, PNTC, Leicester: Apollos, 1999.

Oswald, H. C. (ed.), *Luther's Works*, Vol. 18, Saint Louis, MO: Concordia, 1973.

Padilla, C. R., 'The Unity of the Church and the Homogeneous Unit Principle', *IBMR* 6.1 (1982) 23–30.

Pearse, M., 'Problem? What Problem? Personhood, Late Modern/Postmodern Rootlessness and Contemporary Identity Crises', *EQ* 77.1 (2005) 5–12.

Perriman, A., '"His Body, Which is the Church..." Coming to Terms with Metaphor', *EQ* 62.2 (1990) 123–42.

Perriman, A., 'Church and Body in 1 Corinthians: A Study in Exegesis and the Poetics of Argumentation', PhD Thesis, Brunel University, 1998.

Phillips C. and S. Priwer, *Bridges and Spans*, Abingdon/New York: Routledge, 2009.

Pickard, S., *Seeking the Church: An Introduction to Ecclesiology*, London: SCM, 2012.

Principe, W., 'Toward Defining Spirituality', *Studies in Religion* 12.2 (1983) 127–41.

Rahner, K., *The Trinity*, trans. Herder and Herder, London: Burns and Oates, 1986 (1975, 1970).

Randall, I. M., 'Mission in post-Christendom: Anabaptist and Free Church perspectives', *EQ* 79.3 (2007), 227–40.

Rice, J., *The Church of Facebook: How the Hyperconnected are Redefining Community*, Colorado Springs: David C. Cook; Eastbourne: Kingsway, 2009.

Ricoeur, P., *The Rule of Metaphor: The Creation of Meaning in Language*, trans. R. Czerny, K. McLaughlin and J. Costello, London; New York: Routledge, 2004 (1977).

Ritzer, G., *Globalization: A Basic Text*, Chichester: Wiley & Sons, 2010.

Robinson, J. A. T., *The Body: A Study in Pauline Theology*, SBT, London: SCM, 1953.

Rollins, P., *How [Not] to Speak of God*, London: SPCK, 2006.

Rothschild, C. K. and T. W. Thompson (eds), *Christian Body, Christian Self: Concepts of Early Christian Personhood*, WUNT 284, Tübingen: Mohr Siebeck, 2011.

Runesson, A., 'Placing Paul: Institutional Structures and Theological Strategy in the World of the Early Christ-Believers', *Svensk Exegetisk Årsbok* 80 (2015) 43–67.

Schnackenburg, R., *Ephesians: A Commentary*, trans. H. Heron, Edinburgh: T&T Clark, 1991.

Schrage, W., *Der erste Brief an die Korinther*, EKKNT 7/1–4, Neukirchen-Vluyn: Neukirchener, 1991–2001.

Schreiner, T. R., *Paul: Apostle of God's Glory in Christ*, Leicester: Apollos/Downers Grove, IL, UK: IVP, 2001.

Schreiner, T. R., *Romans*, BECNT, Grand Rapids, MI, 1998.

Schultz, T., 'Why They Don't Sing on Sunday Anymore', 21.05.14, *Holy Soup* website (https://holysoup.com/why-they-dont-sing-on-sunday-anymore/, accessed 18 December 2018).

Sexton, J. S., 'The State of the Evangelical Trinitarian Resurgence', *JETS* 54.4 (2011) 787–805.

Shogren, G. S., '"The Wicked Will Not Inherit the Kingdom of God": A Pauline Warning and the Hermeneutics of Liberation Theology and of Brian McLaren', *TrinJ* 31.1 (2010) 95–113.

Shults, F. L., *Reforming Theological Anthropology: After the Philosophical Turn to Relationality*, Grand Rapids, MI; Cambridge: Eerdmans, 2003.

Smith, B. D., 'The Problem with the Observance of the Lord's Supper in the Corinthian Church', *BBR* 20.4 (2010) 517–44.

Smith, J. K. A., *Desiring the Kingdom: Worship, Worldview and Cultural Formation*, Cultural Liturgies Vol. 1, Grand Rapids, MI: Baker, 2009.

Smith, J. K. A., *Imagining the Kingdom: How Worship Works*, Cultural Liturgies Vol. 2, Grand Rapids, MI: Baker Academic, 2013.

Smith, R. S., 'Joel Green's Anthropological Monism', *CTJ* 7.2 (2010) 19–36.

Snodgrass, K. R., *Ephesians*, NIVAC, Grand Rapids, MI: Zondervan, 1996.

Snodgrass, K. R., *Stories with Intent, A Comprehensive Guide to the Parables of Jesus*, Grand Rapids, MI; Cambridge: Eerdmans, 2008.

Soskice, J. M., *Metaphor and Religious Language*, Oxford: Clarendon, 1985.

Spence, S., *The Parting of the Ways: The Roman Church as a Case Study*, Leuven: Peeters, 2004.

Sumney, J. L., *Colossians*, NTL, Louisville, KY: Westminster John Knox, 2008.

Sweet, L., B. D. McLaren and J. Haselmayer, *A is for Abductive: The Language of the Emerging Church*, Grand Rapids, MI: Zondervan, 2003.

Sweet, L., *Viral: How Social Networking is Poised to Ignite Revival*, Colorado Springs, CO: Waterbrook, 2012.

Tanner, K., 'Creation *Ex Nihilio* As Mixed Metaphor', *MTh* 29.2 (2013) 138–55.

Tanner, K., *Christ the Key*, Cambridge: CUP, 2010.

Tanner, K., *Jesus, Humanity and the Trinity*, Edinburgh: T&T Clark, 2001.

Taylor, C., *A Secular Age*, Cambridge, MA/London: Harvard University Press, 2007.

Taylor, C., *Sources of Self: The Making of Modern Identity*, Cambridge, MA: Harvard University Press, 1989.

Theissen, G., *Biblical Faith: An Evolutionary Approach*, London: SCM, 1984.

Theissen, G., *The Social Setting of Pauline Christianity: Essays on Corinth*, trans. J. H. Schütz, Philadelphia, PA: Fortress, 1975.

Thielman, F., *Ephesians*, BECNT, Grand Rapids, MI: Baker Academic, 2010.

Thiselton, A. C., 'Realized Eschatology at Corinth', *NTS* 24.4 (1978) 510–26.

Thiselton, A. C., 'The Significance of Recent Research on 1 Corinthians for Hermeneutical Appropriation of this Epistle Today', *Neot* 40.2 (2006) 320–52.

Thiselton, A. C., *The First Epistle to the Corinthians: A Commentary on the Greek Text*, NIGTC, Grand Rapids, MI: Eerdmans; Carlisle: Paternoster, 2000.

Thompson, J. W., *The Church According to Paul: Rediscovering the Community Conformed to Christ*, Grand Rapids, MI: Baker Academic, 2014.

Thwaites, J., *The Church Beyond The Congregation: The Strategic Role of the Church in the Postmodern Era*, Carlisle: Paternoster, 1999.

Tickle, P., *Emergence Christianity: What it Is, Where it is Going, and Why it Matters*, Grand Rapids, MI: Baker, 2012.

Torrance, A. J., *Persons in Communion: Trinitarian Description and Human Participation*, Edinburgh: T&T Clark, 1996.

Trebilco, P., 'Why Did the Early Christians Call Themselves ἡ ἐκκλησία?' *NTS* 57 (2011) 440–60.

Turner, M., 'Approaching "Personhood" in the New Testament, with Special Reference to Ephesians', *EQ* 77.3 (2005) 211–33.

Turner, M., 'Ecclesiology in the Major "Apostolic" Restorationist Churches In The United Kingdom', *VE* 19 (1989) 83–108.

Turner, M., 'Spiritual Gifts Then and Now', *VE* 15 (1985) 7–63.

Turner, M., *The Holy Spirit and Spiritual Gifts Then and Now*, Carlisle: Paternoster, 1996.

Unsworth, P., 'Kahaila – Update Jan 14', 6 January 2014, Fresh Expressions website (www.youtube.com/watch?v=eLEEh1K_W8g, accessed 21 January 2019).

Unsworth, P., 'Kahaila', 3 September 2013, Fresh Expressions website (www.baptist.org.uk/Articles/369599/Kahaila.aspx, accessed 21 January 2019).

Vanhoozer, K. J., *Is There Meaning in This Text?*, Leicester: IVP, 1998.

Volf, M., *After Our Likeness: The Church as the Image of the Trinity*, Grand Rapids, MI/Cambridge: Eerdmans, 1998.

Volf, M., *Exclusion and Embrace: A Theological Exploration of Identity, Otherness, and Reconciliation*, Nashville, TN: Abingdon, 1996.

Wagner, P. C., 'Mission and Hope: Some Missiological Implications of the Theology of Jürgen Moltmann', *Missiology* 2.4 (1974) 455–74.

Walker, J., *Testing Fresh Expressions: Identity and Transformation*, Abingdon: Routledge, 2016 (2014).

Walton, S., *Leadership and Lifestyle: The Portrait of Paul in the Miletus Speech and 1 Thessalonians*, SNTSMS 108, Cambridge: CUP, 2000.

Ward, P., *Selling Worship: How What We Sing Has Changed the Church*, Milton Keynes: Paternoster, 2005.

Ward, P., 'Blueprint Ecclesiology and the Lived: Normativity as Perilous Faithfulness', *Ecclesial Practices* 2.1 (2015) 74–90.

Ward, P., *Growing Up Evangelical: Youthwork and the Making of a Subculture*, London: SPCK, 1996.

Ward, P., *Liquid Church*, Peabody, MA: Hendrickson; Carlisle: Paternoster, 2002.

Ward, P., *Liquid Ecclesiology: The Gospel and the Church*, Leiden: Brill, 2017.

Ward, P., *Participation and Mediation: A Practical Theology for the Liquid Church*, London: SCM, 2008.

Webb, W. J., *Slaves, Women and Homosexuals: Exploring the Hermeneutics of Cultural Analysis*, Downers Grove, IL: IVP, 2001.

Webber, R. (ed.), *Listening to the Beliefs of Emerging Churches: Five Perspectives*, Grand Rapids, MI: Zondervan, 2007.

Wikenhauser, A., *Pauline Mysticism: Christ in the Mystical Teaching of St. Paul*, Edinburgh: Herder; Freiburg: Nelson, 1960.

Wilkins, M. J. and T. Paige (eds), *Worship, Theology and Ministry in the Early Church*, JSNTS, Sheffield: Sheffield Academic, 1992, 146–62.

Wilkinson, J., 'The Body in the Old Testament', *EQ* 63.3 (1991), 195–210.

Williams, D. H. (ed.), *The Free Church and the Early Church: Bridging the Historical and Theological Divide*, Grand Rapids, MI; Cambridge: Eerdmans, 2002.

Williams, R., *Tokens of Trust: An Introduction to Christian Belief*, Norwich: Canterbury, 2007.

Williams, R., *Why Study the Past? The Quest for the Historical Church*, London: Darton, Longman and Todd, 2005.

Wilson, R. McL., *A Critical and Exegetical Commentary on Colossians and Philemon*, ICC, London/New York: T&T Clark, 2005.

Winter, B., *After Paul Left Corinth: The Influence of Secular Ethics and Social Change*, Grand Rapids, MI; Cambridge: Eerdmans, 2001.

Witherington, B., *Conflict and Community in Corinth: A Socio-Rhetorical Commentary on 1 and 2 Corinthians*, Grand Rapids, MI: Eerdmans, 1994.

Witherington, B., *The Letters to Philemon, the Colossians, and the Ephesians: A Socio-Rhetorical Commentary on the Captivity Epistles*, Grand Rapids, MI; Cambridge: Eerdmans, 2007.

Wolters, A., 'Head as Metaphor in Paul', *Koers* 76.1 (2011) 137–53.

Wright, N. T., *Paul and the Faithfulness of God: Christian Origins and the Question of God*, London: SPCK, 2013.

Wright, N. T., *The New Testament and the People of God*, London: SPCK, 1992.

Zimmerman, E., 'Church and Empire: Free-Church Ecclesiology in a Global Era', *Political Theology* 10.3 (2009) 471–95.

Zizioulas, J., *Being as Communion: Studies on Personhood and the Church*, Crestwood, NY: Saint Valdimir's Seminary Press, 1985.

Zizioulas, J., *Communion and Otherness*, London: T&T Clark, 2006.

Index of Scripture References

Index of Names

Index of Subjects